Television Entertainment

Television entertainment rules supreme, one of the world's most important disseminators of information, ideas, and amusement. More than a parade of little figures in a box, it is deeply embedded in everyday life, in how we think, what we think and care about, and who we think and care about it with.

But is television entertainment art? Why do so many love it and so many hate or fear it? Does it offer a window to the world, or images of a fake world? How is it political and how does it address us as citizens? What powers does it hold, and what powers do we have over it? Or, for that matter, what is television these days, in an era of rapidly developing technologies, media platforms, and globalization? *Television Entertainment* addresses these and other key questions that we regularly ask, or should ask, offering a lively and dynamic, thematically based overview that offers examples from recent and current television, including *Lost*, reality television, *The Sopranos*, *The Simpsons*, political satire, *Grey's Anatomy*, *The West Wing*, soaps, and *24*.

Jonathan Gray is Assistant Professor of Communication and Media Studies at Fordham University. He is author of *Watching with The Simpsons: Television, Parody, and Intertextuality*, and co-editor of *Fandom: Identities and Communities in a Mediated World* and *Battleground: The Media*.

Communication and Society

Series Editor: James Curran

Television Entertainment

Jonathan Gray

Routledge
Taylor & Francis Group

NEW YORK AND LONDON

First published 2008
by Routledge
270 Madison Ave, New York, NY 10016

Simultaneously published in the UK
by Routledge
2 Park Square, Milton Park, Abingdon, Oxon OX14 4RN

Routledge is an imprint of the Taylor & Francis Group, an informa business

© 2008 Jonathan Gray

Typeset in Perpetua and Gill Sans
by Saxon Graphics Ltd, Derby
Printed and bound in Great Britain
by Antony Rowe, Chippenham, Wiltshire

British Library Cataloguing in Publication Data
A catalogue record for this book is available from the British Library

Library of Congress Cataloging in Publication Data
Gray, Jonathan (Jonathan Alan)
    Television entertainment / Jonathan Gray.
        p. cm—(Communication and society)
    Includes bibliographical references and index.
1. Television broadcasting—Social aspects.
    2. Television—Philosophy. I Title.
PN1992.6.G69 2008
302.23'45—dc22
                                        2007038209

ISBN 10: 0-415-77223-0 (hbk)
ISBN 10: 0-415-77224-9 (pbk)

ISBN 13: 978-0-415-77223-5 (hbk)
ISBN 13: 978-0-415-77224-2 (pbk)

I thank my mother, Anne Margaret Gray, for teaching, loving, and entertaining me even more than has television

Contents

Illustrations

Figures

Tables

Acknowledgments

This book was written with classroom use in mind, and thus throughout its writing I have reflected on the great instruction and guidance I have received from some wonderful, truly gifted teachers both inside and outside of classrooms. The mark of great teachers is that you know they're good at the time, yet the fact only reiterates itself over the years in new situations. All of the following meet this billing, and were constitutive of my development. Going chronologically, let me thank Sheila and Brian Harrod, Julia Wakeling, Jane Morrison, Ms McDonald, Mr Geoffrey Mathews, Mr David Sherlock, Ms Karen Moffat, Mrs Adele Case, Mr Bob Fitzpatrick, Doug Soo, Prof. Susanna Egan, Prof. William H. New, Percy Nacario, Dr David Richards, Bill Schwarz, Prof. Nick Couldry, and Prof. David Morley. Let me also thank the many fantastic fellow students I've had the pleasure of learning from and with along the way – with special thanks to Amita Atal, Bertha Chin, Kerry Day, Boris Ewenstein, Susan Hazan, Kareem Jalal, Leora Kornfeld, Kanisan Nathan, Justin Reis, Rob "Charlie" Stover, and Martin Style – and also my own excellent students who have taught me a lot.

Television studies is a thriving field full of many wonderfully collegial researchers, and I have benefited significantly not only from the field's printed output, but also from discussing all aspects of television with them, and from their friendship. I extend particular thanks to Diane Alters, Ivan Askwith, Martin Barker, Denise Bielby, Will Brooker, Kristina Busse, Mike Chopra-Gant, Lynn Schofield Clark, Melissa Click, Nick Couldry (again), Josh Green, John Hartley, Matt Hills, Henry Jenkins, Derek Johnson, Jeff Jones, L. S. Kim, Derek Kompare, David Lavery, Amanda Lotz, Ernest Mathijs, Matt McAllister, John McMurria, David Morley (again), Allison Perlman, Aswin Punathambekar, Roberta Pearson, Jean Retzinger, Avi Santo, Louisa Stein, and Ethan Thompson. Similarly, warm thanks are extended to my colleagues at Fordham University whom I bounce ideas of various sizes off, and who help to keep me sane, especially Ed Cahill, Margot Hardenbergh, Arthur Hayes, Gwyneth Jackaway, Paul Levinson, Tom McCourt,

Meir Ribalow, Brian Rose, Janet Sternberg, fellow merry rogue Michael Tueth, and James VanOosting. Let me also single out Robin Andersen, C. Lee Harrington, Jason Mittell, and Cornel Sandvoss as superb collaborators on past and continuing projects, whose intellectual generosity, friendship, and good humor have made writing and editing fun.

This book owes further debts of thanks to James Curran, the series editor, who convinced me to write it and who supported me throughout. Low and humble kowtows are offered to Allison, Avi, Derek J, Jason, Jeff, Matt H, and Will (all listed above) for remarkably helpful comments on early drafts. Natalie Foster and especially Charlotte Wood have been ace stewards at Routledge, UK.

Finally, I could revise this paragraph many times and never feel I've adequately thanked my mother, father, brother, and wife. My parents, Anne and Ian Gray, were my first teachers and remain my best teachers. They and my big brother Matthew watched and enjoyed television with me, and encouraged me to watch, think about, and talk about it critically. And all my love and appreciation goes to my wife and frequent watching partner, Monica Grant, who has suffered through many of my rants and enthusiastic raves about television, who has shared a few of her own, whose wide reading and thoughtful insight have informed my analysis far more than I could ever inform her research and studies, and who knows how to tell me when to turn both television and television studies off.

What is television entertainment?

Television: teacher, mother, secret lover.

Homer Simpson

The media have given us the words to speak, and ideas to utter, not as some disembodied force operating against us as we go about our daily business, but as part of a reality in which we participate, in which we share, and which we sustain on a daily basis through our daily talk, our daily interactions.

Roger Silverstone (1999: 6)

television poses a serious danger for all the various areas of cultural production – for art, for literature, for science, for philosophy, and for law . . . and no less of a threat to political life and to democracy itself.

Pierre Bourdieu (1998: 10)

For many of us, next to sleep and work or school, television is the greatest draw on our time. As Roger Silverstone points out, far from just being a shiny box in our living room or a strange "disembodied force," television is remarkable precisely for its "daily" qualities, and for the presence it occupies in our everyday, humdrum routines and lives. Wake up, turn on the television, get ready, leave for work/school, go home, turn on the television, sleep: a fairly standard day in the life of an average person in a developed nation. And when we are watching, all available statistics suggest that entertainment is of particular interest to most of us: whereas Fox News boasts a Nielsen-projected viewership of approximately 1.38 million for the 9–10 p.m. slot in the US (Crupi 2006), for instance, *CSI*, *Lost*, or *American Idol* can bring in twenty to thirty times as many viewers without breaking a sweat, and even *Simpsons* reruns, a daytime soap, or a moderately successful Saturday morning cartoon can easily top such figures too. Many citizens may feel that the news is especially *important*, that such-and-such a documentary is especially *enlightening*, or may realize that the incessant stream of ads is what makes much of television tick, but we still watch entertainment programming in huge numbers.

As such, as Silverstone notes of the media as a whole, television entertainment extends way beyond the living room. If, as infants, we once wondered if television's three-inch tall characters could step outside the box, we soon come to learn that they certainly can, in the words we speak, the things we argue over, the topics of friendly banter, and the things we think about while at work, at play, or asleep. Television entertainment is not as all-encompassing as some critics and alarmists make it out to be – it has not colonized the world, much less our souls and brains – but it is pervasive, and a major entity both to be reckoned with and to be embraced and enjoyed. Storytelling has always been important to humankind, and television entertainment offers us many of today's most successful and loved tribal elders, bards, and raconteurs. As an industry, it is gigantic, with American television alone grossing well over $100 billion per year (*Economist* 2002: 3). As a sociological being, it is capable of touching almost all aspects and institutions of life; indeed, Pierre Bourdieu's (above-voiced) concerns regarding television exist only because television has *access* to art, literature, science, philosophy, law, politics, and democracy, and because most of us experience such things through television. And as a cultural entity, television not only feeds our interactions at the level of its resources, depictions, and information: it is also the substance of many a fear (such as Bourdieu's), and many a dream.

My challenge in writing this book has therefore been to take such a massive entity and make it sensible. Given the powers that some ascribe to television ("television caused Columbine," "television won Bush the election," "television brightened her day," "television fried his brain," etc.), it would be morally and intellectually irresponsible of us not to spend considerable time, effort, and energy examining the intricacies of television. But it also makes it impossible for any one book – let alone any one library full of books – to interpret fully and decode television as object. Nevertheless, this book will cut one path through the terrain of television entertainment. Rather than see it as a "disembodied" force, I will examine the agents involved in its production and consumption – the artists, the network executives, the viewers, etc. – and will present numerous ways in which we can make television tangible, and hence responsive to our desires, fears, concerns, and hopes. I will interrogate Bourdieu's claims that television poses a *danger* to culture, at the same time as I examine what it *offers* culture and society. In doing so, I hope to introduce key methods and concepts for the scholarly analysis of television's place in society for readers relatively new to the area, and to offer new approaches to television entertainment for readers already involved in making sense of this ever-changing entity.

Television entertainment

First, though, we must nail down the item of study: television entertainment. Entertainment is a concept of great familiarity to anyone capable of smiling. While we may struggle to define it in the abstract, we know it when it happens. Nevertheless, the *Oxford English Dictionary* defines entertainment as "the action of providing or being provided with amusement or enjoyment," where enjoyment is further defined as "the state or process of taking pleasure in something." Dolf Zillmann and Jennings Bryant state that it is "any activity designed to delight and, to a smaller degree, enlighten through the exhibition of the fortunes or misfortunes of others, but also through the display of special skills by others and/or self" (1994: 448). To talk of television entertainment is therefore to talk of programs, segments, or channels that enjoy, amuse, delight, and perhaps even enlighten. Or, to be precise, it is to refer to television that *tries* to achieve such goals. Given the vast differences in individual notions of what actually is entertaining and what is not, by television entertainment, I mean programming designed with entertainment as the primary goal.

In this respect, we can make a crude division between programming whose primary aim is to entertain, to inform and educate, or to sell, which subsequently divides the television world into: (a) entertainment programming (b) news, documentaries, and educational programming and (c) advertisements. Of course, ads frequently hope to sell precisely by entertaining, and a rare few – such as public service announcements – sell by informing and educating. The news, meanwhile, is increasingly becoming entertainment driven, with stories on Paris Hilton's or Britney Spears' meltdowns trumping news of diplomatic missions and policy debates. Some of the best educational programming, too, from *Sesame Street* to *Blue Planet*, is wonderfully entertaining, and, as I will argue, entertainment often informs and educates. And at least in ad-driven models of television, *everything* sells at some level or other. These categories are not exclusive, therefore, but they allow us a starting point for examining television. What is odd, though, is how rarely entertainment is a distinct topic of discussion in the world of academic publishing and teaching. Practically any media program worth its salt has a class or more on advertising, and a class or more on journalism. Similarly, the media sections of good academic libraries are full of books on the news, and on advertising; and with most television pundits writing a book a year on their reflections on the news, Barnes and Noble, Waterstones, and Amazon are brimming with books on the state of journalism. Television entertainment, however, is frequently macro-ized or micro-ized: we either see it discussed in books or classes on television as a whole (in which, therefore, the news and ads must play a key role), or we see it discussed tangentially through a smaller case study of a particular program (*Buffy*, *Star Trek*, etc.), genre (reality television, science fiction, soaps, etc.), or audience (fans, teens, etc.). Exceptions exist, some of them excellent, and, of course, some case studies become powerful metonyms and microcosms of the complex whole (see, for instance, Murray and Ouellette 2004). So it is not as if television entertainment is underserved, but there is still the need for more "pan-entertainment" discussion, especially when journalism and advertising have such well-developed publication and teaching niches. Television entertainment is a relatively distinct category to viewers of television – as shown, for instance, by the news' poor ratings next to fictional programs – and it is far and away the most successful category, drawing more production dollars and more viewers more of the time . . . and yet it is underrepresented in scholarship and pedagogy.

To understand why, we should look further at the social connotations and construction of "entertainment." Beyond quoting the *OED* or Zillmann and Bryant, I find it remarkably hard to offer a value-neutral definition of entertainment, since it is one of the most automatically moralized concepts. Entertainment can be a compliment or a profanity, and it can represent transcendence or corruption, salvation or sin, depending upon the speaker. Thus, for instance, even the *OED*'s first example for the word entertainment – "everyone *just* sits in front of the television for entertainment" (emphasis added) – offers an implicit evaluation and criticism of entertainment and of the act of watching it.

Henri Lefebvre (1991) has noted that leisure as a concept is created by the capitalist division of time and space into work and leisure, and we might observe the same of entertainment. Under this rubric, work becomes what we must do, whereas leisure and entertainment are what we want to do. Even before paid labor, though, this division begins and is taught at school, where education, information, sitting in rows, and needing to ask permission to use the toilet often exist in stark contrast to the world of entertainment, holidays, "free" time, recess, and play. Thus, for many of us, entertainment becomes a mental zone distinct from information, education, and duty, a time and space away from the routine and strict order of the nine-to-five world. (We will return later to those who enjoy school, work, and education.)

This social construction of entertainment as distinct from information poses immediate problems for an examination of what entertainment is and how it works in society, for one's approach to the analysis of entertainment can often be determined by one's relative moral evaluation of the importance and nature of work and of leisure. To some, analysis of entertainment risks killing it by dragging it into the cold realm of work, as if a group of teachers showed up on their students' spring break. To others, entertainment is regarded as inherently and always good, based on a strong ethos of hedonistic love for all that is fun, and suspicion of all that is not. Or, reversing this ethos, others see entertainment as itself suspicious precisely because it falls outside the work world, and hence either distracts from or perverts the important work that must be done. Thus, entertainment risks being judged before any evidence can be supplied, and before any books can be written.

For instance, we often hear entertainment talked of in disparaging terms as perverting information. In this version of the story, information becomes the ugly yet noble son, and entertainment (or "infotainment") the handsome yet dangerous bastard brother (Edgar and Edmund from *King Lear*). Arguably the most famous telling of this story regarding television is Neil Postman's *Amusing Ourselves to Death* (1986). Asserting that "television speaks in only one persistent voice – the voice of entertainment" (80), Postman draws a parallel to Aldous Huxley's *Brave New World*, a futuristic novel in which the world's addiction to thrill-seeking drugs renders it helpless to autocratic control. Television is this drug to Postman, entertaining us away from enlightenment. Television, he argues, is the "command center of the new epistemology" (78) that "directs not only our knowledge of the world, but our knowledge of *ways of knowing* as well" (79), producing an attention deficit culture disinterested in complexity and/or nuance, ever enthralled by the latest snippet of news, but never truly processing it. As a world of entertainment, Postman's television aims for "applause, not reflection" (91), lives forever, drug addict-like, in the here and now, with neither access to nor true interest in the past (136), where "serious discourse dissolves into giggles" (156), television-izing a populace into only "knowing *of* lots of things, [but] not knowing but *about* them" (70). He is clear in stating not that entertainment per se is the problem, but rather that in the world of television, everything is presented as only entertainment (87).

Postman is by no means alone in worrying deeply about entertainment's marriage with television. If book sales are anything to go by, the more than 200,000 copies sold of *Amusing Ourselves to Death* (cited in van Zoonen 2005: 2) speaks volumes. Meanwhile, particularly when it comes to lamenting the incursion of entertainment into politics, news, and information, it has become common to look at entertainment as somewhat of a scourge through modern life (see Anderson 2004, Gabler 2000, Meyer 2002, Winn 1985), a "cultural Ebola virus" as Neal Gabler calls it (2000: 6). Oddly, then, while there are too few dedicated books or classes on entertainment, books on journalism and politics frequently discuss entertainment tangentially, setting it up as that which is not journalism and politics. Particularly in the US, a nation still at times somewhat beholden to its Calvinist roots and inherent distrust of that which pleases (whether it be dancing, drinking, poetry, or sex), television entertainment has become a prime topic of suspicion. Just ask someone how much time a day they spend watching television entertainment. In all likelihood, they will either brag of their abstinence, rather shamefully admit the figure, or lie to you with a gross underestimation to save face. Television entertainment is a cause for guilt or shame, so it seems, as if many of us suspect our own desires and pleasures to be the flesh-eating disease that some make them out to be.

What goes hand in hand with this is that it is perfectly acceptable, even expected, to discuss television as "crap." Mark Crispin Miller, himself no great fan, writes that "Everybody knows that TV is mostly false and stupid, that nobody pays that much attention to it – and yet it's on for over seven hours a day in the average household, and it sells innumerable products. In other words, TV manages to do its job even as it only yammers in the background, despised by those who keep it going" (1986: 228). And returning to the image of narcosis, he adds that television is "like a drug whose high is only the conviction that its user is too cool to be addicted" (1986: 228). Over time, television has taken on the moniker of "plug-in drug" (see Mittell 2000), leading to parents' groups and other activists calling for national no-television days, and to the popular concern for "couch potatoes" and "child zombies" unable to pull their eyes and bodies from the all-consuming power of the screen.

Summarizing, entertainment's critics launch three major attacks. First, we see great fear of the incredible powers of television entertainment. Entertainment is posited either as a great ill in and of itself, as capable of masking comparably great ills, or as so completely devoid of content, meaning, and/or value that our culture's love affair with it is seen as the ultimate waste of time and human potential. Second, entertainment is placed in stark and clear opposition to information and education. When writers talk of entertainment "creeping" into information, they employ the imagery of invasion, rival armies, and unlawful occupation. Finally, particularly when metaphors of narcosis are used, entertainment's viewers or "users" are frequently seen as unreliable around such a stimulus, and as slaves to their/our addiction, hence meaning that entertainment plus humans equals a troublesome combination. Witness, for instance, Miller's suggestion that even those who criticize television can't control their passion for it.

In defense of television entertainment, it has become par for the course to admonish critics with the reminder that it's "just entertainment" or "only entertainment." In his book, *Only Entertainment*, Richard Dyer points out that "'Entertainment,' especially preceded by 'just,' is often used as a term to deny or discount something's aesthetic or ideological qualities" (1992: 3), as if the word itself will deflect attention, and as if being meaningful, important, political, and/or artistic stands to jeopardize the whole experience of consuming entertainment media. This is an odd retort, in that it effectively argues for entertainment's banality. It's just fluff (or *should* be fluff), so goes the argument, and television analysts appear no more wise than if they were to criticize cotton wool. The "defense," therefore, proves somewhat similar to the attack, in that entertainment is still seen as banal, and clearly neither informational nor educational. As a defense, then, it is wholly unsuccessful at explaining *why* entertainment is so popular, and so heavily consumed. If anything, by putting its fingers in its ears and refusing to engage with the terms of the debate, this defense only yields the floor to the critics of entertainment.

Taken together, the attack on and the "just entertainment" defense of entertainment work to quash a significant amount of entertainment analysis. Take, for instance, this one-star review of Kevin Glynn's book *Tabloid Culture* (2000), written by "John Q. Public" on Amazon:

> To treat Tabloid TV seriously is like trying to treat Daytime TV as a serious art form. There is no special reason why Tabloid TV has become big business, the Television networks as a whole always wanted ratings [sic] . . . Tabloid news only came about because people liked to read tabloid papers, and with Cable TV taking over like it did, Media excutives [sic] decided to do more yellow journalism shows and put them on cable as fast as they could. Network TV was never all that great to start with. It was called a vast wasteland when it started and it still is. It's sad, ad [sic] it is repulsive, to ignore it is the only sane thing to do.

At no point does the reviewer exhibit any evidence of having read Glynn's thoughtful and interesting examination of the power play in "trash" television; rather, he advocates that we should "ignore it" – both the entertainment and the analysis. But Glynn is by no means alone in receiving such reaction. Not only did John Q. Public have over 200 similar reviews of various films, television shows, and books on Amazon,[1] but as his conveniently everyman nom de plum suggests, his is a common reaction. Anyone reading this present book has no doubt heard many versions of this response, starting with the long line of John Q. Publics who tend to question television and media studies students and researchers about why we would even bother to study television in the first place.

However, his review also renders obvious the *need* for analysis, as he proves unable to account for *why* entertainment has worked as a business or a pastime. His own answer? "There is no special reason." This is inadequate. Saying the Second World War began "for no special reason," or that AIDS is spreading as it is "for no special reason" constitutes nothing close to knowledge: it is the failure of knowledge. And so too with many of the broadside attacks on entertainment. Short of accepting Miller's implicit reasoning that audiences just don't know any better – a patronizingly elitist and similarly unsatisfactory response – we are left without an explanation for *why* entertainment attracts so many of us. What special powers does it have? How does it generate these powers? *Who* generates these powers? How do these powers work? All of these are vital questions for understanding not just television, but society. I return to Roger Silverstone, who notes that:

> We take television for granted in a way similar to how we take everyday life for granted. We want more of it (some of us); we complain about it (but we watch it anyway); but we don't understand very well (nor do we feel the need to understand) how it works, either mechanically or ideologically. Our experience of television is of a piece with our experience of the world: we do not expect it to be, nor can we imagine it to be, significantly otherwise.
>
> (1994: 3)

But it is precisely because of television's, and particularly television entertainment's, relationship to our experience of the world that we must study it, and that we must seek out "special reasons." As Ien Ang observes, "Contrary to other social institutions such as the school or family, television . . . does not have the means to coerce people into becoming members of its audience" (1991: 17–18), and if we return to it, we do so willingly. Why? Television entertainment can inspire us, console us, make us laugh, change us, inform us, include us, empower us, touch us, surprise and shock us, and it can call for action, politicization, and passion. With perhaps the lone exception of our closest loved ones, very few other stimuli are as powerful.

But at the same time, television entertainment can disappoint, disempower, disgust, exclude, and depress us, and it can trigger passivity, apathy, and brainrot. For this reason, the hedonist response to entertainment – that "it's all just great" – is equally inadequate. While one group of viewers are laughing at television comedy, for instance, they may be laughing *at* another group of now alienated viewers, as is the case with racist or sexist television. While one program can cause a viewer to question a corrupt power bloc, another may assure a different viewer's complacence and support. And while one show inspires and uplifts one viewer, another meets a John Q. Public. Postman's distrust in entertainment's ability to work alongside education is too absolute, ironically so for a writer who is praised by cover endorsements for *Amusing Ourselves to Death* as "very funny" and possessing "the wit of a raconteur." But his concerns regarding the marriage of show business with information should not be excused so quickly. John Caldwell rightfully accuses television of too often being an agent of "containment and recuperation" (1995: 335). The wealth of television studies reveals many of the medium's festering sores. Thus, it is just as important to look at why and how television entertainment fails us, how it works against us, and how it falls depressingly short of its potential sadly far too often. It is these failures that have led some to write it off, and to go searching for enlightenment in journalism, or off the medium altogether. But like Lisa Parks, I believe television is too important to ignore: "Simply put, we can't afford to kill our televisions. Instead, we need to turn them on, engage with their blue flicker, and talk more about what we want to see. In other words, we need to care enough about television to fight over it" (2004: 152–3). Or, as the Goldsmiths Media Group offer, "Contemporary, highly dispersed societies need not just (factual) news but (fictional) 'images . . . of what living is now like' (Williams 1975: 9). Entertainment media, as well as news media, are therefore essential to a democratically adequate public sphere" (2000: 45). Television entertainment's moments of success and of failure are too numerous to catalogue, but I will nevertheless attempt in this book to offer six key lenses through which we can examine and evaluate television entertainment, as a collection of aesthetic texts, industrial products, and sociological entities.

Whose television?

First, though, if entertainment proves a difficult concept, television is no less confusing an object. As John Hartley states, to a certain degree, "there is no such thing as 'television' – an abstract, general form with invariable features. Neither does television have any *essential* mode of production, distribution and consumption" (1987: 122). Or, updating Raymond Williams' classic description of American television programming as "flow" – a concept to which we will return in Chapter 3 – Jeffrey Sconce offers his own aquatic metaphor, arguing that it is now more like a "fog – dense, shifting, obscuring, and depthless" (2004a: 258). Part of the problem of definition lies in the trends towards narrowcasting, niche marketing, and both channel and medium multiplication. Television began as a broadcast medium, and most countries had only two or three channels well into the 1970s. Thus, for instance, according to the Nielsen ratings, at its height in 1953, *I Love Lucy* commanded the attention of 21.5 million television households (67 per cent of the approximately 32 million in the nation), whereas, by comparison, though the American population had since grown by almost 140 million people, in 2007 only *American Idol* mustered more viewers, and even *American Idol* could manage no more than 30 per cent of the viewing audience. As John Ellis dubs it, many of us are now in an era of television plenty, having long since left the era of scarcity, and having recently graduated from the era of availability (2000: 39). If I turn on my television right now, I have access to approximately 120 channels. With satellite or expanded cable, I could easily top 300. Add my DVD and VHS collections, YouTube and other online content providers, and a DVR hard drive, and TV grows yet more. Hence, whereas forty years ago, you and I would likely be watching many of the same programs, now we can easily avoid any replication.

Even beyond content, however, we all have different experiences of watching. Some viewers carefully consult *TV Guide*, *Radio Times*, or their cable television guide channel, planning what to watch. Some have television on all the time, an ever-present background (see Lull 1990). Some graze and channel-surf. Some have favorite programs. Some must fight with siblings or roommates to gain control of the remote. Some have their options limited by parents and V-chips. Some watch alone. And some watch in groups, at specialized viewing parties, or in pubs or bars. Or, more to the point, most of us move across most of these viewing positions, an engrossed fan one day, a casual viewer the next. Add the ever-growing assortment of technological paraphernalia that surround television, and the tale gets yet more complex: some viewers are limited to one or two channels; others' cable boxes or satellite dishes give them hundreds; some watch online, downloading from network sites, iTunes, BitTorrent, or a mushrooming assortment of other legal or illegal venues; some rent, buy, or borrow DVDs and watch an entire season at one sitting; some skip the ads with VCRs or TiVo; some watch clips and specialized content on their cellular phones, iPods, or PSPs; some even forego the visuals and watch vicariously through reading recaps online or in magazines, or "spoilers" that reveal plot twists before they happen. Similarly, some watch on tiny black and white screens, while others have their television projected onto massive screens in purpose-built home entertainment centers (see Klinger 2006); some hook their television up to a surround sound system, others stick to mono, and some watch without sound, relying on close captioning. The variations seem limitless, and with each passing year, new options are added to the mix, allowing each viewer to have a different "television" from the next.

Variations in world television systems and content make for vast differences too. Some nations offer public broadcasting services devoid of ad breaks, and such systems also tend to allow shorter runs and more one-off programs; other countries rely on ads for their bread and butter, and so saturate viewers with ads every ten or fifteen minutes, and product placement inbetween the gaps. Differences in global television regulation also produce huge viewing differences, as, for instance, content is more closely policed or scrutinized in some countries, either due to political censorship (as in China), stringent ad regulation (as in the Nordic countries), or dictates on how much children's programming is required. A viewer in England can see full-frontal nudity on television, whereas Janet Jackson's millisecond breast exposure during the 2004 Superbowl resulted in one of the United States' largest media panics in recent history. And cultural flows between countries are by no means equal (see Miller *et al.* 2005, Thussu 2006, 2007), meaning that American television tends to be globally accessible (albeit frequently at a time delay), and that Brazilian, Mexican, Japanese, Korean, Indian, English, French, and German television, for instance, enjoy regional and satellite circulation, whereas most countries' local production stays within their borders.

With so many versions of television, we must never assume that one person's or nation's experience can be generalized. This, of course, presents a problem for a book on television entertainment. I will face this problem by presenting various experiences of television, and by encouraging my reader, here at the outset, never to lose sight of all the variables at play. However, I will focus on contemporary television, not on its history (for excellent studies of this history, see Gomery 2007, Hilmes 2004, Mittell 2004a, Murray 2005, Spigel 1992). I will also focus largely on American primetime programming. I do so not only because the American model of television itself is rapidly becoming the world's more common model (see Miller *et al.* 2005) – hence allowing me to make comments on the system behind such programs that will, it is hoped, have resonance outside America's borders – but also precisely because American primetime shows are available internationally as are few others. I want the case studies and examples discussed in these pages to be accessible, so that local variables can be discussed and debated, and so that the reader is not left in the passive (and *boring*) position of trusting that my descriptions are wholly accurate. To do so necessitates using globally accessible programs, which means skewing towards the big-budget realm of primetime television, and it means skewing American. From *Baywatch* to *The Simpsons*, *Friends* to *CSI*, *Sex and the City* to *24*, much US televisual programming is well-known worldwide. Let me apologize for therefore underplaying some of the world's better programs originating outside US, but I hope the structures of analysis offered will be just as applicable to non-American fare as to the programs discussed here.

Finally, in setting up whose television I am discussing, I should offer a brief note on the author. As Cornel Sandvoss argues, contrary to some critics' contention that it is only fans who should "own up" to their passions when writing on them, we are *all* involved in television: "we can never step outside the system and look on it from above" (2005a: 5). Even those rare few who watch no television have their lives jostled by television's continuing discourse on an almost daily basis. Television exists at a level beyond its programs, production, technologies of consumption, and national systems: it is pervasive. As numerous writers have observed, television happens all over the place, in conversations, arguments, everyday decisions, and so forth (see Bird 2003, Radway 1988, Silverstone 1994, 1999). We all live in a heavily televized, television-ized culture, and there is no escape. So none of us can examine it from a lofty and removed point, which in turn requires me to situate myself. I am Canadian and British by nationality, but grew up in five countries, often with global (particularly American) mediated entertainment as some of the first real ties between myself and the schoolmates of my newly adopted country. As such, television entertainment has long been a language for me, not only a *way* of communicating, but an entity that *allows* communication. And I come from a family in which television was no enemy: I grew up with *Sesame Street*, *The Muppet Show*, *Knight Rider*, *LA Law*, *The Cosby Show*, *The Simpsons*, and so forth. It would be disingenuous for me to pretend I am not involved in television entertainment at a deep level. While John Caughie notes that "Whereas film theory is marked by a sense of people trying to come to terms with their own, almost perverse, fascination . . . television theory always seems to be written by people who see the seduction but are not seduced" (1990: 54), I am part of a "seduced" generation. I do not have the luxury of being able to make disparaging comments about the television audience, since I am part of it. At the same time, though, I am often deeply disappointed and dismayed by what I see on television, and am by no means an unquestioning supporter. I enjoy television entertainment, and think some of it is brilliant, but I am simultaneously amazed by the capacity for many programs to let society (and me) down. Thus, I approach the topic from this conflicted standpoint, as one who watches most of the programs I discuss here, some with pride, some with guilt, some closer than others, but also as one who wants to push the medium to make more of itself, and to live up to its democratic and aesthetic potential.

I was also one of those strange kids who loved school, and am now one of those odd sorts who loves his job. Thus, where above I noted that the entertainment–information distinction springs from an age-old leisure–work binary, in focusing on entertainment here, I encourage my readers to resist the binary themselves. It is beyond the scope of this book to mount a complete defense of entertainment in ads and/or news and educational programming, but whenever entertainment is found on television, whether in fiction, reality programming, the news, an ad, or educational programming, much of my ensuing discussion here can be applied to illuminate what precisely it is doing, other than "just" entertaining. Too often, scholars and pundits have discussed television entertainment simply as *not* television news, constructing along the way an epic battle between information and entertainment, "need" and "want," civic duty and selfish desires, importance and frivolity, wherein entertainment perennially plays the role of bad guy. However, in this book I aim to move beyond a crude caricature of entertainment, and I pose that by studying how television entertainment works within the sphere proper of television entertainment (i.e. not in the realm of news, documentary, or advertising), not only can we improve our understanding of a medium that captivates millions daily, commanding more time from more people than almost any other cultural practice, but we might also develop a better understanding of how entertainment works in a myriad of complex ways in the fields of news, documentary, and advertising.

Chapter summary

Introductory media textbooks are often divided into sections on the media studies' holy trinity of texts (by which is meant programs/shows), industry (production), and audiences (viewers). However, in writing this book, I have instead opted to arrange the chapters thematically. Ultimately, I imagine that most readers seek to understand not the text, industry, or audiences per se, but rather how each of these agents *interact* to construct television as a central institution in contemporary society. Thus, my method of dividing up the material aims to center discussion on the products of interaction and on key powers of television entertainment.

Chapter 1 examines television entertainment's conflicted nature as simultaneously one of modern day's most prominent and loved sources of narrative, art, and creative display, while also frequently being produced as a business intended to attract viewers to advertisements. Television entertainment is therefore an art and an industry, and its producers work towards both innovation and imitation, inspiration to think and inspiration to buy. This duality of purpose has also been responsible for television studies' interdisciplinary nature, since as art, television entertainment requires us to study it with a humanistic toolbox as we might literature, classic film, or sculpture, yet as an industry, television entertainment requires that we also examine the sociology and political economy of its production. Chapter 1 thus raises questions of how and why television entertainment is made, and of how and why it becomes a vehicle for ideas and a vehicle for ads, and in doing so, the chapter inquires into the nature of creativity, innovation, and television's visual aesthetics.

Whether art or industry, though, television entertainment is only as successful as its viewers allow it to be, and so Chapter 2 turns to an examination of affect for and of viewers' emotional relationships to television entertainment. Loving, hating, ignoring, or casually watching television shows are such mundane, everyday acts that we might be led to underestimate the wealth of issues and processes at work in such acts. But it is only through our emotional responses and our varied and varying responses to television entertainment that we can make sense of it. Chapter 2 examines affect and impression as both emotion and as cognitive and rational engagements with programs' meanings, and it studies the often-noted "escapive" quality of television entertainment's fantasies, fictions, and narratives as something that invites and encourages interaction with the world around us. In short, I argue that loving, liking, hating, or disliking television is never just about the show and/or about an engagement with fiction – such responses are intimately about, *and hence can be read to make sense of*, our identity as individuals and communities, and our engagement with the very real here and now.

If Chapter 2 examines how television is about much more than what is in the box, Chapter 3 examines how television's box has expanded. One can now encounter "television" online, on cell phones, on iPods, in movies, on the radio, in posters, in newspaper and magazine articles, in the clothes we wear and the products we consume, in games, and in multiple other venues. Television has also expanded across the globe, not only through the proliferation of sites of production and reception, but also as certain shows reach more nations than did even the European colonial empires. The sun never sets on *The Simpsons*, *Friends*, and *CSI*. Chapter 3 thus charts television's multiple expansions, across lived space, through all manner of media and technologies, and hence throughout our everyday lives. "Watching television" can and does happen almost anywhere, and Chapter 3 examines processes behind this expansion, including the business rationale of embracing such synergy, and the experiences that are thereby created through television "overflow" for audiences, citizens, and consumers.

However, at a time when one can seemingly set foot in the worlds of television entertainment, many critics worry about the degree to which we may be allowing television to create reality. Chapter 4 therefore examines television's constructions and representations of reality, paying special attention to how television represents minorities and minority experiences. The chapter aims to avoid the trap of seeing fiction as patently unreal and untruthful, though, and thus the chapter examines not only how television entertainment augments or bastardizes reality, but also how it can powerfully show us images of reality (or realities), even when fictional or comically exaggerated by nature. Furthermore, the chapter asks questions of whose realities and experiences dictate television and why, and it offers means by which we might be able to evaluate representations and depictions. Much more than a seeing device, television is a mode of transportation, taking us places and bringing places and people to us, and Chapter 4 examines how, and how well or not, this transportation occurs.

As a primary means by which we experience the world around us, television entertainment also holds considerable power and potential to politicize or depoliticize us. What we know of the world, what we feel needs changing or saving, and how we think our various communities should operate are all informed by television, and all determine our political beliefs, values, and convictions. Chapter 5 turns, then, to television entertainment as a political entity, studying both the nature of television entertainment's politics and their determining factors, and ways in which television entertainment can involve us in politics. Television's audiences are often imagined as *consumers*, but we are first and foremost *citizens*, as consumption is only one practice within the broader set of responsibilities that amount to citizenship. Chapter 5 thus discusses television entertainment's address to citizens, arguing that the news and political documentaries alone do not manage our involvement in democratic society. I examine how from reality shows to news satire, television entertainment plugs us into the political world around us.

Finally, Chapter 6 examines televisual power. Each prior chapter focuses on some of television entertainment's key powers – as art and as industry in Chapter 1, as item of affection, suspicion, or dislike in Chapter 2, as expansive entity in Chapter 3, as a painter of reality and fiction in Chapter 4, and as that which connects us to politics and makes politics meaningful or that fails to do so in Chapter 5. But Chapter 6 returns to some of these issues while asking more of how television entertainment gives power, takes it, and channels it. The chapter first braces the issue of television entertainment's normalization and abnormalization of behavior, values, people, and ideas, and later discusses how television can also challenge prevalent scripts of normality, posing new ways of being. Chapter 6 also inquires into the various powers that we as viewers have over television, beyond merely changing the channel, turning the television off, or, as some activists encourage us to do, "killing" our televisions. Television's sheer power and seeming centrality to much of contemporary society can at times convince us that we have *no* power over it, and that it is just there, like it or not. However, Chapter 6 charts various ways in which the industry regularly grabs and hordes power over television, but it also examines ways in which we as viewers do, or at least should, have power over television entertainment, from practices of viewing, to regulation and influence over the regulatory bodies that set the very parameters and framework within which television must operate. In ending on such a note, I hope that readers will leave my book as they might a particularly good television show, for while I am at a disadvantage in being unable to offer explosions, star power, CGI, or "to be continued" cliffhangers, I too hope to leave readers informed, interested, and able to reflect further upon or to use that which has been discussed.

Chapter 1

Art with strings attached: creativity, innovation, and industry

However dirty, compromised, or implicated in operations of power, television is an art . . . the world's most vast, varied, and influential narrative medium.

Jeffrey Sconce (2004b: 111)

Although [American TV] executives may not be allergic to what they deem quality, the networks as a whole aim to create not purposeful or coherent or true or beautiful shows, but audiences. Any other purpose is subordinated to the larger design of keeping a sufficient number of people tuned in.

Todd Gitlin (1994: 56)

Art or industry? Or, how do we study television?

Libraries close, theatres go dark, and webmasters must sleep, but most television channels just keep going. Older viewers remember an earlier age when television stations ended their broadcast day with the national anthem, and some countries such as Iceland used to maintain a television-free day of the week, but increasingly nowadays, television just keeps going. This places the average television channel in the odd position in media history of having to fill every waking and sleeping hour with content. Thus, television experiences an almost unrivalled amount of pressure to be creative. Meanwhile, exacerbating this pressure for many producers is the need to sell. Public broadcasters, such as the British Broadcasting Corporation (BBC) or the American Public Broadcasting Service (PBS), in theory have the luxury of concentrating on what is *best* for their audiences, but commercial broadcasters must always be adding to their audience, scrambling to gain evermore viewers.[1] In many corners of the world, and with the likes of News Corporation, Time-Warner, Disney, etc., buying up great swathes of the world's television channels, cable providers, and production houses (see Chapters 3 and 6), television is one of the world's most successful and fastest-growing businesses, thereby requiring content production to keep pace.

These pressures often create a paradoxical situation for the medium. Television is our world's premier storyteller and artistic creator, as Jeffrey Sconce suggests . . . at the same time as it is frequently a capitalist enterprise. Such is the nature of television's hold over viewers that many readers of the previous sentence may not see the inherent paradox, but for anything to be positioned simultaneously as an art and an industry bucks a centuries-old trend of defining art as precisely not industrial.

Art has traditionally been held to be made of greater stuff than money, fashioned of a nobler, even more *divine*, membrane than is the humdrum, cold exploit of making a buck. A parade of Western intellectuals have looked to art as a balm to cure the soul from the quotidian worries and annoyances frequently created by the world of industry. Admittedly, definitions of art run the gamut from the pragmatic to the sublime. On one hand is Howard Becker's (1984) suggestion that art is whatever the art world says it is. On the other hand is Percy Bysshe Shelley's declaration that poetry/art "awakens and enlarges the mind itself by rendering it the receptacle of a thousand unapprehended combinations of thought," and "enlarges the circumference of the imagination by replenishing it with thoughts of ever new delight" (1991[1821]: 317). But the pragmatists have only recently had their day, as throughout much of Western intellectual history, art has been seen as the result of a divine connection between God, nature, or muse and the individual, becoming a sort of middle kingdom between humankind and enlightenment. Many have defined art with another slippery term, as being "beautiful," whereby beauty can be understood as inspirational and uplifting. And as supposedly above and beyond everyday life, art has been envisioned as a reflective zone, and works of art as those that carve out this space for us, wherein we can step back and analyze the world as it is and as it could or should be. One of the more lasting beliefs of art, echoing Shelley's, is that it "defamiliarizes," in Viktor Shklovsky's terms (1988[1917]). Creation requires novelty – something which was not there before and is thus created – and many have seen art's powers of defamiliarization as creating new ways of seeing and thinking. Many regard art in hopeful, even utopian terms, seeing it as a sign of cosmological order and design, offering evidence that something more important, vital, and meaningful exists beyond the everyday, and given art's longstanding assumed relationship to Heaven, godliness, and enlightenment, the belief in art as sublime is as tenacious as the belief in the glorious afterlife.

Thus, if we were to approach television entertainment as a creative art, we might draw inspiration from Jurij Lotman's comments on the nature of the literary text. Lotman proposes that art uses language (and, in the case of television, let us add image and sound) in a unique, impressionist manner that plays directly on the reader's or viewer's feelings, working in a way that no straightforward exposition ever could. Poetic speech, he argues, "allows us to transmit a volume of information too great to be transmitted by an elementary, strictly linguistic structure. It follows that the information (content) given can neither exist nor be transmitted outside this artistic structure" (1977: 10), existing instead as a special entity and a uniquely enriched form of communication. Lotman further quotes famous Russian novelist Leo Tolstoy, who remarked of his *Anna Karenina* that, "If I were to say in words all that I intended to express by way of the novel, then I would have to write a novel identical to the one I first wrote" (1977: 11). Art, Tolstoy and Lotman intimate, is its own language and mode of communication, full of messages for the taking, yet composed with such precision that those messages transcend mere summary: they are given life and energy by their manner of rendering. As I will discuss in Chapter 2, art works on and speaks to the emotions in ways that hint at transcendence and/or the sublime. Hence, to study television entertainment wholly as art would be to delve into questions of how images, performances, and scripts help and/or inspire us to consider the human experience. What might *The Young and the Restless* or *The Sopranos* tell us about life? How does *Lost* allow us to better understand the struggle of science and faith? How is *The Simpsons'* structure able to comment on the nature of consumerism?

However, a classic account of television, based on numerous interviews with its creators and executives, Todd Gitlin's *Inside Prime Time* (1994) attempts to debunk the idea that innovation or artistry are at the core of television. Instead, Gitlin opens on the note that "innovation is still rare as the networks and their spinoffs and successors relentlessly go on straining after that American icon, Fun," leaving "virtually no place in American television, commercial or public, for a serious writer or director to make a career" (1994: xi). Gitlin concludes that creativity and aesthetics are clearly lacking, as instead television is an industry first, foremost, and often only. Television, he states, represents "the Triumph of the Synthetic" (63). Here, he echoes one of the more famous critiques of modern media as industry, lodged by Max Horkheimer and Theodor Adorno (1972[1944]). Looking at the film and popular music industries of the 1930s and 1940s, Horkheimer and Adorno noted an apparent inability to create new and more challenging modes of thinking. They argued that with such industries we were witnessing a shift from art as innovative, challenging, and new to an industry of mindless repetition. They saw the industrialization of art as the de facto replacement of the work of art by formula, arguing that, "there is the agreement – or at least the determination – of all executive authorities not to produce or sanction anything that in any way differs from their own rules, their own ideas about consumers, or above all themselves" (1972[1944]: 122). Industrial production of culture now followed the wholly familiar, amounting not to art and style, but to the "negation of style" (129). To follow Gitlin, Horkheimer, and Adorno with regards culture industries such as television, the medium has no higher purpose, little artistic expression, and hence provides nothing worth studying *as* artistic expression. Instead, then, our task as media analysts would be to chart the industry's *perversion* of art, and its business aims and practices as constituting a wing of the advertising industry that funds commercial television.

Ultimately, though, as this chapter will argue, neither an artistic nor an industrial perspective is wholly satisfying. Television is not just art, and to ignore its industrial imperatives and the multiple effects of these on the nature of television would be romantic but irresponsible. However, an industrial account provides little explanation as to why we as viewers spend so much time in front of television, unhelpfully implying merely that we are all somewhat mindlessly devoted to repetition, formula, and always more of the same. Clearly, we cannot dismiss Gitlin's painstaking empirical work offhand, but equally clearly, more of the picture exists to be studied. Therefore, this chapter will examine the dialectic – the back and forth – between art and industry, innovation and imitation, originality and repetition, that characterizes television. It will interrogate Gitlin's suggestion, from the quotation that opens this chapter, that industry necessarily *subordinates* art, as I examine television entertainment's capacity to work as an artistic and creative entity. First, I will offer a brief overview of the creative/industrial process of making television, discussing how the television business works. Then I will examine the dance between art and industry that takes place in this system, before, at chapter's end, offering some contextualizing comments on reruns, repetition, and familiarity, lest the chapter fetishize originality and innovation as the only forces of value in cultural production and consumption.

The television industry: who does what?

Television shows are surrounded by various discourses of authorship and creation: on one hand, the list of household name showrunners seems to be growing yearly (Joss Whedon, Matt Groening, J. J. Abrams, David Chase, Aaron Sorkin, Shonda Rhimes, David E. Kelley, Dick Wolf, John Wells, Amy Sherman-Palladino, Rob Thomas, etc.), and on the other hand, viewers are quick to invoke and to blame the specter of the anonymous "producer," "writer," or even "network" when they dislike what is before them. Thus, at times the process sounds intensely human and aesthetic, while at other times it sounds wholly robotic. Precisely *how*, then, is television created, and by whom? Before we can assess the system's capacity for creativity and artistry, we first need to know that system. For illustrative purposes, I will focus first on the American commercial television system, before later in the chapter examining how public broadcasting as model (whether BBC or other) limits or encourages creativity.

The industry can be divided into its three main components: production, distribution, and exhibition/transmission. Beginning with production, a preponderance of primetime programming is produced by one of the five major production houses/studios (see Table 1.1), with Viacom's DreamWorks increasingly active in television production too (having made shows such as *Band of Brothers*, *Spin City*, *Rescue Me*, and *The Contender*). Production is not so simple, though, for behind each program are often numerous production companies. Hence, for instance, Fox Television Studios produces *24* alongside Ron Howard and Brian Grazer's Imagine Entertainment, and *The Simpsons* alongside James L. Brooks' Gracie Films. A production company may be as grand as an entire studio, or as rudimentary as a business name for a single individual, whose involvement with production may range from creating the initial concept, to lending executive help and weight to a project, to keeping an active show running. Most shows, though, require the full force of a studio behind them. Television is an expensive business, requiring poten-tially millions of dollars worth of equipment that only a few studios can afford, and hence, by the end of 2005, production of primetime scripted series for American network television by unaligned, independent producers was simply unviable (Lotz 2007b: 95).

Because of the huge capital investment required to film a television show, however, production rarely if ever begins until a distribution arrangement has been found. As such, while ideas and creativity usually begin at the level of production, distributors make a project real. Distributors take on the task of finding a show a potential audience, both securing a transmission deal and advertising it. Options for distribution in the US include the networks (ABC, CBS, CW, FOX, NBC, or the Spanish-language Univision), a cable station (such as Comedy Central, F/X, Lifetime, or USA), a Pay TV channel such as HBO or Showtime, first-run syndica-tion, and off-network syndication. A network deal guarantees that the network will distribute the show to all its affiliate stations, who agree (with a few restrictions and escape clauses) to play the program at a set time each week, as, for instance,

Table 1.1 Television production and ownership

Corporate parent	Studio	Shows include
News Corp	Fox	*The Simpsons, 24, My Name is Earl, Judging Amy, Buffy the Vampire Slayer, Malcolm in the Middle, Prison Break*
Disney	Touchstone	*Lost, Scrubs, Grey's Anatomy, Desperate Housewives, Criminal Minds* (co-production with CBS Paramount), *The Amazing Race* (co-production with CBS Paramount)
General Electric	NBC Universal	*Law & Order, Crossing Jordan, Battlestar Galactica, House, Heroes, Friday Night Lights, Monk* (co-production with Touchstone)
CBS	CBS Paramount	*Charmed, 7th Heaven, Entertainment Tonight, Frasier, CSI, The 4400, Everybody Hates Chris, Numb3rs*
Time Warner	Warner Bros.	*ER, West Wing, Gilmore Girls, The OC, Smallville, Nip/Tuck, Veronica Mars, The Bachelor, Without a Trace*

when the Warner Bros.-produced *ER* is distributed by the NBC network to NBC affiliates such as WPSD in Paducah, Kentucky, or WNBC in New York. A deal with a cable or pay TV station ensures that they will play the show at a set time or times each week, as, for instance, when the Warner Bros.-produced *Nip/Tuck* is distributed by the cable channel F/X and transmitted through a cable or satellite package by the likes of Comcast or DirecTV.[2] "First-run" syndication refers to when *new* episodes are sold directly to affiliates (hence bypassing the network), and though license fees from networks are substantially higher, several shows in TV history have fared very well in first-run syndication, including *Baywatch* and *The Muppet Show*, daytime talk shows (*The Oprah Winfrey Show*, *The Ellen Degeneres Show*), and most entertainment news programs and game shows playing in the 7–8 p.m. slot, such as *Entertainment Tonight*, *Extra*, *Wheel of Fortune*, and *Jeopardy*. "Off-network" syndication – commonly known as "reruns" – refers to the sale of previously aired programs directly to cable, satellite, or broadcast stations, including affiliates (importantly, a network's contract for transmission is only for one to three broadcasts, and rerun deals are nearly always handled separately).

In broadcast television, the distributor pays license fees to the producer, and in turn the network and/or transmitter makes money by selling ad slots. In each television market/city, television stations may seek affiliation with a network or else run independently. Those that run independently must commission or produce their own programming, or else buy programs on the syndication market. By contrast, affiliation with a network guarantees a station anywhere from two (8–10 p.m.) to twelve (8–11 p.m., national news, morning show(s), late night, soaps, and/or special events) hours a day of programming distributed directly from the network. In any market, only one station can serve as an affiliate, and since the networks still garner the largest audiences and distribute many of the most popular programs, advertising rates are highest on-network. The AC Nielsen company then measures viewing by a combination of: (a) set-top boxes in a small sample of American homes, used predominantly for national viewing figures and ad sales, though also and increasingly in some larger markets for local viewing figures and ad sales; and (b) viewing diaries circulated during the "sweeps weeks" in November, February, May, and July, used for local viewing figures and ad sales. These figures allow advertisers to "purchase" the viewers they want – some opting for the maximum number of eyeballs, regardless of demographics, many aiming for specific audiences, such as the much-desired young highly educated male.[3] During a standard half-hour of television, eight minutes are withheld for advertising, about six of which are the networks' for selling national ads, and about two of which each affiliate sells locally. By contrast, commercial cable and satellite television channels receive anywhere from 5 cents to $2 per subscriber from the cable or satellite provider, although the cable/satellite providers also frequently receive a small portion of ad space in the deal.[4] Pay TV channels (such as HBO, Showtime, and Cinemax) offer no ads, earning the bulk of their money instead by splitting per-channel subscription fees with cable/satellite providers.

With ad dollars flowing fast and furious for most distributors and transmitters, distributors and transmitters frequently garner the largest profits. Hence, for instance, at FOX's 2006 "upfront" (pre-season) sales of ad space, the network notched approximately $1.8 billion, while new kid on the block, CW, earned $650 million (Consoli 2006b). In total, ABC, CBS, FOX, and NBC were projected to earn $17.1 billion in ad sales for 2007 (Consoli 2007). By contrast, producers must frequently rely on "deficit financing." While some producers manage to "barter" for ad space (being paid in ad space instead of money), and while particularly reality television producers have found new revenue sources from lucrative product placement deals, most television entertainment is licensed to primary distributors for no or negative profit. Lotz (2007b: 84) estimates that prior to syndication, an average primetime network drama will lose between $4.4 million and $8.8 million per season. Rather, then, television's cash cow for producers is often the off-network syndication/rerun markets in the US and abroad. Once production has wrapped, and hence costs are already invested, and *if* the show continues to play on television stations worldwide, the producers then reap the rewards. Since syndication works on a station-by-station basis (i.e.: every station in the US – and the world – that plays a rerun must negotiate separately with the producers), it is reruns that make producers and royalty-owning cast members rich. For instance, Lotz (2007b: 85) notes that by 2006, *Friends* and *Seinfeld* had each earned over $3 billion in syndication revenues.

Reruns aside, distributors hold inordinate power: transmitters need distributors for lucrative content, while producers need them for the money that will allow them to *make* content. Consequently, many of the industry's key gate-keepers are to be found at the distribution level. A great idea with a great cast and a great writer means nothing without someone willing to fund and show it. Also, precisely because they are gate-keepers, distributors are inundated with ideas, or "pitches." Network executives in particular are constantly hearing pitches and meeting with would-be producers. From all these pitches, they commission a small few to write a "spec" (speculative) script; from the scripts, they commission a smaller few to produce a pilot episode; and from the pilots, they put an even smaller few on television. One estimate has the average network hearing 5,000 pitches, and commissioning 500 scripts, 50 pilots, and 5 actual new shows each year . . . of which 4 will likely be cancelled by year end (Steemers 2004: 121).

As such numbers suggest, television is risky. Nobody quite knows for sure what will fly and what will bomb, and the volatility of personnel changes at most networks highlights how quickly a master developer can turn into a dud in the eyes of a fickle business. With such risk, many media companies have tried to take the entire process under their wing, so that at least all involved can, in theory, work together and squeeze as much blood as possible from even the hardest stone. Thus, for instance, CBS Inc. produces the majority of CBS Network's programs, and CBS in turn owns numerous affiliates ("O & O" – owned and operated), especially in large markets such as New York, LA, and Chicago. FOX, NBC, and Disney all favor "inhouse" production too, aiming to streamline the process. Only Warner Bros. produces a preponderance of material for other networks (hence, for instance, its *ER* plays on NBC, *The OC* on FOX, *The Bachelor* on ABC, *Without a Trace* on CBS, *Veronica Mars* on CW, and *Nip/Tuck* on News Corp's F/X), largely because its skills (and style) as a production studio exceed the success and budget of first its own WB Network, and then co-owned CW. Nevertheless, the risk inherent in the business is inescapable, and leads to all sorts of attempts to reduce the risk, from excessive testing of new shows (notoriously inaccurate: both *All in the Family* and *Seinfeld* tested poorly), to reliance on stars, proven showrunners, spinoffs, and franchises, to newer methods such as product placement saturation.

There is certainly more to be said of such a system, and interested readers are encouraged to read Robert Kubey's (2004) interviews with television creators, Jason Mittell's (2008) account of the television industry, and Amanda Lotz's (2007b) study of the industry in transition. Many countries, too, offer modifications on this system, most notably for public broadcasters, who we will discuss later. But what does such a system promise vis-à-vis creativity? Artistry on television is often starved by many industrial processes, and yet at the same time critics have often all too easily overestimated the powers of these processes, while simultaneously underestimating the skill of talented artists to overcome or even thrive in the face of such obstacles. Thus the following sections will examine the television industry's dialectic of creativity and innovation.

Scared to innovate: risk adversity and repetition

Television is a risky business, given that seemingly nobody can predict which shows will succeed or fail. As such, it is vital that the industry find ways to reduce this risk. Many such strategies work against innovation. To begin with, since large amounts of money will be wasted on unsuccessful shows, production and distribution staff often find it financially beneficial to work out "golden rules," and stick to them. Golden rules beget formulas, which beget standardization. Horkheimer and Adorno argue that running art as a business squashes it under the weight of such formulas and standardization, and they reason that the "rhythm of an iron system" takes over (1972[1944]: 120), whereby producers and distributors try to condition the audience to accept a highly limited set of products that exhibit no real innovation or artistry – just repetition of the last successful product(s). As television writer Arla Sorkin Manson told Robert Kubey in interview, "The trap with network executives is that they are comfortable with this little mechanical structure. Anything that goes against it becomes too uncomfortable" (2004: 192). Novelty and innovation, by executive logic, are risky, and while they may pay off big (a gamble that executives will sometimes take), it is safer, more "comfortable," to produce more of the same. Consequently, as Jason Mittell (2004b) points out, this leads to a system of "Innovation – Imitation – Saturation," whereby a good idea is imitated ad infinitum, through franchising and outright copies, until finally the public tires of it. Thus, for instance, in the early 2000s, American television experienced a heightened age of imitation/saturation of *Law and Order*-type shows, with the *Law and Order* franchise, the *CSI* franchise, *Without a Trace*, *Criminal Minds*, *Close to Home*, *The Closer*, *Cold Case*, *Navy NCIS*, *Numb3rs*, *Justice*, *Bones*, *Shark*, and so forth. As writer-producer Allan Burns notes, "There is very seldom the desire, on the part of the programming executives, to do something really original on TV. They'd rather you copy something that somebody else has been successful with . . . And if you give them something really innovative it just scares the shit out of them" (Kubey 2004: 180). If art aims to be bold and daring, finances frequently order television to stay cozily familiar.

Beyond pure copying, television has found multiple other ways to hold the status quo. Quite simply, one method is to drag out shows until no longer profitable. Public broadcasters like the BBC can afford the luxury of short runs for new shows, but commercial television will keep a good show around for as long as possible. Hence, for instance, famous Brit comedy *Fawlty Towers* had twelve episodes in two seasons over four years, whereas an American comedy would have been required to produce approximately twenty-two episodes per season, for a total of almost ninety episodes in the same timeframe. Inevitably, this poses a potential problem for creativity, for it may become increasingly hard to keep a show innovative mid-series. As Catherine Johnson has observed of British cult classic *The Prisoner*, "If part of the premise of the series itself was to disrupt conventional forms of storytelling in order to create hesitation and uncertainty in the viewer, then after twelve episodes, this disruption becomes formalised as one of the conventional elements of the series itself, and those stylistic devices that had initially been disorientating become enjoyable aspects of the familiar pleasures offered by the series" (2005: 61–2). Or, for a more recent example, we might note that *The Simpsons*' initial stylistic rebelliousness in attacking the domestic sitcom has by now lost much of its edge for an audience saturated by and having grown up with it and its many imitators.

Even shows with contained timeframes, such as *24* (in which the show's action takes place in "real time" over twenty-four hours in twenty-four episodes), find ways to renew the action, as when *24*'s subsequent seasons showed us Agent Jack Bauer's *second* worst day, *third* worst day, and so forth. The term "jumping the shark" has come into common parlance to describe the moment of death for a long-running show (named after the Fonz's feat of water-skiing over a shark on

Happy Days, a clear sign of the show's deserved death), though "kicking a dead horse" seems a more appropriate zoological metaphor. Or, taking the approach of animal husbandry, executives will often produce "recombinant" programs, as Gitlin (1994) has called them, by uniting two popular shows, as when NBC tried to marry *Grey's Anatomy*'s focus on young interns learning on the job with *Law and Order*, producing the short-lived *Conviction* in 2006. Likewise, spinoffs are another form of inbreeding that sees an established character farmed out to a new program. With these and other strategies, television executives attempt to flatten innovation to a comfortable, manageable low level.

Toward this aim, the sheer cost of making television erects barriers to entry that aid the industry. Innovation in all cultural fields often arises because of the addition of new creators with new ideas and ways of doing things, but television can be a closed shop. Hollywood very rarely trusts just anyone with its expensive resources and large budgets; rather, any potential creator must usually work their way up or across, either paying their dues writing for established shows, or making a name in cinema before transferring over. Hence, Joss Whedon is well known for *Buffy the Vampire Slayer*, but had to work his way up writing scripts for *Roseanne* and *Parenthood*. *Six Feet Under* creator Alan Ball began as a writer on sitcoms *Grace Under Fire* and *Cybill*, then garnered critical acclaim with his script for Oscar winning *American Beauty*, before being handed the reins to his own show. Or *West Wing* creator Aaron Sorkin came to television from film, having already written *A Few Good Men*, *Malice*, and *The American President*. Moreover, such is the nature of scriptwriting for both television and film, that before getting a break, many writers have penned multiple scripts that never became shows. Television is not a welcoming industry in this respect, and any potential creator must be willing to endure years of artisan work before being given a real chance to innovate. Therefore, not only may established practices socialize and tame writers over time, so that when or if they are given creative control, they have internalized many of the industry's golden rules, but also a great deal of the writing that makes television is by writers working on someone else's show, with someone else's characters, and someone else's instructions, not necessarily on projects that they truly care about. Such a system risks more attrition than innovation.

Television, then, can fail abysmally to do anything other than copy itself at times. But as Mittell (2008) observes (albeit optimistically), most wholly imitative programs meet an early death, and a close study of success in television suggests considerable room for innovation. Formulas exist, golden rules are in place, and some genres seemingly live on, barely altered for ever. But perhaps the problem lies in seeing such structures as *wholly* limiting, and here it is helpful to examine novelty in the more traditional, and more widely accepted arts. For instance, take the sonnet, a fourteen-line poem, written in iambic pentameter (a rhythmic scheme whereby each second syllable is stressed in the reading, and each line contains ten syllables), with some form of rhyme between lines, and separated either into (a) an octave, in which a problem or proposition is stated, and (b) a sestet, in which this is resolved; or three quatrains and a final rhyming couplet. Such a form presents the poet with a plethora of restrictions, and yet many wonderful and beautiful poems were created using this form. Even Shelley, so adamant in his essays about poetry as brazenly new and divinely inspired, is most famous for "Ozymandias," a sonnet that, while somewhat rebellious in rhyme, conforms to the rules for sonnets in every other respect. Or, we might think of da Vinci's *Mona Lisa*, which as a portrait of a woman is hardly a generic ground-breaker. Most art is produced not only with plenty of rules and guidelines, but plenty of forerunners and models.

Elsewhere (Gray 2006), I have argued that *all* creation is deeply intertextual, by which I mean that nothing appears out of the ether, transmitted directly from God or muse to artist. Most artists spend considerable time studying other artists, learning both technique and theme from those who have come before them, so that as T. S. Eliot noted in his treatise entitled "Art and the Individual Talent": "we shall often find that not only the best, but the most individual parts of [the poet's] work may be those in which the dead poets, his [sic] ancestors, assert their immortality most vigorously" (1991[1920]: 431). Great artists, Eliot observes, have minds that are "a receptacle for seizing and storing up numberless feelings, phrases, images, which remain there until all the particles which can unite to form a new compound are present together" (1991[1920]: 434), so that "No poet, no artist of any art, has his [sic] complete meaning alone" (1991[1920]: 431). Thus, Shakespeare, for example, took many of his plotlines from Greek and Roman mythology, folk tales, and other literature; and his crowning genre, the tragedy, hearkens back 2,000 years to Greek dramatists such as Aeschylus, Sophocles, and Euripides. The myth of complete novelty is exactly that – a myth – for all great art has been thoroughly recombinant.

Within set parameters, rules, and orders, however, remarkable creativity can occur. Euripides regularly found bold and innovative ways to retell familiar myths, and so it is fair to assume that gifted spinoff, remake, franchise, recombinant, genre, or imitation writers could similarly breathe new life into seemingly dead entities. For instance, *King of the Hill* and *South Park* quite clearly imitated *The Simpsons*, yet both are excellent shows. *All in the Family* and *Battlestar Galactica* are remakes of the British *Till Death Us Do Part* and 1970s *Battlestar Galactica* respectively, yet both are two of the more critically acclaimed shows in American television history. *The Colbert Report* has proven an intelligent and hugely successful spinoff of *The Daily Show with Jon Stewart*, as did *Frasier* of *Cheers*. Even the franchised *CSI: Miami* and *CSI: New York* have offered stylistically unique variants of *CSI*. As such, as in every field of cultural production, television past and present provide ample evidence that television's creators are not totally powerless to innovate within strict limits. Art is often about how best to combine disparate elements (whether words, shapes, images, or sounds), and the artistry usually lies in the combination not the creation of elements. As Sconce argues of television, "the true art is in the algebra of such repetition" and in "the unique integers plugged into the equation" (2004b: 104–5), for this is how *all* art works.

Moreover, though commercial television favors never-ending program runs, dragging out some shows long after they should have died, the television serial's length also potentially offers television its greatest power as an art form. Haikus are three lines, sonnets fourteen, a song about four minutes, a novel about 200 to 800 pages, and a film about two hours. But a long-running television program of, say, 150 episodes (about eight seasons) equals 55 hours if a half-hour (22-minute) show, 110 hours if an hour long (44 minutes). This demand creates the potential for tedium, but in the right hands, it also creates an incredible potential for character, plot, and world development. Thus, the American version of British hit, *The Office*, though derivative of the original in many ways, by a half-way through its second season had eclipsed the total British *Office* episode count of 14, and concurrently its characters were becoming more realized and rounded, and less caricatured, leading many viewers to consider it even better than the original.

Meanwhile, as Sconce (2004b: 95) notes, more and more television shows are exhibiting a knack for "world building," creating elaborate universes full of multiple characters, complex interrelationships, and rich backstory. Such "hyperdiegesis," as Matt Hills (2002) dubs it, allows creators and audiences alike to interrogate closely characters' pasts and motivation (see *Lost*, *Six Feet Under*, *Dexter*, and all soap operas), explore a new and different textual universe (see *Lost* again, *Battlestar Galactica*, *The 4400*, *Buffy the Vampire Slayer*, *Heroes*, *Supernatural*, *The X-Files*), and/or follow and advance a richly developed theme (see *The Wire* and *The Sopranos*). Glen Creeber (2004) adds that such a form may even prove "better able to reflect and respond to the increasing uncertainties and social ambiguities of the contemporary world" (7). Brevity can itself be wonderful, but the potential length of the television narrative – at least in theory, if sadly too rarely in practice – allows a degree of depth rivaled in art and literary history only by the serial comic book. Audience engagement with television is thus phenomenally high for some programs, as I will discuss in the next chapter. Sconce observes that since the last twenty years have brought television all sorts of leisure competition – from computer games to the Internet, iPods to cell phones – television has had to respond by getting better and by learning to "better exploit certain textual strengths it possessed over other media" (2004b: 96), key among these being its power to tell enduring, deeply involving, and complex stories over significant time. Television is slowly realizing its power as an expansive art, using length to its advantage, not just strapping on water-skis to jump the shark.

Artistic interference, or whose art and whose vision?

As both an expansive and a technically complex artform, though, television requires multiple creators. Inherently a collaborative medium (Newcomb and Alley 1983), television brings together directors, writers, producers, set designers, costumers, make-up artists, editors, musicians, lighting technicians, sound designers, and scores of other creative personnel, and the creative act thus relies upon significant synergy and commonality of purpose and vision. Interpersonal problems can easily jeopardize the creative process, as creative personnel disagree with each other, operate on conflicting timelines, bicker, sulk, etc. Part of the problem here lies in uncertain structures of power. From our knowledge of film, we might expect directors to be in charge, but in fact television is sometimes more of a writer's medium, sometimes more of a producer's medium, and sometimes the stars hold significant power. Mix these models, and creativity can suffer, as is made clear by Judith Mayerle's (1994) study of the infighting and tension between Roseanne Barr and other key creative figures on the set of *Roseanne*.

First and foremost, though, creative personnel work for corporations with business agendas, and thus over and above the creative personnel, are potentially hordes of studio executives at all stages of the creative process, interfering, demanding both meaningless and meaningful changes. From the pitch stage to licensing, distributor development personnel surround a project, marshalling an army of past testing axioms, golden rules, intuition, and testing data to force changes in anything from a character's haircut, to the character's gender, the character's existence, or the show's genre. Networks will assign development staff to hopeful shows, but such comments can (and do) come from any stage higher up the corporate ladder too, and merely getting on air acts as no protection from interference, as networks also employ staff to oversee active productions. Paul Taylor quotes a television scriptwriter complaining that only 30 per cent of his scripts see the screen, "because of everybody else's alterations and interference" (1988: 187), with another noting that "On the first script, we had exactly four straight lines left of the original script. They'd even changed the number of the house [the characters] were living in" (188). Echoing these comments, most of the television workers interviewed about their craft by Kubey (2004) complain that network interference is one of the greatest obstacles to their profession. Thus, even before an actor can change a line or two, before a director can change the scene, or so forth, a writer's vision risks being cut to pieces and rearranged by executives. Artistic creation is rarely a solitary act, but "writing by committee" not only jeopardizes the timbre and grain of creativity; it also risks demoralizing the individuals involved, reducing their sense of pride and involvement in their work.

As Gitlin notes, "In headlong pursuit of the logic of safety, the networks ordinarily intervene at every step of the development process. It is as if there were not only too many cooks planning the broth, but the landlord kept interfering as well" (1994: 85). His metaphor here is illustrative, for much of the interference comes from executives, whose prime concerns are those of costs, not quality per se, leading them to make changes to save money here, or make money there. In particular, executives often prove hostile to ideas that require any real change in routines of production, for as Richard Caves notes, "If an innovation in creative activity rejects existing conventions and requires that a new set be learned, it suffers from high costs of adoption" (2000: 204). Meanwhile, executives are likely to approve of any change that could substantially *lower* the costs of production. Therefore, as Chad Raphael (2004) has documented, one of the key forces behind the rise of reality television was purely economic: reality television requires neither actors, their agents, nor unionized writers, allowing for vastly reduced production costs. Rather than leaving the cooking to the cooks, then, executives often interfere for wholly economic reasons.

Another form of interference is television scheduling, since the industry requires weekly or daily delivery of most programs, hence rushing the creative process. Some artists are blessed with the ability to create at speed and under remarkable time pressure. Shakespeare, for instance, is believed to have written most of his best tragedies in a few short years. But art and creativity can also take time: a resource that television often lacks. Admittedly, many new shows may have lived in their creators' heads for years before hitting the screen, but once they are on screen, the pressure for script after script, and season after season, is immense. Writer-producer Susan Harris states, "What makes for a poorer product is the fact that you have to turn a product out every week . . . Given the time factor it's almost impossible to do terrific work" (Kubey 2004: 132). And this is one of the key reasons why, unlike film, television is *not* a director's medium: television directors aren't given the time to compose scenes, retake, and craft them the way they might like. As a result of such time pressure, as Jane Feuer (2001: 70) notes, for instance, we often see American sitcoms begin strong, but weaken over the years. Or, equally unfortunate, many veteran shows come to rely on larger-than-life events and (sweeps weeks) stunts to keep the writers, cast, and audience busy. Creative burnout becomes one of the leading causes of jumping the shark. Burnout is also a significant problem for the executives who try to keep the 24/7 world of television running, resulting in rushed decisions and a tendency to fall back on formulas to save time. As agent Ray Solley observes, "One of the biggest problems in television is time. You never really have a chance to sit and talk, and more importantly, you never have a chance to sit and analyze something. Things are happening so fast; there are so many deadlines" (Kubey 2004: 427). Or, as producer Dave Bell explains, "television executives are stretched thin. Television executives read 8, 10 scripts on a weekend, read them in the car, read them on airplanes, read them on boats, read them every goddamn place except sitting down in a nice quiet spot. As soon as you give them a complicated script, they lose track" (Kubey 2004: 263).

When executives interfere, they act out of concern, and frequently out of fear. Allan Burns' above-quoted comment on executive discomfort with innovation continues that "It doesn't have anything to do with their lack of intelligence; it has to do with fear" (Kubey 2004: 180). What they fear are the Nielsen ratings. After all, green-lighting an Emmy award-winning show or somebody's favorite program means very little for job security at a network: ratings rule. Consequently, producers, distributors, and transmitters must play all sorts of games to inflate the viewing numbers. Especially in a remote control era, shows must "front-load," starting each episode with a bang or hook, in order to capture audiences' attention before they can change the channel (see Bellamy and Walker 1993: 190). Notoriously, sweeps weeks are filled with stunts, from guest stars to wild premises, weddings, and deaths, so as to spike viewing numbers when they matter the most (see Caldwell 2004: 61). And equally notoriously, shows cannot afford the luxury of time in finding an audience, lest they be cancelled after only two episodes; as a result, not only have many wonderful shows been cancelled prematurely, but producers and distributors must be ever-mindful of the Nielsen guillotine poised above their shows' necks, forcing many to internalize a suspicion of potentially ratings unfriendly textual qualities, such as narrative complexity. If a longstanding axiom states that artists' fame and fortune usually arrive posthumously, commercial television avoids such geologic notions of time: success should be immediate, leading to the intrusive presence of ratings and testing data – or simply the fear of ratings and testing data – in the creative process.

That said, art is often born in a context of pressure. Shakespeare also had sponsors to impress, monarchs to appease, casts of actors to work with and around, and a more immediate form of Nielsen ratings with which to contest – projectile vegetables. Other famous sculptors and painters spent years in schools with masters, had their own students complete work for them, and had their work curtailed or determined by the vagaries of finances, sponsorship, and available materials. But key here, and an important principle for understanding innovation, is that many artists find a way. Economist Richard Caves' tome *Creative Industries* opens with several overarching and characteristic properties, and one of these is the "art for art's sake property," which states that "the creator . . . cares vitally about the originality displayed, the technical prowess demonstrated, the resolution and harmony achieved in the creative act" (4). To satisfy this creative impulse, continues Caves, "the artist may divert effort from aspects of the task that consumers will notice (thus affecting their willingness to pay) to those they will neither notice nor value," hence creating a situation whereby "artists turn out more creative product than if they valued only the incomes they receive" (4). Admittedly, Caves also contrasts artists to "humdrum" craftsmen, implying (not wholly convincingly) that the latter will care only for the assigned and contracted task. But true artists *care* about their art, and surrounding them with a group of executives, itinerant cast and/or crew, budgets, technology, deadlines, ratings, and so forth may make their job harder, but is unlikely to drain their creative impulse altogether. World history is full of tales of artists creating in odd and hostile environments, and while many artists have failed in the shadows of such successes, adversity and obstacles alone are not always enough to stop artists who care.

Here we reach a key problem with structural accounts that treat transnational media organizations as grand machines, for such accounts can often forget the human elements within. Interviews with television personnel suggest a range of worker "types," with some television staffers caring little about their work or craft (see Taylor 1988, or Gitlin on Aaron Spelling (1994: 137)). But most interviews reveal individuals who have lived and breathed television from an early age, who work long hours at low pay for much of their career to rise to a position where they can realize their own creative visions, and who are both savvy of industry structure and keen to work around it to the best of their abilities (see especially Kubey 2004). Not only, then, should we expect that many creative personnel will try actively to overcome structural obstacles, but we should also not be so quick to assume that executives merely create obstacles. All creative industries are surrounded by businesspeople, and while some are there for the business, some are (also) there for the art. Hence, for instance, many bookstores and publishing houses are filled with those who love books and literature, and many art dealers and agents love art. Doubtlessly, then, some television executives work in television because they love television, and want to participate in the creative act. Many of Kubey's industry insider interviewees expressed concern about the growing number of mindless "suits" in the industry, populating especially the upper echelons (see 2004: 37, 196, 263, 421), but television is also still home to many executives who have been around for a long time, whose decisions will be guided by both financial *and* creative imperatives, and whose tenure in the business may well prove of assistance at times, rather than being pure interference.

Moreover, as David Hesmondhalgh points out, creative industries must give their artists some room if they want them to create. A key strategy for managing the industry's inherent risk is to cultivate top talent, treating them well, so as to encourage their loyalty and their creative output. To get shows and ideas out of artists, Hollywood brass must frequently grant "considerable autonomy within the process of production – far more, in fact, than most workers in other forms of industry" (2002: 22). "This point about creative autonomy," he later notes, "is absolutely crucial for an understanding of the cultural industries in the late twentieth century. It shows that the metaphor of the traditional factory production line, often used in critiques of industrial cultural production, entirely misses the point" (56). Hesmondhalgh explains that the industry exerts considerably more pressure over the stages of reproduction and circulation (as we will revisit in Chapter 3), and will often exert tight control over non-key creative personnel, so clearly not all creators enjoy loose control all the time. But certain latitude must be given precisely for the sake of innovation. Simply put, Hollywood *needs* its successful creators, and those with proven track records can frequently parlay this into more creative control, and into a defense against many structural obstacles. Thus, for instance, James L. Brooks' prior success in television allowed him to negotiate a "no notes" policy for *The Simpsons*, effectively allowing his writers freedom from FOX's demands for change (see Figure 1.1). Similarly, given *Lost*'s success, Carleton Cuse and Damon Lindelof were able, in 2007, to negotiate an end date for their show, a rare concession from the industry. All creator power has its limits, but television is perhaps more free, even more *keen*, to give it away, and many creators are more keen to use such power, or to carve it out, than many critics might think.

Figure 1.1 The power of past success: producer James L. Brooks's prior television success ensured that for the production of *The Simpsons*, Homer and the writing staff had the remote, not FOX

Television's granting of creative license is particularly evident in its continual development of visual aesthetics. As Johnson observes, too little work in television studies examines visual style (2005: 147), instead focusing obsessively on plot, theme, and industrial structure. A notable exception is John Caldwell's *Televisuality* (1995), a book which examines television in the 1980s and its cultivation of given "looks," noting that "one of the chief directorial tasks in primetime is to construct coherent stylistic worlds, on command, and from a wide variety of visual styles" (77). Television as industry may fear all sorts of innovation, but particularly starting in the 1980s, a key and encouraged way to differentiate one's own program was to make it *look* and *feel* different. Michael Mann's crisp "MTV cops"-style *Miami Vice* paved the way, with loud and popular music overlaying most scenes, and bold colorization making it instantly identifiable in a channel-surfer's universe. Industry mythology has it that Matt Groening colored *Simpsons* characters yellow to make them stand out for channel surfers. Beyond merely having a set look and feel, though, as Caldwell states, many shows cultivated the art of changing their look weekly or for sweeps weeks episodes (see also Caldwell 2004), Hence, for instance, *Quantum Leap* played with visual generic style on a weekly basis, as its lead character time-traveled into various people's bodies, *Moonlighting* filmed an entire "Shakespearean" *Taming of the Shrew* episode, and subsequent television shows have gone on to film live episodes (*ER*, *Will and Grace*, *The West Wing*). Meanwhile, today's visual avant garde is led by the likes of the *CSI* franchise and *House* – both of which make use of computer effects, and the former of which differentiates its members by color scheme (*CSI: New York*, for instance, frequently filmed in a cool, cold blue in its first season, *CSI: Miami* making heavy use of warm oranges) – but includes many programs, from *Buffy the Vampire Slayer*'s gothic-meets-*90210* mix, to *Lost*'s crane-cam work, and from *The West Wing*'s visual style to *Scrubs*' magic realism.

Somewhat dismissively labeled by Caldwell (1995) as "stylistic excess," such visual style is often a venue for significant creativity and artistry, and one that is encouraged and welcomed by the networks. A show can easily risk becoming reduced to its visual style if its other creative levels are vacuous, but we should not underestimate the role of a show's look in engaging its audiences, not merely as bright lights and spectacle, but as visual art. While I have by necessity discussed mostly fiction as the key locus of creativity in television entertainment, visual style is improving in all sorts of entertainment genres, from reality television to sports programming.

Other culprits: advertising and "the masses"

Less supportive executives, Nielsen data sheets, repetition, and recombinance may pester the creative process, or at times shut it down altogether, but they are mere symptoms of what to many is the prime obstacle to commercial television's dreams for artistry: pressure from advertisers. Ratings, after all, are both powerful and meaningful in the television business not because they say which shows are popular per se, but because they tell advertisers who is watching. And even high ratings alone are no guarantee of a show's livelihood. Producers must deliver the *type* of audience that advertisers want. Therefore, for instance, *The Beverly Hillbillies* was still a popular show when CBS cancelled it in 1971, but increasingly sophisticated ratings data had suggested that its audience skewed older and rural, the kiss of death for many advertisers. CBS yanked the program, replacing it with younger, more urban fare (Gitlin 1994: 205–6). Then again in 1996, CBS first rescheduled then later cancelled *Murder, She Wrote*, even though it had been winning its timeslot, because ratings revealed an older audience (Napoli 2008). In recent years, with Nielsen data getting more sophisticated, with the advent of "psychographic," "niche" style advertising pinpointing certain consumer "types" (see Turow 2006), and with most television channels specializing in particular audience types, knowing one's potential advertisers and giving them the kind of content they want is becoming a necessary survival skill for many creative personnel. Hence network television's long-time love affair with domestic sitcoms, filled as they were with good little consumers (see the kids' rooms in shows like *Full House* or *The Cosby Show* for a vivid display of conspicuous consumption) . . . until *The Simpsons* and *Roseanne* spoiled the party in the early 1990s by satirically undercutting the supposed normality of such families. Hence the networks' fondness for shows like *The OC*, with lots of young, pretty, and affluent characters and viewers. And hence the fact that dark, depressing, and brooding shows like HBO's *Six Feet Under* or Showtime's *Huff* or *Dexter* survive best away from advertising, where their down-beat tone won't poison the buying mood.

Advertisers do not just occupy ad breaks: they exert considerable pressure, both direct and indirect, on television to become an ad-friendly environment, demanding and rewarding consumerism friendly shows, and as we will examine further in Chapters 4 and 5, often requiring a flattening of a show's politics, so as to avoid controversy, boycotts, and viewer displeasure. Recently, too, the incident of product placement has increased dramatically (see Chapter 3), so that savvy, budget-minded producers and executives now think not only of how to please spot advertisers, but also of how to woo product placement. Reality television in particular often sells its soul quite openly to such deals, given its relative failure in the rerun market, and thus its reliance on alternative modes of funding (see Magder 2004). As with "regular" advertising, the rise of product placement risks encouraging producers to keep things light, happy, fantastical, and advertiser friendly, thereby narrowing the scope of creative possibility.

The pressure of advertisers' wishes is not an easy one to circumvent, for in commercial television, funding begins and ends with advertising. Chapters 4 and 5, too, will examine further the wide-ranging effects of advertising on television programming. That said, its strength is more evident on some shows than others, for advertisers will at times ultimately support shows that bring them their desired demographics, regardless of those shows' content. Also, television's advertisers are not as uniformly hostile to good content as critics contend. Some advertisers simply want the best quality show to which they can attach their name, and as Lotz (2007b) has illustrated with the examples of ABC's short-lived *The Days*, and CW's *The Gilmore Girls* – both of which were born in large part from advertiser involvement – advertiser involvement is not necessarily synonymous with bland conservatism. Even advertisers for *The Simpsons* and *South Park*, two shows that often mock and gouge at crass consumerism (the former doing so before its ad breaks on many occasions), have stayed with the programs to keep attaching their products to the shows' hip reputations, showing that in time some shows can master their advertisers. But *The Simpsons* and *South Park* are exceptions to a business that is still controlled in many ways both conspicuous and inconspicuous by advertising.

If some critics posit advertisers as the root cause of televisual problems, others have blamed "the tyranny of the masses," arguing that ratings hold smart shows ransom to the supposedly lowbrow, simplistic tastes of "the average Joe." Readers of this book might therefore try an experiment: find someone who believes that television, particularly commercial television, is hostile to creativity, ask them why, and start a stopwatch. Stop the clock when they use the phrase "lowest common denominator." Considerable fear of the supposed masses exists in many of television's most outspoken critics, especially fear that these assumed-to-be simple and easily entertained beings will always prefer their bright lights, slapstick humor, and women in bikinis to anything more substantial, noble, and artistic. Hence, for instance, the BBC's refusal for many years to use audience research, since it was assumed that any form of asking the audience what it wanted was bound to put the broadcaster on a slippery slope to 24/7 *Wheel of Fortune* (see Hilmes 2003). As I will argue in Chapters 2 and 4, ratings often prove a sloppy way of measuring audience desires, and as I discussed above, ratings-led systems encourage some producers to fill their programs with bells and whistles. But blaming the masses, while convenient – since "the masses" are always other people – is rather spurious, especially since much television judged high quality by cultural critics has commanded high ratings (as with *All in the Family* or *Lost*).

As television moves towards narrowcasting, with cable channels and even networks specializing in particular audience types, there will always be an audience for smart and innovative television. Repetitive television based on familiarity, as I will later discuss, should by no means be dismissed lightly, nor should its audiences be easily pathologized, so "smart and innovative television" is not all that we should wish for. However, when "artistic innovation" often serves as a codeword for high art, and with high art the distinguishing cultural exploit of the upper middle class (see Bourdieu 1984), artistic innovation stands to deliver precisely the audiences that many advertisers want (the wealthy, or upwardly mobile, educated upper-middle-class) and that flatter a public broadcaster's sense of job performance. Television has long since become an acceptable medium in upper-middle-class homes, perhaps the object of a few snide comments, but rarely excluded altogether. And while the upper middle classes often watch their *Jerry Springer Show* and *Fear Factor* as much as anyone, a certain expectation of creativity and artistry also emanates from this audience, an expectation that is convincing more and more shows to aim high and go after this group. Certainly, though, this trend warrants study for the consequences on meaningful programming for other classes, and so I will return to this in Chapter 4. Suffice it to say now that television's "mass audience" contains all sorts of tastes, some of which demand innovation. Gitlin's study of television executives also found many programmers blaming bad television on the masses, but this move is a disingenuous way of deflecting attention from advertiser interference and executive and/or creative failure to audiences, albeit without audience.

Case study: *The Sopranos*

Many shows illustrate the lack of creativity in television, but let us examine a creative show to see what innovation and artistry can look like. *The Sopranos* first aired in 1999 on HBO, enjoying seven seasons before ending in 2007. Based around patriarch and New Jersey mob boss Tony Soprano and his family, it followed the Sopranos' familial relations, mob operations, and, famously, Tony's sessions with his psychologist. Being on HBO, it never needed to fawn to advertiser wishes, and creator David Chase has been unswerving in discussing his extreme dislike of network television, stating in one interview that "I loathe and despise almost every second of it," elaborating that "I considered network TV to be propaganda for the corporate state – the programming, not only the commercials," since it continually hammers home the message that American life is wonderful (cited in Lavery and Thompson 2002: 19–20). Nevertheless, Chase had worked in network television for many years, with time writing and producing for both *The Rockford Files* and *Northern Exposure*. Thus, Chase is one example of many of a creator who spent years paying his dues before being given a chance to envision truly his own show (his earlier attempt to create a show, *Almost Grown*, ended in cancellation).

If Chase expresses considerable disdain for the message that American life is great, however, *The Sopranos* offers a compelling image of the US in crisis. The show begins with Tony Soprano suffering anxiety attacks that require him to see a psychologist. Here, then, a mob boss – arguably one of the last fifty years' key symbols of virile and aggressive American masculinity and power, of the American dream and entrepreneurial spirit, and of American libertarian distrust of the government – is depicted on the edge of a nervous breakdown. *The Sopranos* is a

Figure 1.2 A *Sopranos* Season 6 advertisement highlights the lifelessness of Tony's home, and his alienation from others – a stark contrast to American television's more familial bliss (see Figures 1.3 and 2.2)

dark tale, not suited for interruption by Trident chewing-gum ads, and is somewhat Shakespearean in tone and even structure. It plays an interesting game with its audience, sometimes luring them in to the mob life and romanticizing it, other times playfully mocking it and satirizing it, and occasionally horrifying the audience with brutal and shocking violence. As such, the show defamiliarizes the mob genre, for as Creeber notes of the therapy sessions in particular, they "self-consciously fragment the serial's narrative dynamic, forcing the viewer to stand back for a moment from Tony's exotic (and perhaps essentially 'cinematic') lifestyle so that they can briefly distance themselves from the genre's historically seductive appeal" (2004: 107). At the same time, moreover, it moves between intense and warm identification with the nuclear family, and significant suspicion of it (see Figure 1.2). As David Johansson (2006) points out, the show's opening credit sequence inverts the frequently idealized sitcom moment of dad coming home after a day at work, making it foreboding, disturbing, even somewhat dystopian, for Tony's grim countenance, and for the lack of life in the urban landscape that surrounds him. Thematically, *The Sopranos* is rich with commentary on its televisual and cinematic forbearers, and on American life.

Visually, the show is a tour de force, filmed with great care and attention to minute details from shot composition to light play and contrast. Moreover, Chase's scripts often make use of dream sequences, rich with symbolism and foreboding, and Tony's shrink sessions quite often follow their own impressionist and symbolic path. In a medium often scared of the non-representational, and long weary of telling a story on any level other than the obvious surface, *The Sopranos* habitually strived to challenge and push the medium. And Chase's efforts have been largely rewarded, as *The Sopranos* ranks as one of the more touted and revered programs in American television history. Contributing to this are the performances of James Gandolfini (Tony), Edi Falco (his wife, Carmella), and Lorraine Bracco (his shrink) in particular. Between script and actor, Gandolfini, Falco, and Bracco offer nuanced and meticulous portrayals, approaching each episode with the precision that is often more characteristic of cinema. Indeed, it was *The Sopranos'* cinematic feel that helped HBO considerably with its brand mantra, "It's not television, it's HBO." Ultimately, then, from thematic interests to acting, writing to filming, *The Sopranos* is a bold and innovative show. It draws from obvious intertextual forefathers, such as *The Godfather* and *Goodfellas*, and cop/detective shows, but its creative spin and commentary on these all add further to its novelty. Ironically, *The Sopranos* began with Chase's hatred of television, but it has played a significant role in showing television what it can be and aim for.

HBO enjoys a commercial-free production process and a creator-centered philosophy, and so it is no surprise that it has produced such outstanding shows as *The Sopranos* and *Six Feet Under*. But network television has provided its own moments of creative brilliance, from the filming and complex narrative of *Lost*, to the visually stunning *CSI: Miami*, from remarkable performances on *The West Wing* by Martin Sheen and Allison Janney, to the tone, suspense, and "feel" of *24* and many competitive reality shows, and from the witty and clever satire of *The Daily Show with Jon Stewart* and *South Park*, to the dazzling animation of children's shows such as *ReBoot*. Gitlin states that in network television, "Everything emerges at the end of a chain of *ifs*" (1994: 273), but more and more shows are circumnavigating this chain, finding ways to create in spite of their many structural limitations. Television systems internationally must now play catch-up with the likes of *The Sopranos*, and some surprisingly good results are being achieved.

Hitting pause on the advertiser button: public broadcasting

Above, I have described the situation for American commercial television; some differences exist for other national commercial systems, but many of the key barriers to creativity remain. Public broadcasting, by contrast, may seem to offer a more open, welcoming system, especially since advertising dollars, the ratings guillotine, and the wanton lust for profits do not hang so heavily over a public broadcasting system, funded as it is by taxes, television ownership surcharges, and/or contributions and donations, and charged with the task of educating and enlightening as much as entertaining. Public broadcasters occasionally enjoy the luxury of reduced risk, and in this respect, they can afford to be more daring and overtly innovative in their programming. Shows need not run for multiple seasons, nor even for multiple episodes. New ideas can be tried out, as the lack of adver-tiser-induced standardization allows creators the option of riskier endeavors. Namely, shows can last for various lengths, and need not build in cliff-hangers in preparation for commercial breaks (as is the case with Pay TV too). Admittedly, executives still care about obtaining sizeable audiences (see Ang 1991), but there are less structural requirements placed on who must be *in* that audience: the BBC's fondness for gardening programs and the Second World War era nostalgic retro-spectives, for instance, exhibits an interest in senior friendly programming that the advertising-driven, and hence youth-obsessed, American networks will never match. In many ways, then, a public broadcasting system is one that allows more innovation. Indeed, commercial television has long used public broadcasting as a cheap research and development division, learning from (i.e.: copying) its successes. Reality television, nature documentaries, quality children's program-ming, and cooking shows are just a few of the genres that commercial television has poached from public broadcasting. American PBS and the alleged elitism of international public broadcasters such as the BBC are frequently the subject of jokes, but the truth is that PBS and the BBC in particular have played as important a role as has anything in keeping American television watchable.

Public broadcasting is by no means an open zone of unbridled creativity, however. As does commercial television, it can suffer from too many cooks – what Caves (2000) calls the "Motley Crew" principle of innovation in the creative indus-tries. Inhouse production and favoritism are frequently just as prevalent in public broadcasting as in commercial television (see Tinic 2005: 86–7). Long-running shows can suffer from a similar lack of innovation. Executives can cause just as much grief for creators. The industry can move at a similarly breakneck speed, not allowing time for analysis and reflection. And, as Ang (1991) has documented, when PBS works alongside a commercial system, executives and creative person-nel alike can easily internalize the logic of ratings, audience shares, and commercial production, becoming virtual commercial broadcasters. Also, while public broad-casting frees the distributor from the whims of the market, many of the production companies working for the public broadcaster may still be operating wholly within the market.

Hence, we must avoid the urge to romanticize public broadcasting, especially since for all that it offers its creators, it often cannot provide what commercial television can: a vast infusion of money. Television is a remarkably expensive art form, from the film stock, to the lights, rigs, microphones, editing equipment, cameras, sound stages, and sets; to actors, directors, writers, directors of photography, and countless other crew; to location costs, catering, electricity bills, and so forth. Creativity in television requires much more than supplying a writer with blank paper and a pen, and commercial television, when it works, and when the sponsors and executives are happy, can grant creators vast sums to realize their artistic or creative vision. This money, for instance, allows *Lost* to film on location in Hawaii, to employ an orchestra rather than use canned music, and to maintain a large ensemble cast. It allows *The Amazing Race* to send twenty people plus crew around the world. It allows game shows to award big prizes. It allows shows like *House* or *CSI* to experiment with high-quality computer graphics. And especially in recent years, it has acted as a talent magnet, allowing many shows to woo leading film actors, cinematographers, and writers over to the small screen. Thus, as Jeannette Steemers notes, many of the world's public broadcasters struggle to fund quality fictional programming in particular, leading to a situation whereby two thirds of the international trade in television programming is of fiction, much of this from the cash-rich American commercial broadcasting system (2004: 32). Commercial television throws plenty of obstacles in the way of outright creativity, but it also offers the capital frequently needed to "televisualize" many creative visions.

Déjà vu: reruns and repetition

As I hope to have shown, creativity, innovation, and art must be fought for in television, especially commercial television, but they are by no means absent from the box. However, in our haste and eagerness to discuss novelty in television, we must not forget that much of the medium is devoted to pure repetition, through the form of the rerun. On one hand, of course, any given rerun may be "new" to an audience member who has not seen it before, and thus "reruns" are sometimes no more repetitive than is a book in its second printing, or a film playing on its second day. On the other hand, they populate television with repetition, and hence their prevalence demands that we examine both for how they mitigate television's capacity for creativity, and what they might tell us about the audience for creativity and/or repetition. Reruns, as noted earlier, are cash cows for production companies: Kompare notes that *The Cosby Show* netted $600 million for its first syndication cycle alone (2005: 143). But they are also vital to the television system as a whole. No television station can afford 24/7 creativity and new production, and so all stations devote at least part if not a significant amount of their time to reruns, and/or to replaying films, both of which cost less than creating something new. Similarly, if television executives fear change and must limit risk, we could well understand their love of a rerun-filled system: even in the face of generic copies, spinoffs, or remakes, after all, the rerun is "the ideal product of U.S. commercial television: the perfect incarnation of stability in an often unpredictable programming game" (Kompare 2005: 69).

Structurally, reruns' relationship to creativity is deeply ironic and contested. The first irony of reruns, as Steven Johnson notes (2005: 159), is that in recent years, as producers have stood to gain more and more not only from reruns on television but also from DVD and VHS sales and rentals, producers have had to make shows better. Mediocre shows from the 1960s or 1970s, for instance (such as *The Brady Bunch* or *Hart to Hart*), may enjoy limited success as nostalgic or camp reruns, but the real money, nationally and internationally, lies in creating a program that can stand up to multiple viewings. *Seinfeld* and *The Simpsons*, for example, enjoy remarkable success on the worldwide syndication market, partly because, Johnson suggests, people *can* and desire to watch each episode several times. Thus, it may be that the growth in syndication and DVD markets has forced producers to make their programs better, so as to transcend their otherwise ephemeral nature: repetition has led to innovation. The second irony of reruns, as charted by Derek Kompare, is that they may have played a key role in validating television as a cultural form. Kompare notes that television's constant repetition of itself has created a "television heritage" – a nostalgic record of the nation, and our place in it, in which television figures prominently, so that, for instance, *I Love Lucy* has become as endemic of the 1950s, *Miami Vice* of the 1980s, and *Beverly Hills 90210* of the 1990s as anything from outside television. This heritage "validated the medium in ways that it had never been before, giving it an acknowledged role in the recent life and memory of the nation, and thus an assured place in American cultural history" (2005: 105). He speaks here of the US, but we may note the same for any nation. Hence, reruns, as the "*lingua franca*" of the television industry (Kompare 2005: 93), have arguably done for television what new but ephemeral first-run shows never could.

At the same time, however, reruns have also hurt television's prospects for creativity. Cheap and often successful, they risk encouraging lazy executives and particularly owners to eschew creativity in favor of yet more *Who's the Boss?* More importantly, there is a notable international component to the trade in reruns, whereby the resource-rich American television industry produces a significant amount of the reruns for the world, contributing to a stark and worrying imbalance in global cultural flow, and a crisis in local creativity (see Miller *et al.* 2005, Steemers 2004). Meanwhile, as much as the lust for rerun profits may encourage deeper shows, this lust may also lead to a flattening of immediate cultural relevance, and to less plot development. David Grote charges that comedy in particular has been hit hard by the rerun-ification of television, noting that because the sitcom "has to be comprehensible at any time period, in reruns . . . it has lost almost all contact with daily events in the outside world" (1983: 95). In addition, since sitcoms are often run out of sequence as reruns, writers are wise to limit character development or the need for any extra-textual knowledge that may confuse the rerun viewer.

Beyond reruns' many effects on televisual creation at the level of individual shows and writers, we must also discuss their effects on the very nature and ontology of television. After all, if so much of television is repetition, can we truly call it a creative medium? Kompare charts the rerun's fascinating history in American television, from its forerunners in the publishing industry, to its triumph over television in the fifties, and its mass-proliferation with the advent of cable in the eighties. In spite of particularly early television's promise of liveness, he notes, we could see the medium as "instead a machine of repetition, geared towards the constant recirculation of recorded, already-seen events" (2005: xi), and of nostalgia (see Figure 1.3). Early programmers feared that audiences would eventually rebel against the rerun, Kompare records, but the rebellion never occurred, leaving us to wonder why not.

The answer should serve as a sobering reminder should we wish to lionize creativity as the necessary cornerstone of any televisual art: as Kompare notes, "American television – both as an industry and a culture – needs repetition" (2005: 169). First, let us add that the US is not alone. Repetition in entertainment is vital and important, and repetition is an important function of art. Not only can a piece of art *allow* multiple viewings, listenings, or readings, but it often *requires* them. Let

Figure 1.3 Full House and its reruns offer viewers the chance to return to a safe, familiar environment

us not get carried away here, for multiple viewings of any given *Full House* episode are hardly likely to reveal deeper and deeper layers, but some shows warrant and reward repeat viewing. Not only will viewers be able to analyze and think through an episode with greater ability upon subsequent viewings, but also, as they gain more extra-textual knowledge and context, whether through viewing other episodes, other shows, discussing the program with friends (or in class), or simply aging and gaining new life experiences, they can perhaps see and understand more in the episode. For instance, in *Buffy the Vampire Slayer's* Season 4 episode entitled "Restless," while the characters sleep in front of a movie, we watch their odd and imagist dreams unfold. Each dream offers an oblique key into understanding the character, and into future events on the show, but they require multiple viewings, and open up more as the series progresses. Here, then, the meaning is buried deep, and subsequent viewings help the viewer decode it more effectively.

Beyond repetition as consumption of art, however, repetition opens up multiple other pleasures of consumption. Writing of the pleasures of watching certain films multiple times, Barbara Klinger (2006) offers a variety of rewards. By bringing viewers back to a familiar and beloved text, repeat viewings can either "operate subtly to confirm individual identities" or "introduce more volatile dynamics into the mix, inciting reassessments of the viewer's self or worldview" (2006: 139). They can bring "enjoyment via a combination of both mastery and solace: mastery of the narrative and one's own world; solace in the sense of control that predictability brings and in the way the screening of the same narratives can transform a space into a secure environment" (2006: 155). Or they could serve as a photo album of sorts, allowing us a view and an experiential trip back into our past (where was I when I last watched this? What was my life like then?) (2006: 174–5). And, of course, they open up considerable space for fun, via play and performance in allowing viewers to learn scripts, and hence repeat lines, "karaoke-like" (2006: 182). Thus, the range of pleasures embedded in the seemingly simple and mundane act of watching a show for the umpteenth time are anything but simple and mundane. As Klinger writes:

> Choosing the same coffee shop or restaurant to frequent, the same sneakers or T-shirt to wear, or the same family stories to retell is a commonplace of life. Like such choices, watching the same film or TV show acts as a guarantee of pleasure or satisfaction as well as a way to give a controllable shape to everyday existence. In this way, an inevitable daily dance takes place between the known and the new. Too much of either would be unsettling or displeasing. Thus, familiarity is just as key to experience as novelty. To deny the pleasures that one finds within the precincts of the familiar text is to ignore the intrinsic and necessary place that the known occupies in broader social circumstances.
>
> (2006: 155)

Klinger, then, provides us with a good place both to end this chapter, and to start the next. She reminds us that as important as novelty, creativity, and innovation are – and as much as we should insist on them from television producers – the absence of innovation often holds its own pleasures. Hence the rebellion against reruns never occurred, and hence the importance of various entertainments: some new, bold, and artistic, others repetitive, comforting, and familiar. But this moves us into the territory of the viewer, and of viewer love, hate, admiration, disgust, casual approval, and disinterest, and it demands that we now turn to an examination of affect and television.

Chapter 2

Broadcasting identities: affect, fantasy, and meaning

Television is more than just a technology – more than a composite of wires, metal, and glass. It possesses an essence that is bound up in its context, in how the box is most commonly used, in where it is located, in what streams through it, and in how most use it, despite the possibility for broad variation in all the factors.

Amanda Lotz (2007b: 29)

fandom has become an additional realm of identity construction alongside other long-standing factors such as religion, the nation-state, ethnicity or work.

Cornel Sandvoss (2005a: 62)

the outlawing of "want" as excessive is an arrogant move. Out with the bath water of greed and garden gnomes goes art, entertainment, body adornment, culture and creativity. After all, we don't need any of these things to stay alive. Herds of wildebeest manage well enough without them, why shouldn't we?

Kathy Myers (1986: 7)

The whimsical 1980 film *The Gods Must Be Crazy* begins when, flying high above the Kalahari Desert, a pilot throws an empty Coke bottle from his plane, sending it hurtling downwards to a remote tribe. There, the tribespeople find many uses for it, beating maize and smoothing animal skins with it, using it to entertain the children as a toy and an instrument, and using it as a weapon, as both a club and a sling-shot. Just as the bottle introduces the tribe to a consumer society, it offers viewers a fundamental rule of this society: use changes essence. Coca-Cola makes bottles to store its sugary beverage, but having served this purpose for the pilot, the intended use becomes irrelevant for its subsequent life in the Kalahari. By contrast, televisions (we hope) do not fall down on us from the sky, nor do they arrive in our livingrooms without any clue as to their appropriate uses. As with the Coke bottle, too, we can only use television and television entertainment in certain ways (for instance, we cannot easily use a 32-inch plasma screen HDTV to beat maize). Nevertheless, as Amanda Lotz suggests, television is never just about wires, metal, and glass, nor is its entertainment just about production, industry, and intent: its essence is what we make of it. Television entertainment only becomes important to any individual or community when it is used. Consequently, to understand television entertainment's many roles in society, we must understand why it is consumed, how it consumed, and with what affective relationship.

As Cornel Sandvoss suggests, our fandoms are frequently as integral to us as identity markers and as communities of belonging as are more traditional cultural units, such as nations, religions, and ethnicities. Thus, when someone reveals what programs they love and watch religiously, they perform aspects of their identity, and potentially give listeners a glimpse into who they really are and what makes them tick. Similarly, though, if they were to list what they detest or what they watch with either disinterest or only casual interest, once more they could reveal a great deal about themselves. Affective relationships to television entertainment quite often act as key identity markers, coloring our experience of television entertainment, not only as individuals but also as communities and as an entire society. But we can love, hate, or ignore television and its programs for many different reasons, and in many different ways, again coloring their overall significance. As such, affect is the fundamental complicating factor in any examination of television entertainment, for affect can amplify textual properties, erase them, or otherwise modify them. Affect determines what television is and what it does. To love *Desperate Housewives*, for instance, and to watch each episode several times over, post at online fan sites, and buy related merchandise is to render *Desperate Housewives* a markedly different entity than it is for those who have seen half an hour of the show and never come back.

By "affect," I invoke the realm of feelings, emotion, and impressions. Following George Marcus (2002) and Sara Ahmed (2004), though, I do not see affect as divorced from cognition and rationality. As Ahmed notes, after all:

> we do not love and hate because objects are good or bad, but rather because they seem "beneficial" or "harmful" (Descartes 1985: 350). Whether I perceive something as beneficial or harmful clearly depends upon how I am affected by something. This dependence opens up a gap in the determination of feeling: whether something is beneficial or harmful involves thought and evaluation, at the same time that it is "felt" by the body.
>
> (2004: 5–6)

In this chapter, then, I will examine our cognitive yet simultaneously affective, *emotive* reaction(s) to a program. These reactions may take any number of forms – some programs make us laugh, others scare us, worry us, excite us, make us cry (whether in sadness or inspiration), calm us, make us cheer, or fill us with anger. Television entertainment can invite and/or trigger any number of emotive reactions and may attract and repel us for this very reason. As a result, whole sub-genres of media studies have sought to study the psychological meaning and workings of affect (see, for instance, Hockley 2003, Mulvey 1989, Zillman and Vorderer 2000). As informative as such work might be, here I am interested in how affect changes the *social* and *cultural* not solely individual/psychological roles of television, transforming programs from yet more products into texts that elicit love, hate, fear, elation, and other emotional responses, and thereby layering their relevance to analysis, and fundamentally changing how they are consumed. As such, in this chapter, we will turn to affect, love, dislike, and casual interest to ask how they change the very nature of television entertainment, and to ask how television entertainment is *used*.

To focus on affect is to change focus from a term that is more prevalent in studies of television: effect. Since Plato (1974[390 BC]) first dictated that poets should be expelled from his ideal republic, out of concern for poetry's effects on humankind's emotions and rationality, Western society has been fond of effects discourse. Other modern media such as videogames, films, comics, and music have attracted their fair share of effects panics, but television and particularly television entertainment quite frequently figure heavily in effects discourse. Television entertainment, we have been told, has made us more fearful, and has caused eating disorders, ensured the continuance of patriarchy, made us more liberal and more conservative, dulled us to the gravity of war and violence, made us mindless consumers, and shortened our attention spans . . . to list but a few of its alleged crimes. Meanwhile, television entertainment is often at the center of plans or at least hopes to create other effects, such as increased literacy, tolerance, and/or education (think *Sesame Street*). Certainly, when television makes news (outside of entertainment news, that is), and when academic studies into television are publicized, the stories are often about effects.

By focusing on affect, not effect, in this chapter, I do not mean to belittle either concerns or hopes regarding effects. Effects research is notoriously hard to conduct, especially in such a media-saturated environment as our present day, and is too often marred by sloppy methodology and dubious assumptions of what constitutes an actual effect (see Barker and Brooks 1998, Buckingham 1997, Gauntlett 2005), but we would be foolish and naïve to believe that television is anything other than able powerfully to create numerous effects. Chapters 3–6 assume outright that considerable effects battles are occurring. However, at some level or other, effects must go through affect and cognition (and in turn, affect will often follow effects), and so a detailed understanding of what affect (and the cognitive processes behind it) can do to effects is important. Too much effects research, and too much public discussion of effects assumes that television entertainment's uses are preordained and hence wholly predictable, as if, notes Silverstone, the television audience is little more than "plankton floating on the surface of the Gulf

Stream and the North Atlantic Drift – alive but entirely impotent to affect the dominant direction of the current" (1994: 140). But in examining affect, the powers of television entertainment fantasy, and instances in which viewers "affect" meaning themselves, we move away from a belief in the preordained to a study of the everyday uses of television entertainment. After all, we are not plankton, nor, as Kathy Myers notes, are we as simple as wildebeest crossing the Kalahari: as humans, we demand other things from television, and we use it in often stunningly complex ways. Moreover, as Ang reminds us, despite a pervasive and impressive faith in effects and the like, in a world verging on communicative overload, the *failure* to communicate may actually be the more normal state of affairs (1994: 198); therefore, in this "new world (dis)order" (1994: 199) of communicative feedback loops, boomerang effects, and dead ends, it becomes all the more imperative to examine how communication *does* succeed. This takes us to the realm of affect.

The chapter will begin with fans and followers,[1] as those viewers who are seemingly most involved and most actively implicated in their consumption. We will see how textual love works, focusing on such issues as fantasy, the construction and performance of identity, play with and construction of meaning by fans, and the social pleasures of texts. Then we will shift to anti-fans, trying to understand what is involved in textual hatred or dislike, and interrogating what such equally strong feelings tell us about our multiple relationships to and uses of television entertainment. Then, lest the affective world seem divided wholly into love and hate, we will examine non-fans, casual viewing, and hence the experience of television that is likely most common for most viewers most of the time. Finally, we will discuss producers' attempts to harness and control audiences, through measurement and surveillance. Precisely because affect and use change televisual essence, producers and advertisers alike are increasingly going to great lengths to tap into the central nervous system of audience affect, and their attempts to do so warrant close attention. I will return to writers', producers', advertisers', and audiences' attempted uses of affect throughout this book, especially in Chapters 4 and 5, and their strategies of corralling it will form the basis of Chapter 3.

Ultimately at stake in an examination of television entertainment and affect is a better understanding of how contemporary subjects experience, cope with, and inhabit modernity. In a seminal essay on the pathologization of fandom, Joli Jensen (1992) argues that stereotypes of fans as obsessed losers tell a reassuring, if wishful tale: that the rest of us have a wholly healthy relationship to modernity and to the media. As the strange other, *they* – the Trekkie, or the soap fan, for example – may have (supposedly) lost sight of reality, but *we* imagine ourselves to be unaffected by media powers. Thus, such stereotypes have circulated so freely because their presence normalizes the rest of "us." However, updating Jensen, Hills notes that increasingly, fans "are no longer viewed as eccentric irritants, but rather as loyal consumers to be created, where possible" (2002: 36), and Henry Jenkins (2007) has even suggested that fandom is now so common, so mainstream, and relatively unproblematic that perhaps the term "fan" has no further currency. Regardless of whether Jenkins is correct, fandom or the lack thereof (and hence anti-fandom and non-fandom) still tell tales of "normal," abnormal, and ideal relationships with mediated modernity. Hence, as Gray *et al.* (2007b) argue, to study fans (and anti-fans and non-fans, or affect in general) is to study many basic structuring principles of modernity: how we create identity, how we relate to each other, why we watch so much television entertainment, how we envision a better society, and so forth. Studying affect tells us about television entertainment, but it also tells us about the society that television is in.

Scratching the surface: soap and sports fans

To begin our examination of fans, let us consider two of fandom's more stereotypical representatives: the soap fan and the sports fan. Both types of fans are regularly subject to demeaning jokes and caricature. Thus, popular impressions of soap fans often rely upon conjured-up images of bored housewives and gossip-mongers falling hopelessly in love with square-jawed stars and sending flowers to newly married fictional couples – social misfits living vicariously through Nikki and Victor, the Watts, and the Mitchells. Meanwhile, many televised sports fans have been pathologized as drinking, eating, and farting to excess, screaming at the screen, and recalling batting averages or starting lineups from the 1950s over wives' or children's birthdays. Fandom is often imagined in terms of aberrant gendering – as with the "too feminine" soap fans and "too masculine" sports fans – and abnormal identity construction and psychology. However, might soap, sports, and other fandoms not only have more in common with each other, but also point to quite mundane or even universal needs and social practices?

As numerous studies show, much soap, sports, and other fandom is about community, and specifically communities of interest (see, for example, Brooker 2002, Harrington and Bielby 1995, Hellekson and Busse 2006, Jenkins 1992, Sandvoss 2003). Sometimes, the fan object will appear a mere alibi for the establishment of community. Hence, to entertain the caricature images of a group of men watching "the game" together at the pub, or the women in an extended family watching "their" soap together, in either situation, the activity may be enjoyed largely as a way to facilitate community. Analyzing these or other fan groups through the lens of community, many of their practices cease to appear as strange as some critics and cruel jokes contend. In particular, fan-related activities may serve primarily as investments in that community, so that, for example, reading up on a star's reflections on his or her character or on a goalkeeper's past record in games played in the rain offers one knowledge to share with the community, a visible sign to others in that community and to oneself of involvement, interest, caring, and belonging. Or the additional knowledge might allow one to jockey for relative power in that group, just as does knowledge capital in any (fan or non-fan based) group. And because television programs and their audiences are often gendered in the popular imagination – as evident in the caricatures of who watches soaps or most sports – one's public or secret attraction to various fan communities may amount to a traditional performance of gender, or to a contestation of those traditions, and thus community membership can say a great deal about one's individual process of identity construction and performance.

Fandom, though, is not just about community, nor just about gender. Instead, it is also about specific meanings, and thus fan groups are rarely interchangeable. Soaps, for instance, privilege the domestic sphere, valuing familial and friendship bonds and deeply layered knowledge of social relationships and history, and so we might imagine that such elements attract many soap fans and fan groups, their resulting fandom a testament to belief in such values. Sports fandoms, by contrast, may focus more on a love of competition, individual physical prowess, and geographic rivalries. Of course, however, we cannot plot a simple concordance of fan objects and values or meanings: given that all fan objects are rich with possible meanings, the nature of a fan community's bond or bonds may surprise us. Sports fans may focus on the team and the collaborative aspect of play more than competition, for example, or many fandoms of serial dramas focus on a single character or relationship, and on what s/he or they represent to the fan(s), excluding much of the rest of the program in the process. What this proliferation of meanings points to, therefore, is the danger of falling into the trap of assuming one understands any given fan's or fan community's practices and/or of judging either that fandom or fan object based on one's own interpretation or reading of the show in question. Rather, we will always need to find out what the fandom means *to the fans*. It is not the fan object, program, or genre per se that attracts heightened affect as much as its meaning, or aggregate of meanings and uses. To "know" or understand soap, sports, or any fandom requires considerable study.

Seeing between the pixels: active fans

Since the late 1980s, however, an increasing number of academic studies have taken up this challenge and have examined fan communities and culture, allowing us empirical data and informed analysis well beyond the easy stereotypes and extremes. Frequently, this work has examined particularly involved communities and individuals, such as creators of fan fiction, 'zines, and videos, fan convention attendees, and so forth, but their findings point towards pleasures and uses of fandom that exist for us all, regardless of our level(s) of fandom.

Much of fan studies' early work focused on the notion of "audience activity." Earlier mass communications researchers (see Blumler and Katz 1975) had already posed a "uses and gratifications" "down-up" model of media consumption (whereby power begins with the audience member seeking media content for specific "uses and gratifications"), rather than the top-down model of much effects research (whereby audiences passively consume whatever is given to them). But the wave of "active audience" studies of the late 1980s and early 1990s (e.g.: Bacon-Smith 1992, Buckingham 1987, Fiske 1989b, 1989c, Jenkins 1992, Radway 1987) greatly elaborated on the varied powers of audiences, and also showed the degree to which audience resistance to programs could be communal, not simply individual. Two of the classic examples of active audiences come from Janice Radway (1987) and John Fiske (1989b). Radway began by noting the highly patriarchal content of romance fiction, yet her conversations with romance readers suggested considerable resistance to patriarchy, as women would read alone, away from familial/"womanly" duties, and then form reading groups that would discuss and sometimes play with the content. Fiske looked at teen-girl consumption of Madonna, a performer who in the late 1980s seemed to exist largely as a sex symbol, and yet whose fans, Fiske argues, admired her as a powerful woman who could be controlled by no man. Both writers, then, found evidence of audience members using programs actively and in ways other than those seemingly proscribed by the texts themselves.

As with the above examples, active audience studies often sported a strong feminist vein, not least because women had often been coded as the most passive and mindless of consumers, a demeaning assumption that feminist cultural studies researchers set out to disprove. This mindlessness was seen to crystallize in the form of the soap fan, and thus fan research of soap fans has been particularly strong, offering careful study of ironic and knowing consumption (see Ang 1985, Buckingham 1987), of identity construction (Harrington and Bielby 1995), of the pleasures of soap watching (see Modleski 1984), and even of resistive international consumption of the über-capitalist *Dallas* (see Katz and Liebes 1990). While feminist media studies have often been at the forefront of pointing to the patriarchal, hegemonic meanings embedded in programs, feminist audience studies researchers have also been careful to show how mindfully, even *creatively*, some women have been in reading these and other programs.

Feminist and feminist-inspired active audience studies such as these greatly sophisticated our understanding of female consumers, and of how women wrestle with problematic programs, not as thoughtless wildebeest, but often as wise and savvy consumers, working with some textual elements and excluding others. If earlier assumptions of fans had often posited them as loner individuals or as thoughtless members of a "mass" audience, active audience studies often showed the importance of communities of viewing and interpretation, focusing on how these communities repurposed programs through use. As Henry Jenkins would argue in his seminal work, *Textual Poachers*, fans "cease to be simply an audience for popular texts; instead, they become active participants in the construction and circulation of textual meanings" (1992: 24). Following Michel de Certeau (1984), Jenkins wrote of fans as "poachers," taking what they want from popular texts and leaving what they don't want. Similarly, Fiske wrote of consumption as a process of "excorporation," whereby an audience would pull those pleasures and meanings that they liked from the body of mass cultural texts, in the process domesticating and taming mass culture into popular culture, an entity which Fiske saw as always inherently personalized to the individual community. Popular culture, Fiske argued (1989c: 23), is culture (active), not consumption (passive). All texts, as such, are "incomplete," requiring reader/viewer involvement to complete them (1989c: 123). Fan reading, stated Jenkins, "is a social process through which individual interpretations are shaped and reinforced through ongoing discussions with other readers" (1992: 45), meaning not only that individual readers' use affects the program's essence (what it is, what it means), but also that communities will continue this work of textual creation in how they talk about a show, and in how they choose to make sense of it. Television shows thus become a form of "silly putty," as fans stretch their boundaries "to incorporate their concerns, remolding its characters to better suit their desires" (Jenkins 1992: 156).

Take, for example, the hugely successful *Sex and the City* and *Grey's Anatomy*. A traditional feminist reading of either might point to their female lead character's obsession with finding a man, and the subjugation of her professional life to the

Figure 2.1 Sex and the City: feminist or not? A question for the viewers

often titillating details (and video) of her sex life. Carrie and friends may be seen as often depending upon men's interest in them to provide a sense of personal value, while Meredith Grey's famed address to her beloved "McDreamy" in Season 2, plaintively calling on him to "pick me, choose me, love me," may similarly be read as demeaning herself to the level of an object to be selected. But fans of either show might discuss such shortcomings, actively using the programs – two of the only primetime shows in American television history to privilege the lives and loves of young women – to "poach" what they want, fully self-aware and critical of limitations, while grasping to the programs' more progressive moments, characters, and potential (see Figure 2.1). Just as we might love yet be critical of a sibling, liking or even loving a show never requires us to love everything about it. However, whereas siblings rarely let us change them, at the level of consumption and through poaching, television programs are more malleable.

As will be discussed further in Chapter 6, such a model of consumption offers a radically different notion of textual power than does the top-down model of passive audiences. Constance Penley offers that "No one knows the object better than a fan and no one is more critical . . . The idea is to change the object while preserving it, kind of like giving a strenuous, deep massage that hurts at the time but feels so good afterwards" (1997: 3), suggesting knowing fans who can correct a show's problems at the same time as they enjoy other elements of it. As should be evident, though, such a view of consumption also shifts how we think of textual ownership. Harrington and Bielby pose the idea of the fan as "moral author," "a person who feels that a [text] is morally or emotionally theirs, regardless of who might have actually written the text" (1995: 155). As much as anti-piracy discourse would like us to believe that the programs we consume belong to others, Harrington and Bielby, and many other fan researchers, suggest that they very much are *ours*. With their many characters, themes, plotlines, images, sounds, and ideas, television shows are spaces of play, into which we can enter relatively empowered to do with them and take from them as we would like.

That said, active audience work – and John Fiske as its de facto figurehead – have been heavily criticized for overstating the case. First, as Celeste Condit concludes after interviewing two viewers, one anti-abortion, one pro-choice, of a relatively pro-choice *Cagney and Lacey* episode, audience activity takes substantial *work*, and "We need to investigate how much more this costs them" (1994: 434). Working against a show takes mental energy, and while individual viewers might find this "cost" acceptable if a show has multiple other pleasures on offer, the cost will be prohibitive to most viewers, resulting in a failure either to resist, watch, or enjoy. Therefore, while all of us may be capable of resisting a program, and giving it a "deep massage," many of us simply will not bother. Moreover, as William Seaman's (1992) broadside attack on active audience scholarship notes, *your* act of resistance by no means entails *my* act, and thus we must beware extrapolation from a small group's textual play to believe that *all* viewers will resist. Finally, as Sandvoss (2005a: 7) notes, a Fiskean model presupposes viewers who are disempowered by a program, and displeased with (aspects of) it, whereas in fact many viewers will happily read with the program. Sandvoss points to E. Graham McKinley's (1997) study of *Beverly Hills 90210* viewers, in which McKinley finds no evidence of oppositional reading. After all, many of us are fans of shows precisely because we feel no or little need to resist them. Popular culture would be considerably more chaotic if more viewers actively resisted more shows than at present. Resistance is an option, and all programs are open to a reader's participation, opposition, and/or play, and as the wealth of fan studies suggest, considerable pleasure is created for many viewers by doing so; as Roland Barthes (1995) wrote of literature, one of the great "pleasures of the text" is to *play* with it. When doing so, viewers may well bypass or override effects, but we must not make the mistake of thinking that this is the only pleasure of television entertainment, and hence that affect will always allow us to sidestep effect.

TV connections and identity creation

Fan research signals to us how volatile meaning construction is, so that even once clever and creative writers have dodged their ways through the many creative obstacles that particularly Hollywood throws in their way, no guarantees remain that their programs will say and mean to audiences what the writers intend them to. However, while we can see this play with meaning in terms of audience activity, it also creates significant creative potential for consumers to construct personal and community identities. Genres such as the news and documentaries are used for identity construction purposes too, but television entertainment is particularly useful for constructing identities. While I wrote in Chapter 1 of creativity as a writer/producer's pursuit, considerable creativity takes place in consumption.

As David Chaney has argued, today's self has become "an object of cultural mapping" (2001: 83), a "project articulating who [we] are" (2001: 83). Both Chaney (2001) and James Lull draw a distinction between culture that is willed to us, and that reflects where we come from – what Chaney calls "ways of life" and Lull (2007) capitalizes as Culture – and culture that we create, choose from, and that reflects who we want to be – what Chaney calls "lifestyles" and Lull calls "superculture." Both writers see modern subjects as empowered to draw from a seemingly endless palette of popular culture in constructing lifestyles and superculture. "Symbolic creativity," as Lull dubs it, is an art form in which we all engage, dressing in this shirt to send this message, consuming this program to satisfy this part of ourselves, and so on. Inevitably, this process entails much more than the consumption of television entertainment – it is also about how we dress, speak, and dance, where we hang out, what music we listen to, etc. – but given the huge amount of time that many of us spend either watching television entertainment or talking about it, frequently television entertainment serves as a centerpiece to this identity project, as each of our favored programs tells both us and others something about ourselves.

Key to understanding how television entertainment can offer such symbolic creative powers is an appreciation of television's ability to move us. Here, I use the word "move" in both senses, for it is both our emotional involvement with television entertainment, and the medium's stunning capacity to take us places that combine to make it such a rich tool for identity creation. As a form of travel, television can take us far from our homes and our lived environments, geographically and experientially. Thus, on one hand, for instance, we can travel to Borneo or the Pearl Islands with *Survivor*, but the program also transports us into an elaborate game of, as the byline says, "Outwit – Outplay – Outlast." Or, as we will examine in detail in Chapter 4, programs can introduce us to people we might otherwise never meet, and introduce us to lives and ideas foreign to us. Having transported us elsewhere, television can then lure us in, interest us, and make us care with characterization and narrative hooks. Moreover, much television entertainment returns us to these foreign places with such regularity (once a week, or even once a night) and potentially over many years, that bit by bit the foreign may come to seem local. Mayberry, Stars Hollow, Albert Square, Springfield, the Tardis, Wysteria Lane: these are places that empirically "don't exist," but that many of us feel attached to, and sometimes inhabitants of. When such locations and/or structures of feeling become so familiar, they become personal, and – when shared with others – communal, making their subsequent movement into identities wholly understandable.

Ironically, for all that beloved shows can move us *away*, many of them also create a veritable sense of *home* (see Morley 2000, Sandvoss 2005a: 64). Curling up on the sofa, under a blanket, with a familiar program is a calming experience for many of us. Matt Hills (2002) uses D. W. Winnicott's object relations theory to make sense of the fan object, writing of it as a "primary transitional object." Winnicott (1974) writes of the key period in a baby's development when it must be separated from the mother, a period of uncertainty and risk for an infant whose mother has until then always been its provider. To cope with this transition, infants often embody the warm, comforting feelings of motherly safety and belonging into a transitional object, whether a beloved teddy bear, a blanket, or a favorite toy. However, ours is a world of strife and risk, and thus Silverstone (1994) has pointed out the continuing need for and use of transitional objects by adults. With their mother-like ability to calm us at the end of the day, turning our attention away from serious problems and towards light fare, certain programs such as *Late Night with David Letterman*, *Sports Center*, or late night reruns are particularly efficient transitional objects. Beyond these, though, as Hills notes, objects of fandom frequently serve a calming role. He writes:

> A fan culture is formed around any given text when this text has functioned as a *pto* [primary transitional object] in the biography of a number of individuals; individuals who remain attached to this text by virtue of the fact that it continues to exist as an element of their cultural experience.
>
> (2002: 108)

Particularly many longrunning or rerun shows remind us of our youth, and hence serve a nostalgic purpose, both individually and communally, and many favorite shows remind us of their past success in transporting us away from an unpleasant here-and-now to that warm (mother-like) place that we call home (see Figure 2.2).

Interestingly, then, television entertainment's affective powers construct both ways of life and lifestyles, both culture and superculture. On one hand, its programs can show us new ways to be, think, look, and feel (superculture) that

Figure 2.2 Television's place called home: perfect family Ricky, David, Ozzie, and Harriet Nelson enjoy another perfect Christmas in the perfect sitcom world of *The Adventures of Ozzie and Harriet*

move us away from more ingrained identity markers such as gender, ethnicity, religion, or nationality (culture). On the other hand, the tendency for fan texts to serve as primary transitional objects can encourage us to hole up in our past. As we will discuss further in Chapter 4, television narratives have played a sizeable role in constructing a sense of national home and national history that while cozy and saccharine for those included, often reveal a worrying exclusionary xenophobia and fear of change in their core. Hence, for instance, family dramas and sitcoms such as *The Waltons* and *The Andy Griffith Show* create ideas of an American home and nationality that are trapped in a whites only, women-in-the-kitchen suburban mentality (as toyed with so wonderfully in the film *Pleasantville*). Ultimately, then, television entertainment offers affective wonderlands for both sides of the cultural equation, serving as inspiration for lifestyles and superculture, at the same time as it can work alongside ways of life and culture.

In this way, we can start to see television entertainment as providing us with a language for communicating our complex identities. Despite the vast array of programs on offer, this language lets us down at times, for television entertainment will always fail to communicate some of our most important feelings and beliefs, so this language has not *colonized* our identities, as some fear (see Miller 1986: 186). Nevertheless, the utility of fandom or textual love for play and for the performance of our identities is a key reason why fandom is so prevalent (and why stereotypes of fans miss a great deal). If programs can transport us places, whether backwards in time or to another place altogether, play with such programs can allow us to revel in such travel. Play, as Jurij Lotman notes, "makes it possible for a man to enter into situations that are beyond his reach in real life, and thus it is play which permits man to discover his true essence" (1977: 63). Hence, television entertainment allows us to play with the world, experimenting with ways of being or thinking, watching others deal with issues (as yet) unknown to us, and so forth. Meredith Grey struggles so that we need not. Much as children use play to think their way through different actions, reactions, and states of being (see Fleming 1996), so too can we all use the emotionally engaging characters and programs of television to map out potential experiences. The first stage of such play may well occur alone, in solitary reflection, but it will likely include communities of others at a later stage, as we debate characters' decisions and ethics with other viewers. Play carries with it the risk that the logic of the playworld will be superimposed onto the real world (see Chapter 4), but when we play with others, they bring their own life experiences with them to the playing field, and together, they can help us to bump a play logic and its laws of causation up against those of the real world. In some small way, then, anytime we discuss a show with others, we are playing, as we transform the media into a central framing and organizational tool for discussing all matters of experience, longing, and relationships (Bird 2003: 17). Borrowing from Pierre Lévy (2000), Jenkins (2006) writes of fans' construction of "collective knowledge" of a show's minutiae, but part and parcel with this is the knowledge fostered by general collective *play*.

Where there is play, there is performance, and thus Abercrombie and Longhurst (1998) have posited performance as a key lens through which we should aim to understand contemporary audiences. By performance, they do not suggest inherent falsity, but merely that audiences are "constantly drawing from the endless media stream that passes them by a set of diverse elements out of which they can construct imaginative worlds that suit them" (1998: 107). Identity, in Stuart Hall's words, is a production, "a matter of 'becoming' as well as 'being'" (1990: 236), for we must constantly be creating ourselves. However, we cannot be ourselves only to ourselves, for we must perform our identity for others to see, and with television entertainment forming part of the wellspring from which performances are put together, its imaginative worlds quite literally help us work out who we are. As such, Abercrombie and Longhurst note, "everyone becomes an audience all of the time" (1998: 68); television on or off, we constantly use it for the most intimate task of performing the self, both to the self and to others (see also Sandvoss 2005a: 48). Given the central role that fandoms play in this performance, as Hills writes, this indicates that "fandom is about more than just 'interpretive communities' or a rational(ised) system of meaning; it is also about the dialectic of value – the interplay between intensely subjective, personalised value and objective/communal accounts" (2002: 129). Discussing Jack and Kate, Lorelai and Rory, Jerry and Kramer may be significantly more important than it sounds to some. Some performances will boldly challenge the individual with difference, otherness, and new ideas, whereas others (those that seek a comfortable, known "home") risk merely reflecting the self back upon itself, Narcissus-like. Sandvoss' (2005a, 2005b) recent critical work on fan psychology and textuality suggests that some fan's reading practices impose meanings upon programs, as they make the progam slave to the Narcissistic performance rather than learn from its inherent otherness. Thus, fans' and others' often exhaustively creative uses of television entertainment should not be inherently celebrated, but their central role in identity construction should nevertheless be evident.

Watching between worlds: fantasy and escape

Such an understanding of fan uses of programs helps us to highlight the errors in commonplace notions of television entertainment that regard such programs as all about escape and escapism. As we have said, television does indeed allow us to escape, but the space to which we escape is often reflective at some level of our ongoing production of identity: rarely are we escaping "reality" entirely (as if such a feat is even truly possible). To others, we might seem to be merely sitting mindlessly in front of the television watching Jack Bauer kill another bad guy on *24*, for instance, and no doubt our enjoyment of this spectacle is likely predicated on our understanding that Jack, Jack's life, and Jack's US are far from our own everyday experiences (see Figure 2.3). But our mind is actually performing some complex tasks of learning and comparison, even as we reach for yet another handful of munchies — it is bouncing our world off against his, evaluating both his choices and his decisions against those that we might have, and comparing his US to our own. We can only recognize something as fantasy or escapism in the first place if we have already computed that its logic and laws of action and reaction, and its narrative set-up, are sufficiently different from our own to allow us to feel as if the narrative has transported us. Having already made these subtle calculations, our mind is thus poised to analyze them, albeit simplistically at times, and with significant complexity at other times. Affect always works hand in hand with cognition, and as any good science-fiction writer or reader could tell us, all good "escape" narratives tell us about the point of departure as much as, if not much more than, the point of arrival.

Fantasy and the fantastic, then, bring together many of fandom's other qualities, as, to varying degrees of power and importance, fantasy can force reflection on the world in which we live, it can open a textual space in which we can either experience otherness and difference, or reaffirm a connection to the comforting and the

Figure 2.3 Another hour in the life of Jack Bauer: "escaping" into the world of *24*

known, and its very difference from "reality" allows room for subsequent challenging of either the logics of that fantastic world or the "real" world, in either instance
inspiring "audience activity." The world of the fantastic is one in which we can
perhaps safely reflect upon our world and our selves from a critical distance. For
this reason, Lawrence Grossberg has described fandom as potentially offering a
"site of the optimism, invigoration and passion which are necessary conditions for
any struggle to change the conditions of one's life" (1992: 65), and Richard Dyer
offers that entertainment's greatest power may be one of utopianism, giving us
"the image of 'something better' to escape into, or something that we want deeply
that our day-to-day lives don't provide" (1992: 18). Whereas the news' discourse
of the real, the here, and the now, can depress, worry, and scare us, perhaps its
most frustrating quality is its frequent failure to pose a way forward. Television
entertainment, by contrast, may well pose simplistic or even impossible or naíve
ways forward, but it provides us with images of difference that enable both play
and performance. For this reason, we will return to the powers of fantasy in
Chapter 4, when considering representation and reality, and in Chapter 5, when
considering television entertainment and politics. After all, fantasy brings us into
contact with discourses of utopia and dystopia, but ultimately it is what we *do* with
them that matters.

A danger of discussing fantasy alongside fandom in a book about television
entertainment is that we risk perpetuating the notion that fandom and fantasy
attach themselves *only* to television entertainment, and hence that the news, politics, and other "important" topics work in wholly different ways. However, news,
politics, and even academic theory fans exist (see Gray 2007, Hills 2005a, McKee
2007), and as I will argue in Chapter 5 (see also van Zoonen 2005), fandom can
often facilitate and enable citizenship, not simply turn it off in favor of another car
chase or cheap sexual pun. For now, though, let us remember that even when we
do not, say, "export" *24*'s Season 5 thematics regarding the dangers of presidential
power and ignorance into a political campaign in the real world, these notions
contribute to our identity construction and to the narrative building blocks that
circulate throughout society. Hence, it is impossible to restrict wholly the flow of
ideas between fantasy and reality.

Of course, here I speak only of television entertainment's *potential*; many television stories create utopias of no note whatsoever. Similarly, while some fantastic
narratives and spaces encourage reflection on issues of considerable gravity and
importance, others will do little more than make us consider what kind of shoes
to buy, or what to buy a friend for her birthday. Surely, such choices contribute to
our ongoing production of identity, but not all will give us great reason to get
excited. Audience theory can offer us windows into what shows *can* do, but not all
shows and not all audiences will play along. As such, it becomes important to
study audiences in the trenches, so to speak. Assuming one knows how audiences

interpret a program, based on anecdotal evidence and casual supposition, is easy but also frequently wrong, and if we are serious about wanting to understand how any television show is consumed, we must be willing to engage with actual audience research.

Hate, dislike, distaste, and disgust: anti-fans

The love of a good program, its characters, and its world may guide some of our interaction with television entertainment, but dislike, disgust, disappointment, and derision also form the basis for many other interactions. Most of us have programs we eagerly anticipate, but we also have programs we do our best to avoid. Some programs remain personal pet peeves, whereas others garner communal or even societal disapproval. It may seem rather odd to pause here on such programs, given the supposition that we are not watching them anyway, but anti-fan discourse surrounding television programs can be just as constitutive of their meaning and relevance to the individual or society as can fan discourse. For instance, Mittell (2004a) notes that anti-fan discussion of the talk show as smutty, depraved, and exploitative plays a key role in determining what "the talk show" means to society as a whole. Not only are talk show fans therefore required to defend the genre and themselves against such allegations, but the anti-fan definition of talk shows frequently serves as a general frame through which fans, anti-fans, and non-fans alike will look. Similarly, all genres and their viewers must bump up against anti-fan discourse, whether it is of science fiction (as "escapive geek TV"), family dramas ("sappy chick flicks"), sitcoms ("formulaic sterile humor"), game shows ("dumb contestants, flashing lights, and peppy hosts"), or so forth. Encompassing all anti-fandoms, meanwhile, is the suspicion of television entertainment in general.

Moreover, anti-fans can be just as active and productive as can their fan counterparts (see Gray 2005). All censorship campaigns are, of course, instances of anti-fan activism, as a group of anti-fans attempt to erase the offending program from the public sphere. And due to particularly the networks' desperate attempt to keep all viewers, many such campaigns *work*: in early 2006, a threatened boycott of NBC by various conservative Christian groups forced the cancellation of *The Book of Daniel*, a program with a drug-addicted episcopal priest, two gay characters, a gay creator, and a rather iconoclastic Jesus; following Bill Maher's post-9/11 comments on *Politically Incorrect* suggesting that, by lobbing missiles and bombs from afar, the US showed equal or greater cowardice as did the 9/11 perpetrators, angry listeners (and non-listeners) encouraged FedEx and other advertisers to boycott the program, resulting in its cancellation; and the outrage surrounding the 2004 Super Bowl Janet Jackson "wardrobe malfunction" forced a time-delay on all live broadcasting from the major American networks, and produced a remarkably boring, sterilized half-time show in 2005. As the last example here suggests, and as researchers of censorship have long noted (see, for example, Sandler 2007), not only does anti-fan discourse work in the trenches when faced with a specific grievance, but it can also become the two-ton gorilla in the room around which production and programming decisions must operate, whether in fear or by brazenly violating them. One should never underestimate the importance that the fear of offending plays in dictating all sorts of decisions within the television industry, whether in the field of programming, casting (due to, say, an actor's previous "morally questionable" roles), or brand identification. Anti-fan discourse surrounds most television entertainment – if sometimes for no other reason than it is television entertainment! – and works as a force field through which much action must work, or else fail in the process.

Anti-fan discourse also proves conclusively that our reactions to and engagement with television entertainment does not always require actually *watching* its shows. Those who lead anti-fan campaigns are often quite proud that they have not watched the offending program; rather, they have heard *of* it, and object based on the scant (and perhaps highly selective) information to which they have access. But such is the case with non-campaigning anti-fans too: often, one's deepest felt televisual prejudices and dislikes are of programs whose premises alone cause revulsion. This revulsion may be aesthetic, moral, or rational–realistic (see Gray 2005), as we may, respectively, feel that the program or genre constitutes poor art, that its morals and ethics are reprehensible, and/or that its premise is patently absurd. As with all of the cultural industries, television is structured in a way that gives us plenty of pre-viewing time of any show: we might see previews, read articles about it, hear interviews, hear other viewers' reviews and criticism, and so forth. Television entertainment is categorically too vast and voluminous for any of us to even attempt to consume but 1 per cent of it, and thus we are forced to prejudge constantly, in order that we might filter out a viewing shortlist. Our choices of what not to watch and why not to watch it are thereby as constitutive of our identity, of the show's public meaning, and of the show's powers and effects, as are our televisual desires and fandoms. Moreover, the distinctions we draw between what we dislike or hate privately, what we dislike or hate publicly, and what we hate with an active vengeance work to construct both ourselves and the world around us. After all, in stating what is not wanted, anti-fandom can be markedly political, and at the very least is highly revealing of our individual and communal criteria for what television should be.

Moreso than fandom, though, anti-fandom can move into the realm of dictating what *others'* television should look like. Thus anti-fandom also reveals societal panics regarding effects. As many audience studies have recounted, audiences tend to think only of others as likely pawns for effects. This type of "third person effect" is most amusingly discussed by David Buckingham, who notes of his qualitative work with children "a kind of infinite regression here, as children in each age group claim to have already attained the age of reason some years previously" (1997: 38). Anti-fan discourse, then, becomes a way to have conversations about what other people should watch: you may not feel that this instance of sex or violence, for example, will affect you, but you may worry greatly for others. Anti-fandom involves watching with an imagined community of fellow watchers, and it reveals the extent to which many of us are deeply aware of, and worried by, television entertainment's "massness." Television entertainment is not just about engaging with a plot or characters, and reveling in the different worlds presented to us; it is also, and sometimes instead, a massive cultural database and vocabulary we can access to discuss society – what it is, what it could be, what we wish it was not. Thus, battles and debates over what is on television are often battles and debates about "the real world" and about what choices/"vocabulary" we want made available to those in this real world.

Confusingly, then, while anti-fandom may often seem to express both a reaction to television, and considerable fear of others' reactions to television, anti-fandom may actually be more important for what it says about viewers' use of television *as a reaction to the world around them*. Hence, for instance, many campaigners against violence on television may posit television as the initiator of violence, but clearly, from Vlad the Impaler to Hiroshima, humankind has proven supremely capable of horrific violence without television, and few but the most deluded of campaigners would honestly blame all violence on television. Such campaigners are correct to question television's possible exacerbation and amplification of violence, but we should also understand their anti-fandom as simply a plea for less violence in the world outside of television. These campaigners use television as a vocabulary, and we would be mistaken to hear them as talking only *about* television, for they are just as much talking *with* and *through* television about a more endemic issue. Worst and best television shows lists therefore often tell us a lot about citizens' fears and wants for the world around them.

Anti-fandom from 'Television Without Pity' to Monday night football

Though anti-fandom can be about anything from different values to different aesthetics, a prominent form of anti-fandom can be seen in political objections to a show. For instance, in the *Grey's Anatomy* forum at popular television discussion site, *Television Without Pity* (www.televisionwithoutpity.com), one poster states that a viewing of the show:

> pissed me off no end. It was blatant pandering to a low brow male audience (or the one they were trying to make watch after the game) point of view, of

women as whiney, cry babies who really can't hack it when the going gets tough. But the male characters were all depicted as gung ho and take-chargey. Ok I know that is not a real word, but its [sic] been 3 days and I am still pissed off about it.

The poster here expresses considerable reservations about *Grey's Anatomy*, based on her/his reading of its gender depictions. Her/his comments serve not only as commentary about the actual program, therefore, but also about gender in real life. Concerned with how women in particular are regarded, s/he uses the program as a resource and tool to open up discussion regarding preconceptions of gender and "femininity." In doing so, s/he also "performs" a sense of what a woman is, and of how viewers and readers *should* see women. In such a way, anti-fandom and the dislike of television often allows important discussion about society as a whole.

Complaints regarding the politics of depiction are rife throughout the pages of this site, sometimes solitary missives, but other times giving rise to extended and hearty discussion among hundreds of posters. For example, during Season 1 of the American *Apprentice*, African-American contestant Omarosa Manigault-Stallworth became the center of a firestorm of criticism that was still generating debate three years later on the site. Omarosa had her fans, but she also had legions of anti-fans, many of whom worried that viewers would see her as representative of both women and African-Americans in the workplace. As one poster wrote:

there is and always will be prejudice in America, so there will be people out there who may view her as a sick woman, but also will lump all black women together into a group and say "This group is delusional" and will base hiring decisions on that. Open-minded people won't do this and will instead just look at [Omarosa] as sick and shrug it off when an African American woman comes into their office to interview, but there will be some that use her as a benchmark for all African American women. It's inevitable.

In time, this anti-fandom built to fever pitch among the community, reaching its climax with the initiation of a letter-writing campaign to Clairol, who were rumored at the time to be hiring Omarosa as a spokesperson for their Herbal Essences shampoo. Posters shared their letters with others from the site, with one noting, for instance, "Ms. Manigault-Stallworth is not a role-model for any sort of positive behavior, and it is baffling why any well-respected company, such as Clairol, would feel the need to do business with her." Eventually, Clairol announced that they had no intent to hire Omarosa, suggesting that this anti-fan campaign had seemingly succeeded in imprinting its desires onto the public sphere. If one reads through the hundreds of pages of comments surrounding this affair, however, it is clear that few felt the campaign was about advertising or Clairol – it was about the politics of representation, and about who should serve as role models, two key concerns for a mediated era.

Anti-fandom can similarly allow one to perform all sorts of aspects of one's identity. Hence, for instance, we might observe the range of identities that televised sports allow their anti-fans to perform. Heavily gendered sports are prone to disparaging commentary from viewers of the other gender seeking to announce their masculinity or femininity, and thus comments about a son or husband watching "his stupid football" or the same son or husband's groans when the television is turned over to a figure-skating competition, allow for considerable performance of gender roles. National sports also become victim to criticism from those seeking to perform national identity, resulting most prominently in the widespread English conviction that baseball and American football are stupid, with cricket and rugby being touted respectively as more cerebral and tougher. For their part, Americans often counter that cricket is for silly old aristocrats, and that American football is considerably more exciting than either rugby or soccer. Such national performances crescendo when national teams play – as when Scottish viewers in pubs worldwide cheer any English team's defeat – or when fans discuss the relative virtues of national broadcasters' coverage – as when, during the FIFA World Cup 2006, many non-Americans working in the US frequently expressed disdain and contempt for ESPN, turning instead to Telemundo. And criticizing certain sports can similarly allow one to perform an intelligence and class sophistication, or a sense of grounded everyman-ishness, so that, for example, a distaste for wrestling or American football is firmly expected of the upper classes. Whether in the pub, at home in the living room, or typing away on the computer, in these and other ways, anti-fandom allows us to construct an image and identity for ourselves and the world around us.

Between "meh" and "hmm": casual viewing and non-fans

All of us are fans at times, and anti-fans at others. However, much viewing time is likely spent somewhere in between: as casual viewers, perhaps somewhat interested but not particularly so, willing to change the channel or turn the television off if need be, and perhaps even talking, eating, napping, or doing homework while watching. One of the greatest traps in studying audiences lies in automatically assuming that they have turned on a specific show with purpose. As Ron Lembo notes, frequently the turn to television represents simply "the path of least resistance" (2000: 5): one comes home from school or work and needs to switch one's brain off, one's family is arguing, there are twenty minutes to spare, it's either television or chores, the house feels safer with some noise in it, or, as programmers eagerly hope, one favorite program has finished (or yet to begin) and so the television just stays on. Lembo argues that too little work has examined "the turn to television" – why we watch in the first place – and his ensuing empirical analysis evocatively illustrates the many reasons (or seeming lack of a reason and "purposelessness" (27)) behind turning on the television. Show choice, too, is a sticky topic, for as Webster and Phalen note:

> If, as is sometimes the case, people select media offerings without a full understanding of their options, the interpretation of choice as an expression of preference is complicated. How many times have you missed an interesting magazine article because you did not know it was there? How often have you discovered a favorite program or song long after it first aired?
>
> (1997: 36).

Or, they could add, how many times have you watched a program only because your family or friends had control of the remote (see Morley 1986)? Beyond the programs that we purposively seek out or avoid are hordes of shows that we arrive at by chance. Thus, as much as choice may tell us about television and how it is being used, often an audience member's choices are severely limited, or made randomly and rather disinterestedly.

Anna McCarthy (2004) offers a particularly clear example of non-fan consumption in her study of waiting room television. Here, doctors, government offices, department stores dressing rooms, and so forth install televisions in the hopes of distracting those who are waiting, "producing not an absorbed spectator but a temporarily occupied one" (195). Waiting room television becomes symbolic of boredom, the lack of anything better to do, and of being trapped in a bureaucratic vacuum cycle, just as its occasional tendency to loop back on itself creates a "no exit"-like setting of tedium and anxiety. Rather than serve as an isolated exception, though, waiting room television and its correlate of non-fan consumption is representative of much television in other sites too. First, it reminds us that much of television is "ordinary" (Bonner 2003), warranting neither the engrossed fandom or anti-fandom of more spectacular television. As McCarthy notes, moreover, "When considered as a televisual affect, waiting seems to be the opposite of the liveness so often ascribed to television – and in fact is closer to deadness" (2004: 194). This "deadness" leads to a second point: that much of television may be as boring and as anxiety-inducing an experience as is waiting room television: "we may think we're having fun or relaxing, but actually our leisure is just another way of waiting to go back to work" (201). Hence, the "turn to television" for some may suggest much about the absence of other alternatives, and about a pervasive boredom and proclivity to live in stasis, between other activities, that has made television a waiting room for many viewers at many times.

As normal and regular as non-fandom may be, though, its ramifications are often underestimated. For instance, if Bobby is a fan of 7th Heaven, and watches it closely, and Christine misses the first ten minutes, and even then flips back and forth between 7th Heaven and numerous other programs, our analysis of these two viewers' textual interactions must diverge. Our non-fan, Christine, may have missed half or more of the plot, may have missed the moralized speech at the end of the program, and may never have seen the show before, giving her little context or background information. Christine's 7th Heaven is a different aesthetic entity, therefore (closer to a series of images, and including only snippets of dialogue), it is a different rational–realistic entity (she may have missed key arguments or points), and it is a different political, moral, and/or social entity. Particularly if we want to draw conclusions regarding 7th Heaven's effects or power over its audience, we are faced with the conundrum of working out how Christine's casual viewing mode has refracted or otherwise misdirected any effects. Thus, for instance, Mittell's (2004: 114) research into how viewers and non-viewers define talk shows suggests that anti-fans did not even see the genre's educational/informational role, while fans highlighted it, and non-fans sometimes discussed it. Or, to offer arguably broadcasting history's most infamous example of non-fan effects, subsequent research into the panic that embraced some listeners of Orson Welles' radio program, *The War of the Worlds* (see Cantrill 1966), suggested that most of the panicking listeners had missed the opening minute, which framed the program as fictional. Here, casual listeners experienced a different set of "effects" than did close listeners, but in other situations, perhaps they would experience *none*, the program flying by them at speed. Indeed, albeit from different perspectives, Joke Hermes (1995) and Jean Baudrillard (1983a) have both put forward the possibility that some media use may be meaningless, empty of any other signification.

Ultimately, however, audiences do not so easily divide themselves into fan, anti-fan, and non-fan "teams" with respective jerseys. Instead, a great deal of television consumption involves floating between categories. For instance, Hills (2005b) has examined what he dubs "cyclical fandom," whereby a viewer becomes fannish about a text for a brief period of time, before leaving the object and moving onward. When shows disappoint us, or simply when our evening schedules shift, we can lose touch with old favorites and become lapsed fans. Or sometimes our fandom may include room for ironic distancing, or for the love of shows that we acknowledge are awful. We may even be fans or anti-fans only because we feel obliged to by our peers, in spite of ourselves, and/or by our evaluation of a show's political worth in the face of its aesthetic failure (or vice versa). In these and many other ways, fandom, anti-fandom, and non-fandom cross wires. Yet when these are the wires through which effects, televisual powers, meaning, personal and communal identification, and politics must run, as analysts we are left with a daunting task before us of sorting through the resulting mess. Through the humdrum, unremarkable nature of non-fandom, too, television entertainment can cross wires with everyday life itself:

> Television has become inextricably part of, and often indistinguishable from everyday life. We often do not remember whether we learnt of a certain fact from a friend or television, we fail to notice that our images of the elderly, for example, derive more from television than everyday interactions, and when we recount an anecdote or interesting observation, does it matter if it came from watching television or from a personal experience?
>
> (Livingstone 1990: 4)

Ultimately, then, any examination of television entertainment should at some level attempt to account for the audience's varying levels of affect, and for the degree to which these levels refract what television entertainment is, why we watch it, and how it works.

Tracking the audience

Clearly, affect matters to an understanding of a show's role in society; however, we need also to ask how it feeds back into the structure of the industry, and into the production of programs. In Chapters 4, 5, and 6, we will discuss how the powers of affect have been harnessed for particular political purposes. But at a generic level, how (or) do producers and network executives learn from fans, anti-fans, and non-fans? (How) do they program for these varying viewers? Or, in short, how does affect matter to the industry itself? The disturbing answer is that affect has often mattered far too little, or, rather, it has often mattered in the wrong way. But why?

First, in answering these questions for a public broadcasting system, we should note that traditionally this was a system built on the suspicion of affect, or at least suspicion of mass affect. Public broadcasting has aimed to broadcast what its audience *should* see and hear, not necessarily what they *want* to. Public broadcasting has also proven remarkably elitist at times, programming only or mostly to the highly educated upper classes. Admittedly, many public broadcasters have of late become more populist, but their intended audience is still an odd construct, patched together from intuition, ratings data, and projections of an ideal audience.

By contrast, for a commercial system, ratings data *is* the audience. We may be deluded into thinking that our personal regard for a program matters to the industry, but under a ratings-driven system, the sad truth is that in and of itself, our affect and our viewing choices have little or no *direct* effect on a show unless we form part of the measured audience. In the United States, measurement is handled exclusively by the A. C. Nielsen company. As discussed in the previous chapter, Nielsen measures audiences both by people meters (installed in approximately

5,000 family homes for their national sample, measuring approximately 13,000 people) and sweeps week journals.[2] In the United Kingdom, the Broadcaster's Audience Research Board (BARB) handle ratings, with 5,100 homes and 11,500 people in their sample, and other countries either have their own system, or make do with Nielsen and/or BARB figures (foreign though they be). Viewers with people meters or journals matter, but the rest of us matter only insofar as we can affect these viewers' consumption behavior. Hence, if I watch and adore the entire ABC line-up, for instance, unless I am part of Nielsen's sample, or unless I create buzz around this line-up that might influence a Nielsen sample member's viewing behavior, my act of watching is meaningless to ABC, and my tastes will be inconsequential to programming decisions. Of course, the creative personnel may be happy to hear of my adoration, but structurally and financially, I remain deadwood.

However, even a Nielsen or BARB sample member's *affect* is undervalued. As Philip Napoli explains, "In selling audiences to advertisers, media firms essentially deal in human *attention*" (2003: 5 emphasis added), not affect. Whether a Nielsen audience member has their eyes closed while listening to an iPod while "watching," or whether they watch with baited breath, the people meter records their viewing the same. Equally important to understanding the "audience commodity market" (see Meehan 1990), though, not all Nielsen audience members are created equal in the eyes of advertisers. Despite the industry's fondness for touting its inherent "democratic" quality, not only do most "citizens" of a media nation have no vote, but some votes count double, or triple. Not all advertisers, after all, care about all audiences. Poor audiences are particularly unattractive for some advertisers, as are the elderly – whose consumption often proves lower than younger generations, and whose brand loyalties already assumed to be accounted for (see Napoli 2003: 104–5). Similarly, since men, and especially young men, have proven harder for advertisers to reach, their attention is coveted, and valued above that of women (Napoli 2003: 105). Furthermore, many minority audiences have proven easier to reach (Napoil 2003: 106), or substantially overlap with poorer audiences to the point that they too are less valued. As a result, many (though by no means all) advertisers seek only the attention of a select few, and with their dollars or pounds funding much television, networks and producers must obey.

Nevertheless, as will be discussed further in Chapter 3, new changes in the industry may be forcing networks to care more about affect, and particularly about fans. First and foremost, channel proliferation has changed the nature of audience measurement. In an era of three or four channels, audiences had less options, but with 74 per cent of American families, for instance, having access to forty or more channels (Lotz 2007b: 55), executives must now put more time into keeping their audiences, and must fight more viciously to please them. Thus, as Jenkins notes, "Cult works were once discovered, now they are being consciously produced, designed to provoke fan interactions" (2002: 164). In the moment of watching, a fan may mean exactly the same as a non-fan, but fans are proving important for their loyalty – since they will count next week too – and for their proclivity to buy product-related merchandise or texts, which increases revenues outside of the audience commodity market. Many television producers are looking to synergy, multi-platforming, and secondary markets to stay afloat, and the fan is, as such, a powerful being to court, especially since fans are more likely to become "inspirational consumers," bringing other new viewers into the fold (see Jenkins 2006). Second, as Napoli (2003) explains, channel proliferation has also caused a crisis in audience measurement. Sample sizes must always increase as do available options being tested for, since asking one hundred people to choose between two options, for instance, produces more reliable data than asking them to choose between fifty options. Our current era of endless channels has thus rendered Nielsen's sample a paltry sum. Ratings acquisition has long been deeply problematic, suffering from a host of problems (see Meehan 1990, Napoli 2003), but with advertisers and media firms alike needing an industry standard, the industry has just accepted the current system, warts and all. However, with sample size issues making it particularly hard to measure cable channel audiences (Napoli 2003: 91), and with DVR/TiVo, off-television, and outside-of-home viewing on the rise, advertisers' patience with the system may finally run out. In such a situation, evidence of a sizeable fan audience can sometimes supplement Nielsen data, so that, for example, both *Family Guy* and *Futurama* returned from cancellation due to high DVD sales.

Third and finally, Pay TV channels such as HBO and Showtime make their money by subscription sales, not ads, and thus they have realized the importance of fandom and of affect more than their commercial or public broadcasting counterparts. Pay TV outlets need viewers to want to watch their shows enough to justify subscription fees, and so affect is remarkably important to them. With HBO's shows winning multiple accolades, other channels are quickly trying to imitate them, and thus may similarly take on their interest in fan cultivation. Affect is still nowhere near the gold standard by which the entire industry works, and viewers are still frequently forgotten or ignored outright, rarely even warranting a mention in some trade fairs, for instance (see Harrington and Bielby 2005: 904). But perhaps our new televisual era of overflow promises a recalibration of the system to care about fans.

Ultimately, though, and as we will also discuss further in Chapter 3 (and 4), many of the industry's changes, along with many of its current problems, point to a continued, or even exacerbated, devaluation of minority, women, poor, and elderly audiences. Fans may matter more in years to come, but the question will be *which* fans. Might we be approaching a television that caters to an educated, high-income young white elite as its fans, leaving much of the rest of the viewing populace to inhabit the role of non-fan or anti-fan, or else conform to the educated, high-income young white elite's tastes?

Meanwhile, as much as recent developments in television promise a new prominence for some fans, these and other developments also create concern for the ways in which such fans will be used. The increasing power and coverage of cable providers and of TiVO/DVRs may in due course lead to a Nielsen or BARB rival. In theory, cable or DVR boxes can record everything we do with our televisions, reporting this data back to Time-Warner, Comcast, TiVO, Sky, or whomever consumers have signed their contracts for service with. While this freeflow of data could immediately solve many of Nielsen's and BARB's recording errors and sample size problems, we should also worry about the ensuing access that media firms have to our viewing practices. Precisely because our viewing is often a highly personal act, constitutive of identity, we must ask if we *want* media firms to obtain such information about us with the click of a mouse. Already, fandom is fast becoming "recordable," and while we may occasionally enjoy the perks when TiVo or Amazon recommends something else we might enjoy, the tradeoff is yet more personal information going to media firms about our consumption habits (see Turow 2006). Thus, as Mark Andrejevic (2007) poignantly argues, a significant battleground between audiences and media or advertising firms exists at the level of privacy and (un)acceptable surveillance (see also Lyon 2007).

As such, we find ourselves at an interesting crossroads: media firms have often cared far too little about our affect, but now they are becoming interested – albeit only in *some* affect, as described above – and are developing the technologies to record it. As Henry Jenkins explains, this "caring" gives rise to a central paradox of television affect:

> to be desired by the networks is to have your tastes commodified. On the one hand, to be commodified is to expand a group's cultural visibility. Those groups that have no recognized economic value get ignored. That said, commodification is also a form of exploitation. Those groups that are commodified find themselves targeted more aggressively by marketers and often feel they have lost control over their own culture, since it is mass produced and mass marketed. One cannot help but have conflicted feelings because one doesn't want to go unrepresented – but one doesn't want to be exploited, either.
>
> (2006: 62–3)

Thus, if corporations and advertisers alike are now starting to realize the power of "affective economics" (see Jenkins 2006), and are increasingly calling for affective television, not just television that puts (possibly disinterested) bums in seats, we are forced to ask, do we now *want* them to care, and how can we ensure that they "care" in ways that are acceptable and are not invasive to us?

Meanwhile, however, if surveillance is increasingly a key battleground issue, this is in part because today's audiences are so hard to pin down, between our iPods, DVDs, BitTorrent downloads, spinoff toy purchases, incessant clicking of the remote, and so forth. And it is thus to this world of televisual expansion and over-flow that we now turn.

Chapter 3

Television unboxed: expansion, overflow, and synergy

the new integration/synergy model can be seen as a sort of pinball machine. The principle behind it would be something like this: you launch with great force the little steel ball, shoot it to the top, and then you watch it bounce off the different contacts, pass through the different gates, and whenever it touches a contact, your winning figures go up. The media entertainment business is such a pinball machine: the challenge is to "own" not only the steel ball, but also as many of the contacts as possible because the same "ball" gets you even higher scores, that is, profits. The contact points are the cinema screens and video stores, theme parks and toy shops, restaurant chains and video arcades, bookstores and CD record shops.

Thomas Elsaesser (2002: 18)

We are at a point where we have to consider what it means to engage with a television programme, to "follow" a specific show.

Will Brooker (2001: 457)

Television is an ever-expanding entity, showing no sign of slowing down. It is becoming an entity that transverses time, space, and multiple technologies and viewer practices, each year growing larger yet. Television can be found on or in cell phones, DVDs, TiVo hard drives, PSPs, iPods, bedspreads, clothes, toys, videogames, podcasts, CDs, novels, role-playing games, official websites, spinoff websites, fan sites, YouTube and iFilm, magazines, newspapers, radio talk, VCRs, and likely many more sites by the time you are reading this. Television is even the topic of movies (such as *The Truman Show*), novels (such as Don DeLillo's *White Noise*), magazines (*Entertainment Weekly*), and other television shows (*Entertainment Tonight*, *Studio 60 on the Sunset Strip*). As Will Brooker (2001) notes, television is now accompanied by significant "overflow," as we are invited to "live" such-and-such a program, interact with its characters in games and online spaces, wear the clothes of the show, and so forth. Television, in other words, "is no longer limited to the television medium" (Brooker 2001: 457), has overflowed from the box, and is frequently *off*-TV. Ours is a transitional era (see Lotz 2007b) in which each week brings new ideas, experiments, and lawsuits that set the parameters for the television of the future. In the meantime, though, the barrage of changes and expansions of television that have already taken place must be accounted for.

This chapter will examine these changes and will interrogate some of their innumerable ramifications on television and on society. First, by way of introducing some of the changes, I will examine the expansion and overflow of ABC's *Lost*, one of the growing number of programs that is experimenting with televisual form, economics, and delivery. Then, I will turn respectively to television producers, advertisers, and audiences, to study how each group is contributing to televisual expansion, and how such a newly developing system of television entertainment changes the nature of each group's interactions with the medium. For producers, the last ten years have brought intense industrial shifts, ranging from conglomeration and its ensuing pursuit of "synergy" (textual ventures that can reap profit in various media, from television to merchandise, film to food, etc.), to instability at the ontological level of what television producers really "do" as producers. As Elsaesser suggests above, today's media corporations no longer concentrate on the text ("pinball") itself; rather, the task now is to fill the playing field with yet more points of televisual contact. For advertisers, the continued evasion of ads has forced more cunning strategies, and has also forced them to restructure their business relationships with producers. And for audiences, today's television programs, as Brooker suggests above, are different beings. Technological shifts are allowing programs to become more accessible, their commercial context more easily evaded, while textual shifts are layering programs, sometimes making them less accessible and more requiring of our time and effort, but offering larger, more complex storyworlds to step into. They also allow greater personalization of the program and of its consumption process. But for all their benefits, such changes in televisuality not only threaten the culturally cohesive qualities of yesterday's age of broadcasting – they have also occurred unevenly, leaving some audiences behind. Thus, in inquiring into audience relationships with television expansion and overflow, I will concentrate first on uses and meanings of the program, but will then discuss the prospects for broadcasting – as opposed to narrowcasting – and the reality of a growing digital divide between televisions old and new and their viewers. Finally, television's global expansion, while by no means new, is accelerating, with *Friends* reruns, new episodes of *CSI*, versions of *Pop Idol/American Idol*, *The Office*, and *Who Wants to Be a Millionaire?* and many other instances of television entertainment populating the planet; hence, I will examine issues related to global televisual expansion.

Lost in television's future

On 22 September, 2004, *Lost* premiered on ABC. A bold, genre-bending program, the show opened with Oceanic Airways Flight 815 from Sydney to Los Angeles crashing on a remote island in the South Pacific. This island, though, was far from normal, with, for instance, a mysterious creature in the trees, an equally mysterious group of "others" on the island, and a hatch leading to a bunker with a lone inhabitant engaged in an unspecified experiment with a wealthy but enigmatic corporation behind it. *Lost* is part drama, part science fiction, part fantasy, part mystery, and stood out for its use of flashbacks – each week focusing on the pre-crash life of one of the characters – and for its signature reliance on cliffhangers, mystery, and a complex narrative involving multiple characters and set across a very long story arc and multiple timeframes. It is an innovative show, and a clear example of American network television producing aesthetically rich material. But it is also an example of television in transition, as the writers, producers, and marketers have, from the beginning, made frequent use of other storytelling and/or marketing platforms. Thus an examination of *Lost* stands to illuminate many expansive strategies of today's producers of television entertainment.

Lost's arrival was by no means unheralded. Early buzz for the show was seemingly everywhere going into the 2004–2005 season. ABC showed what goes into television before it is even *on* television. To begin with, the program had a host of well-known figures associated with it: producer J. J. Abrams was much beloved for helming ABC's *Alias*, actor Dominic Monaghan was hot off the *Lord of the Rings* trilogy, actor Matt Fox had starred years earlier in the critically acclaimed *Party of Five*, actor Harold Perrineau had starred in HBO's gritty *Oz*, and Terry O'Quinn, Daniel Dae Kim, and Ian Somerhalder had all been supporting actors on cult favorites *Alias*, *Angel*, and *Smallville* respectively. Thus, the producers understood well the need for resonant and "trustworthy" actor-intertexts, and they played to past fan–star relationships. ABC then farmed this group out regularly to entertainment magazines and programs, renewing these fan-star relationships where possible, and using the significant good-looks factor inherent in the cast to fish for new fan–star relationships pre-release. Furthermore, previews left a series of baited hooks of suspense for viewers-to-be, showing this attractive cast stranded on the island, trying to cope with the crash, before building up to a sequence in which strange noises are heard from the jungle, before the camera closes in on a concerned looking Monaghan, who asks, "Guys, where *are* we?" Hence ABC offered viewers a *Survivor*-like beginning of beautiful people on an island, and then, almost playing with the overblown rhetoric of *Survivor* trailers ("This year, everything changes!"), threw in a twist that *Survivor* guru Mark Burnett could never craft. The preview is pregnant with intertextuality, with links to previous shows and texts – *Lord of the Flies* meets *Survivor* – at the same time as it seems so obviously divorced from most previous network fare – set on an island. In an era in which many programs are cancelled before their fifth or sixth episode, the production and marketing personnel clearly appreciated the importance of making their program stand out against the general clutter of a new season, even going so far as to fill a beach with bottles with *Lost* ads in them as a bold and quirky form of viral marketing (Finkle 2005).

Soon after *Lost* was up and running, its producers and fans found multiple other ways to make it "overflow" its television boundaries. *Lost*'s official website was fairly boring, given other television-related websites: the website for *Invasion*, for instance, took the form of a blog about alien conspiracies supposedly authored by one of the show's characters, *Smallville*'s website purported to be the local Smallville newspaper, the website in early seasons of *24* included links to the show's fictitious White House, and *Dawson's Creek*'s website gave its viewers access to the title character's computer desktop. Nevertheless, *Lost*'s site included diary entries from an anonymous, yet-unmet "Lostaway." More innovatively, though, ABC also commissioned a website for the show's fictitious airline (see Figure 3.1), and another for the show's elusive Hanso Foundation.

Figure 3.1 Care to book a flight? *Lost*'s doomed airliner, *Oceanic*, overflows from television to Internet

Humorously or forebodingly, depending upon one's outlook, the Oceanic site's supposed flight search engine includes the Flight 815 information, and the string of numbers at the bottom are *Lost*'s "cursed" numbers. Similarly, the notice of flight cancellation in lieu of the plane crash is slightly interrupted by text printed underneath that reads, "I survived a horrific plane crash and am stranded on an island somewhere Northeast of Australia and Southwest of Hawaii. In the event that I am never found, please forward word of my fate to my parents," an ominous message that leaves the mystery of its writer (and of how s/he managed to hack into Oceanic's site) wide open, its own mystery outside the border proper of the program.

For its part, the Hanso Foundation site gave information, albeit oblique, on the foundation's various projects, ranging from electromagnetic research to aging and life prolongation. It included video messages from Hanso staff, and an odd section that promised to allow one to send a message to a monkey (!) before shorting and freezing. While the site was up and running throughout the summer hiatus between Seasons 2 and 3, by summer's end, navigation to the homepage brought one to a short message saying that the site had been hacked into, and hence was now offline. Interestingly, too, in the final weeks of Season 2, ad breaks during *Lost* contained an ad for the Hanso Foundation. Rather insidiously, though, these also directed viewers to websites for sponsors (such as a www.sublymonal.com link that led directly to a Sprite site); playing along, though, one of the sponsors, Monster.com, offered a supposed search page for jobs at the Hanso Foundation (see Figure 3.2). The page only offered five vacant positions, but in themselves, these added folds to the mysteries of *Lost*, provoking viewers to ask what sort of organization has needs for an organ courier, an art therapist, a Simian veterinarian, an anger management director, and a personal assistant. Since Season 2 had ended with viewers aware that Hanso and its Dharma Initiative were somehow behind the secrets of the island, not only were such sites playful, but they were also studied and debated in great detail by fans eager for answers. Though the distinction may have been lost on many viewers happening upon one or more of the above examples, many of these overflow sites were part of an ongoing "ARG" (alternate reality role-playing game) designed to keep fans engaged during the summer hiatus with a clue-based game promising (yet ultimately failing) to unlock some of the island's secrets (see Brooker 2008). Other clues in this ARG even included a limited release of Apollo chocolate bars – a sweet from the *Lost* universe. *Lost*'s ARG was particularly inventive, but by no means unique, as other television shows and films (most famously, *A.I.* (see Jenkins 2006: 123–7)) have also used the form.

Beyond websites, ARGs, and chocolate bars, though, *Lost* produced yet other off-TV platforms. Several tie-in novels have been released by Hyperion Books (owned by ABC parent company Disney), including most notably a detective novel by "Gary Troup," called *Bad Twin*. Not only was Troup said to have been a victim of

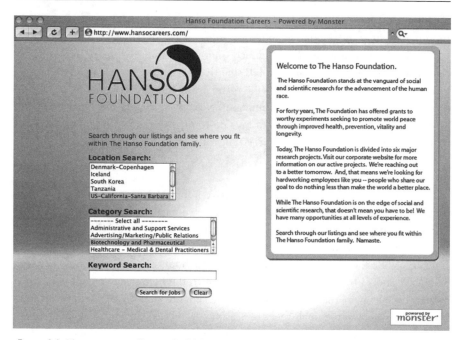

Figure 3.2 Monster.com offers a playful form of sponsorship, offering job information for *Lost*'s Hanso Foundation

the Flight 815 crash, but two characters on the show have read his manuscript, and the book also makes allegations regarding Hanso, leading to website refutations in "the real world," and even to the appearance of "Hugh McIntyre" on ABC's *Jimmy Kimmel Live!*, who claimed to be a Hanso representative out to clear the company's name! *Bad Twin* even made it to the *New York Times* bestseller list. Yet *Lost* writers Carleton Cuse and Damon Lindelof were disappointed in the real writer behind the fictional one (see Zeitchik 2006), illustrating how overflow and synergy can produce creative tension and confusion, not just streamlined textual expansion, and showing the significant potential for chaos in a sea of overflow.

With all the mysteries surrounding *Lost*, and all this material to decode and debrief, *Lost* fandom is in hyper-drive. The show has many dedicated fan sites and discussion boards, which attract thousands of viewers worldwide who discuss the program, its meaning, its secrets, and their reactions. Occasionally, too, *Lost*'s producers and cast members even appear on the sites. Or, although promising less direct interaction, writers Carlton Cuse and Damon Lindelof produce a weekly free podcast which teases the program, discusses production, usually offers an interview with a cast member, and answers some questions from viewers. All the while, of course, the producers and cast are regularly interviewed in more main-stream publications as well, often make appearances at Comic Con (an annual multi-genre fan convention that regularly attracts over 100,000 attendees), and present a bevy of bonus materials on the *Lost* DVD packages, including documentaries on the show's beginnings, audition footage, cast and crew commentary, Matt Fox's on-set photographs, and extra scenes. However, arguably attracting the most fan attention are the "spoilers" that are either leaked by production personnel (whether intentionally, to lead fans off the scent or to tease them, or against the producers' wishes) or by fan bystanders. Spoilers include any information regarding what will happen on the show, and their careful analysis and discussion takes up many a webpage (see Gray and Mittell 2007). Some spoiler pages, for instance, include uploaded photographs of the set from viewers who live nearby in Hawaii, while others luck on to insiders willing to share snippets of information. Other fans have proven highly creative, penning fan fiction, creating fan videos, and creating their own *Lost*-world websites. For instance, alongside Oceanic's and Hanso's websites is a fan-designed site for Drive Shaft,[1] the fictitious band of *Lost*'s Charlie, played by Monaghan. The site gives background on Charlie and his bandmember brother Liam, along with album designs, lyrics to three albums worth of songs, pictures of the band, supposed articles and reviews of the band (including one from the French *Rolling Stone!*), interviews, downloads, a guestbook, and more. As a fan initiative (and as does fan fiction or video), it therefore represents an instance of the show's viewers penning backstory and fleshing out a character, unofficially and non-canonically, yet still contributing to the construction of *Lost*'s wider world for those who visit the site.

Lost can be watched in various ways. Beyond watching it via television broadcast or recorded on a DVR, VCR, or DVD, North American viewers can go to ABC's website and watch episodes online. In 2006, ABC began experimenting with offering episodes of *Lost*, *Alias*, *Commander in Chief*, and *Desperate Housewives* free with some ads on their website, and by the end of the summer had judged this experiment a success and hence expanded the service (Shields 2006). *Lost* is also available for purchase at iTunes, hence allowing viewing on a computer and/or video iPod, British and French viewers can access episodes on Channel 4 and TF1 websites respectively, and episodes can easily be obtained for free on file-sharing sites using BitTorrent software. Despite being held up by legal problems, by mid-2006, announcement came that Verizon Wireless' V-Cast direct-to-cell phone delivery systems would, in late 2007, release short video diary sequences of new material not released in the show itself. And while ABC as yet is not offering the show On Demand, CBS and NBC are planning experiments with On Demand delivery of their own shows (Crupi and Consoli 2005), suggesting this next step may be close by. For its part, Nielsen is now attempting to measure media consumption on iPods, cellphones, etc., hence acknowledging that television consumption has changed fundamentally. In early 2007, media buzz around *Lost* expressed concern for its reduced ratings, yet if we account for its popularity in many non-network television venues, the show may not have actually lost viewers – rather, they may simply have migrated to other viewing platforms, hence showing the Nielsen ratings' inadequacy at measuring total audiences *across* venues.

As for spinoff merchandise and the like, in 2008, a *Lost* computer game was released by Ubisoft, allowing players to set foot vicariously on the island and explore it daily. A *Lost* boardgame was available in 2006, as was a set of jigsaw puzzles that, when connected, reavealed a "secret" drawing on their flipside if a UV light was directed at them. Meanwhile, the games joined countless other official and unofficial *Lost* merchandise – from the uninspired, such as posters and keychains, a luxury action figure line and trading cards, to the more inspired alarm clocks fashioned after the island's 108-minute clock, Oceanic luggage tags, and Dharma brand hats that seemingly place the viewer partially inside the *Lost* universe. In sum, *Lost* has become a truly expansive program, existing in and across multiple media. It is a free-floating entity that inhabits various bodies, some of them which contribute to the *Lost* storyline and mythology, some of which merely circulate images of the characters, and some of which contribute to viewers' play and identification with, and decoding of, the show. Importantly, though, rather than merely being a loosely put-together assemblage of texts, merchandise, and afterthoughts, many of *Lost*'s various bodies are connected by the thematic focus on the island's mysteries: from spoilers to *Bad Twin*, the Hanso website to DVD bonus materials, many work together in sync.

In an age of televisual expansion, *Lost* is a standard-bearer, but it is not alone. Many years before Flight 815, for instance, *The Simpsons* rewrote the playbook for television merchandising and expansion, unifying most of its outgrowths, from video games to beer can-openers, with the irreverent parodic ethos for which the program became famous. In 2007, *The Simpsons* was at it again, with a long-estab-lished form of overflow and synergy – a movie – but also with a competition amongst the US' various Springfields to host the official premiere and thereby "be" *the* Springfield for a day, and the conversion of twelve 7–11 stores across North America into Kwik-E-Marts full of *Simpsons* characters (see Figure 3.3) and selling the show's fictional Buzz Cola, Krusty-O's cereal, Squishees, *Radioactive Man* comics, and signature pink donuts. Other shows, too, have led the way with other forms of expansion, as with *Battlestar Galactica*'s illuminating and information-generous podcasts and "webisodes" filling in gaps in the story, soap operas' long-standing use of dedicated magazines to manage and bait anticipation and release, and sports programming's innovative development of fantasy leagues. And other developments offer multimedia television:

- Warner Bros. and AOL launched IN2TV, a service that offers free downloads of old shows no longer in syndication (including *Chico and the Man*, *Scarecrow and Mrs. King*, and *Growing Pains*).

- In 2006, NBC chose to premier their much-hyped *Heroes* free at iTunes a full three weeks before its televisual debut, and their San Francisco O & O KNTV chose to distribute a new documentary on the 1906 Earthquake free at iTunes a week before its televisual screening.
- HBO and Showtime have led the way in developing On Demand services, complete with old and current episodes, "making of" mini-documentaries, and films.
- Sprint's GoTV and Verizon's V Cast, along with numerous other wireless companies and television channels, are now offering either live-to-cell phone television, or DVR-to-cell phone services.
- In 2005, FOX and V Cast (or Vodafone in England) partnered up to bring customers *Conspiracy*, a spinoff narrative from FOX's *24*.
- With the development of HDTV and state-of-the-art home entertainment systems, more and more movie-goers are bringing their movies home, leading to a whopping $118.7 billion video sale and rental business in 2001 (Wasko 2003: 125).
- In the UK, the BBC's Creative Future blueprint has called for sweeping changes for a digital-age public-broadcasting identity, including more dedicated use of the Internet, blogs, and other media.

All the while, too, European cable providers have for several years now been offering innovative uses of digital interactive delivery in order to "layer" programs,

Figure 3.3 Inside the Kwik-E-Mart with Ralph and Homer

allowing viewers to change camera angles for sporting events or surveillance-style reality television, for instance, or providing polls and extra information. Alongside these newer developments, tie-in magazines, merchandising, and spinoffs are, of course, nothing new for television, so *expansion* is not new. But *overflow* is on the rise: merchandising rarely aimed to expand and/or develop the storyworld as do many examples from the last ten years of television, and what we are witnessing in *Lost* and many of its peers are not only attempts to distribute the same content across media, but also to produce new kinds of content and to fashion grander transmedia storyworlds that take television out of television.

The business of expansion

One may find it tempting to view such changes as the industry's reactions to technological innovation, but as David Hesmondhalgh points out, "we need to be particularly cautious in addressing technology as a causal factor. For technologies are themselves the effects of choices, decisions, contingencies and coincidences in the realms of economics, politics and culture" (2002: 98). European cable providers' development of digital interactive delivery serves as a reminder that particularly American television can and frequently does resist the pressure to respond to technology. In 2000, in England, I was able to select from multiple Olympic events while watching one channel of the BBC, but seven years later, I still cannot receive such services from Time-Warner in New York, dubbed the world's media capital. The American networks have also dragged their heels on upgrading to broadcast digital transmission and to HDTV (see Castañeda 2007), even though the American NTSC standard has long been the world's most inferior delivery system in terms of pixilation, with 525 scanning lines, as opposed to European PAL's 650. So why has the industry embraced so many other bells and whistles of the digital age? Or, rephrased, why expand, and why overflow?

Hesmondhalgh (2002: 19) argues that synergy can be a clever response to risk within the industry.[2] As was discussed in Chapter 1, television is risky business – thus, despite its good luck with *Lost* in 2004, ABC lost millions in 2006 when they surrounded *Emily's Reasons Why Not* with an advertising blitz, only to cancel the horrifically bad show after one episode. Quite simply, however, synergy allows a company to profit as much as possible from its more successful content, on as many platforms as possible: as Elsaesser suggests in this chapter's opening quotation, synergy is about owning the pinball machine. Hence, rather than just profit from *Lost* on network television alone, ABC owner Disney profits on multiple platforms, allowing it to make up for several *Emily's Reasons Why Not*s. Some of its profits come from licensing fees alone – as with the action figures, made by MacFarlane Toys – or are collected by third-party organizations – as when iTunes sells episodes – but some are wholly inhouse – as when Disney's Hyperion sells copies of *Bad Twin*. Particularly as fan cultures have thrived and developed (though who begat whom is, of course, the chicken-and-egg debate of contemporary television), today's media conglomerations have realized the immense prospects for profit in expansion. Indeed, Disney has long understood the wonders of synergy and spinoffs, having made millions from toy, VCR, and DVD sales of its children's films and programming. Synergy's early days may have been for kids, but, for instance, as *Star Wars* fans grew into adults and kept buying *Star Wars* paraphernalia, though Twentieth Century Fox had negotiated away merchandising rights to series creator George Lucas, they and its corporate colleagues realized the power of textual expansion, and FOX is now singing all the way to the bank with their synergy diva *American Idol*, as they profit from *Idol* CD releases, tours, pay-per-call votes, the computer game, and an ad-supported website (see Jenkins 2006).

The desperate attempt to keep profits inhouse, while expanding programs onto ever-more platforms, led in part to the massive wave of media conglomeration that hit the world in the last decade. When the buying and merging dust settled, each English-language American television network in particular belonged to a fully integrated media multinational. In 2006, the struggling WB and UPN networks merged to form CW, while Viacom split into Viacom and CBS (with Sumner Redstone still in control of both, however), leaving the media landscape as is depicted in Table 3.1.

Each of these companies has multiple other holdings in addition to those listed below (see Bagdikian 2004, McChesney 2004). Thus, to varying degrees, they can all easily move products across their plate of companies, multiplying revenues at every step of the way. Caldwell (2004) notes that companies no longer tend to use the word "programs," instead preferring "content," hence perhaps flagging the degree to which synergy has become corporate common sense and logic, so that television is now expected to expand into and across a company's integrated family of producers. Conveniently, too, synergy is free advertising: the *Lost* videogame advertises *Lost*, which advertises the books, and so forth, just by being branded under the common *Lost* title. Media conglomerates are investing large amounts of advertising space to promote their own materials, both on their own channels and on sister channels under the same conglomerate umbrella.

In Chapter 6, we will examine further the implications of such an ownership structure on the power and control over television. At this point, though, we must avoid overstating the expansive powers of such conglomerates. First, with size come greater logistical nightmares in arranging cross-media campaigns, and thus most conglomerates only have a few *Lost*-sized campaigns in them per year. Second, with size come confused and conflicting goals. In *theory*, one hand should be able to help the other; in *practice*, though, the managing officers of the helping hand will likely do so only if they too can profit. Freebies are not common in such a ruthless business as the media, and so favors will not always be forthcoming.

Table 3.1 Media ownership (partial listing)

Corporate parent	Network(s)	Studio(s)	Other TV channels	Print holdings	Other
CBS	CBS CW (50%)	Paramount (TV)	Showtime	Simon & Schuster	CBS Outdoor advertising, CBS Records, radio stations
Disney	ABC	Disney, Touchstone, Buena Vista	ESPN, Disney Channel, SOAPNet, Lifetime (50%), A&E (37.5%)	Hyperion	Disney resorts, Go.com, Movies.com, Buena Vista Music Group, radio stations
General Electric	NBC	Universal	USA, SciFi, CNBC, MSNBC, AMC, Bravo, Chiller, Sleuth, Telemundo		Universal Studios Resort, radio stations
News Corporation	FOX MyNetwork TV	Fox	FX, Fox Sports Net, Fox News Channel, Fuel, National Geographic Channel (67%), Speed	HarperCollins, Zondervan, *TV Guide*, *Wired*, multiple newspapers	Sky & BSkyB, DirectTV, FoxTel, Canal FOX, MySpace
Time Warner	CW (50%)	Warner Bros., New Line	HBO, CNN, TBS, TCM, Court TV, Cartoon Network	DC Comics, *Time, People, Entertainment Weekly, Fortune, Sports Illustrated*	AOL, Netscape, Moviefone, MapQuest, TMZ.com, Time Warner Cable, New Line Records
Viacom		Paramount (Film), Dreamworks	MTV, BET, Nickelodeon, Comedy Central, VH1, TV Land		iFilm, Xfire, Atom Entertainment, GameTrailers, Bubba Gump Shrimp Co.

Thus, *Lost* action figures are made by MacFarlane Toys due to the company's high reputation for making edgy adult toys, rather than by one of Disney's more common toy-making partners that specialize in plush, cuddly, and cutesy toy production. At times, one part of a conglomerate or corporate partnership will even clash with the other. Certainly, Time Warner's merger with AOL has been widely considered a failure, and perhaps a difference in business ethos lies behind this failure. Taking illegal downloading, for instance, as a content producer, Time Warner regularly rails against piracy, but as an Internet provider, AOL profits from piracy. As Jenkins notes, although "[p]olitical economists and business gurus make convergence sound so easy . . . from the ground, many of the big media giants look like great big dysfunctional families, whose members aren't speaking with each other and pursue their own short-term agendas even at the expense of other divisions of the same companies" (2006: 7–8). Third, as Jennifer Holt charts (2003), when artists stand to gain royalties from lucrative licensing deals, they have proven ready with attorneys at hand to sue for unfair trade practices if a corporation offers a show to its corporate cousin at a bargain price. Thus, total synergy and integration for all shows is an unlikely eventuality, as much as *limited* synergy is an important way of battling risk, and raking in profits.

Meanwhile, as much as one company's plans for synergistic expansion may succeed, in an expanded television full of channels and parent corporations scrambling to come out on top, all expansion comes face to face with competing textual expansion. One *can* consume *Lost* across the media world, but likely, many audience members do not. To begin with, transmedia expansion and overflow have reached the point that it is often hard even to find out about much expansion. Thus, for instance, I expect that many *Lost* viewers were not aware of all instances of its overflow and expansion detailed earlier in this chapter. Media synergy plans can sound almost megalomaniacal in the abstract, but in the actual media landscape, they run up against constant and relentless competition. Megalomaniacs, in other words, must do battle with countless other megalomaniacs. As must programs themselves. Many of us watch television ready to change channels at the slightest displeasure, and hence as much work goes into programs and synergy, today's television shows are fundamentally and perpetually under threat of viewer cannibalization and destruction (see Gray 2006). Despite synergy, expansion, and overflow, we are still relatively free to consume the version of the program that we want to consume, whether that means skipping episodes, refusing to play the ARG, watching when we are busy, or so forth. Networks and channels therefore are spending increasingly more time and energy in branding and promoting themselves, encouraging us to never leave them or their products (see Caldwell 2004: 55–6). Lotz notes that in 1999, ABC and NBC were devoting a full five extra minutes per hour to promoting their own programs than in 1989, amounting to approximately 30,000 promotions per year, at an estimated loss of $4 billion worth of advertising time (2007b: 108). Some network executives still remember a time when they had only two counterparts, but now their shows must do daily battle with hundreds from other channels, not to mention with the many alternate technologies and media available to today's citizens.

Against this expansion and competition, then, it seems pertinent to ask about the future of television as a business. Especially since, as we will soon discuss, many new platforms for television consumption offer chances for viewers to avoid ads, the networks and cable companies are spending increasingly more time dealing with non-advertiser-funded delivery. When, for instance, *Lost* sells to an iTunes customer for $1.99, no ads are factored into the deal. Some have even floated the possibility of *complete* off-network delivery of programs, as Mittell (2005), for instance, poses that the much beloved but ratings-doomed *Arrested Development* could have survived financially using iTunes alone, and Lotz (2007b: 147) points out that ABC might even be making more per episode on iTunes than on their ad-supported network. With iTunes, HBO, Showtime, On Demand, Netflix, and various other pay TV options flourishing, moreover, many consumers are clearly being acclimatized to a pay-per-view model, which, along with the possible lucrative nature of Pay TV models, might eventually provoke more producers and channels to give up on advertisers completely. That said, the economics still make such attrition wholly unlikely. First, pay-per-view bypasses affiliates, not only important players in the television economy of today, but frequently (in the form of the O & O) the most lucrative cog in the corporate machinery. Second, when network television and its associated syndication cycles can garner billions of dollars, the lure of the ad-supported model is still too strong for most. Third, as will later be elaborated upon, networks serve a vital role as viewing hub, and many audience members may find watching television without this hub confusing or alienating. Fourth, as will also be elaborated upon later, not all audiences can afford a pay-as-you-go model: television's "freeness" is still a large element behind its mass popularity. Nevertheless, an interesting sea change is occurring, whereby television channels in commercial systems such as the US, who have long been in the business of selling audiences for singular programs, are now relying upon multiple other revenue sources, doing more business directly with consumers, not solely with advertisers. Whether this will lead to a television system that is more *responsive* to audiences and less beholden to advertisers remains to be seen.

Selling in the synergy

However, if expansion, synergy, and overflow are potentially transforming the industry into a less advertising-dependent entity, surely advertisers themselves might have reason for concern. When viewers can get their weekly *Lost* installment off iTunes, a DVD, file-sharing programs, a VCR, or a DVR, they can easily skip ads. Only 7 per cent of American households had DVRs as of 2005, and VCR use had reached near complete saturation as of 2003 (now lower, but balanced off by 66 per cent ownership of DVD players) (Lotz 2007b: 55). Studies have suggested that TiVo users spend only 30 per cent of their television-watching time watching television live, a number that decreases the longer the TiVo is around (*Economist* 2002: 10), and thus advertising's placement within the flow of television can clearly be disrupted for owners of recording devices. Industry and academic speak about "The TiVo Effect" on advertising is admittedly overstated (see Mandese 2005), but nevertheless a harbinger of times to come. Meanwhile, watching online or on an iPod, or simply changing the channel during a commercial break, effectively erases ads from the viewing experience. Furthermore, when producers can now gain large profits away from advertiser-supported platforms, spot advertisers arguably have less power over the types of stories that can be told, and the types of programs that will populate our various televisions. Nielsen Media Research has responded to many of the huge shifts in television viewing by announcing its bold new Anytime Anywhere Media Measurement (A2/M2) initiative, as they have promised to develop systems for measuring viewing on iPods, cell phones, and online, and as they try to overcome their longstanding failure to measure out-of-home television viewing. A study by The Total TV Audience Monitor in 2006 suggested that Nielsen was missing approximately 44 million American viewers who watch in unmeasured places such as off-campus housing, the workplace, hotels, restaurants and bars, and second homes (Consoli 2006a). If we add viewers on other media, we have a sizable population of unmeasured viewers. Even if Nielsen can manage to track such viewers, though, the question remains to what degree, if any, will they *count* to advertisers. After all, why should an advertiser pay for an audience member who will not watch their ad in the first place? On-television viewing at least offers the hope of ad exposure (although even this hope is being challenged by channel-surfers and channel proliferation), but how are advertisers responding to the loss of their purchased audiences?

One strategy entails the expansion of advertising itself. If viewers are on the move, advertisers are now chasing them. Thus, ours is an age of advertising clutter. In 2005, for instance, ABC sold 17 per cent of hit show *Desperate Housewives'* "hour" to advertisers, 12 per cent more time than the primetime average (McClellan 2005). CBS has experimented with digitally embedding advertiser logo "watermarks" on the bottom of the screen (Consoli 2005). And, in general, ads now go anywhere an advertiser can place them (see Klein 2002, McAllister 1996). While synergy or expansion might hurt some advertisers, synergy can also inflate audience size, hence delivering new audiences to advertisers, not only taking audiences away. For all the potential "woes" of advertisers, no less, media advertising forecaster Bob Coen, senior vice president at Universal McCann, projected that the big four American networks would earn $17.1 billion of advertiser money in 2007, up 3 per cent from 2006, and that all of cable television would share $20.1 billion in ad sales, up 4.5 per cent from 2006 (Consoli 2007). Thus, advertisers are clearly still pumping vast amounts into television proper, let alone into advertising in all other venues. Advertisers may at some point flinch in the face of audience attrition to new technological platforms for viewing, but for now they seem to be dealing with the potential by advertising ever more in ever more locations. This advertising overflow is cause for multiple concerns, many of which are beyond the scope of this book to discuss (see Jhally 1987, Klein 2002, McAllister 1996), but quite simply, it potentially detracts from the viewing experience for many viewers. It should also force us to reconsider the notion of "free" television, for as Janet Wasko explains, due to the exorbitant advertising prices that commercial television commands from corporations, "Consumers ultimately pay higher prices for products and services, to which advertising expenses have been added" (2003: 90).

Another instance of advertising overflow, and another strategy for facing an expansive television, is product placement. Here, ads overflow into programs, becoming inseparable, and hence inescapable. Being set on a remote island, to date, *Lost* has included relatively few instances of product placement in the main program, though, as previously explained, their Hanso Foundation ads directed viewers to a Sprite webpage, and Hanso's "job page" was sponsored and "powered" by Monster.com.[3] Other programs have more shamelessly sold out to advertisers, so that, for instance, *The Amazing Race* prominently features cars, airlines, and tourist destinations, while *American Idol* plasters its set and shots with all things Coke, and finalists produce a different music video for a sponsor each week. Reality programming in general has become a vast playground for product placement, with *The Apprentice* in particular largely paid for by product placement (see Jenkins 2006: 69–72, Magder 2004), at the expense of making each episode an extended infomercial. Children's shows have also fallen victim to product placement, with most episodes of *Pokemon*, for example, essentially describing the wonders of such-and-such a card in the Pokemon deck. Another experiment in product placement saw Ford sponsor the Season 2 premiere of *24*, allowing for no ads other than two book-end *24*-themed three-minute spots, but trading this off for rampant product placement throughout the episode and series. NBC, meanwhile, included a one-page introduction advertising Nissan in their *Heroes* tie-in graphic novel, proving that product placement can "overflow" too. Recent years have even seen the rise of companies specializing in adding products digitally after the fact (see Boddy 2004: 121). Product placement also allows advertisers to make all of television fair ad game by invading the supposedly ad-free realms of pay TV and public broadcasting, as is most evident in HBO's *Sex and the City* and *Entourage*'s revolving door of "must-have" glamour purchases. As with clutter, advertisers must tread carefully, and they risk turning the volume up too high with overt product placement – so that, for instance, anti-fan discussion of *The Apprentice* online makes frequent reference to it having "sold out" – but it is poised to become the advertising of the future, not least of all because advertiser money usually goes directly to the production company, rather than to the network (as is the case with regular spot advertising). As such, television has by no means escaped the grasp of advertisers, and to overestimate

the effect of new technologies as providing a plan for such escape is to underestimate the savvy of Madison Avenue.

Advertising also remains a lead weight tied to the foot of televisual innovation.
As was described in Chapter 1, advertising can force networks to favor repetitive,
low-grade fare. Moreover, in an era of particular advertiser risk, reruns in particular can save the advertiser's day. Admittedly, reruns do not attract the big ad dollars
of new shows, but they have become the daily bread and butter for most cable
channels. With the ever-decreasing reliability of ratings information, advertisers at
least know that they can fall back on safe bets like *The Cosby Show*, *Friends*, *The
Simpsons*, *Seinfeld*, *Law and Order*, *CSI*, and so forth. Similarly, in an international
market (to be further discussed later), when American ratings and popularity soar
for such programs, local advertisers in other countries can easily become attracted
to the solid reliability of shows that have already proven themselves. In the US, too,
many such programs are surrounded by intense feelings of nostalgia, as they
become our televisual past, "heritage" (see Kompare 2005), and "home," all of
which are feelings into which many advertisers eagerly seek to buy. Thus, as much
as synergy, expansion, and overflow might excite one with the possibility of innovative, interesting, and involving programs, and as much as advertiser involvement
in such processes may even lead to innovation, as with the *Lost* ARG, funded in
large part by the sponsors' dollars, synergy, expansion, and overflow can also
provoke intense economic conservatism on behalf of advertisers who then slow
innovation down to a gentler pace.

Consuming the overflow

In many disparate ways, then, expansion and overflow are often profoundly changing many people's experiences of and with television, sometimes limited by corporate and advertiser imperatives, but at other times significantly developing the
prospects for fandom, affective play, and identification. The sheer number of channels, programs, and venues for television alone offer greater potential for more
viewers to engage in a personally involving experience. Thus, on one level, a
greater variety of programs are on offer, as television is growing what Chris
Anderson dubs a "long tail." Anderson notes that many media content providers are
not only selling mainstream fare to the masses, but are realizing how lucrative sales
of more specialized, less popular content (the medium's "long tail") can prove. For
example, he notes the case of Rhapsody, a subscription-based streaming music
service, who stream each of their top 400,000 titles at least once a month.
Similarly, he notes that each of American chain bookseller Barnes and Noble's
stores stocks approximately 130,000 titles, yet more than half of online bookseller
Amazon's book sales come from outside the top 130,000 titles (Anderson 2006:
2). Television cannot brag of such gargantuan numbers, but it is still developing its

own long tail, as boutique cable channels, Netflix, On Demand, IN2TV, BitTorrent sites, and so forth offer viewers many more titles than just hits like *Lost* or *CSI*. Being a cult television fan has never been so easy.

Furthermore, on another level, a second long tail of viewing *mode* is growing. Given the many platforms on which *Lost* exists, for instance, there are many combinations of how one can watch: with or without ads, on a television, computer, or iPod screen, with or without online chat afterwards, and so on. Many of these viewing practices attract only a small percentage of viewers (how many *Lost* fans own Oceanic or Drive Shaft merchandise, for example?), but attract enough to prove economically viable. Hence viewers not only have more to watch, or more to choose from, but also more control. Jason Mittell (2006) writes eloquently of his family's various uses of TiVo, and particularly of his wife's and his use of the technology to control what their young children watch and when they watch it, and to offer him a built-in library of quality children's programming. Meanwhile, DVD, On Demand, iPods, and downloads allow viewers to watch entire series in a weekend, disrupting the slow drip of network television's week-by-week delivery system, so that as Kompare writes, "DVD box sets provide the content of television without the 'noise' and limitations of the institution of television; 'television' removed from television" (2005: 214). Many such services also encourage archiving and collection, complete with their own pleasures (see Bjarkman 2004, Klinger 2006, Kompare 2005: 208), so that increasingly viewers are creating their own libraries of television, whether on a hard drive or a bookcase. Downloading even allows viewers to transcend their local broadcaster's delivery schedules, so that, for instance, many European viewers were eagerly downloading *Lost* months before local broadcast, while American sci-fi fans were downloading new *Doctor Who* episodes when no deal for local broadcast had even been made. While traveling in Miami in the 1970s, Raymond Williams famously wrote of the televisual "flow" from program to program, but as I have discussed elsewhere (Gray 2006), today's television is rife with competing, random, and chaotic flows. We are also now able, within limits, to create our own flows.

Writing before television's digital age, Fiske noted that television's "nowness" lets us feel that we "have both the right and the ability to influence the future narrative" (1989a: 67), that "Because of their incompleteness, all popular texts have leaky boundaries; they flow into each other, they flow into everyday life" (1989c: 126), and that "the pleasures of television lie not just in the meanings it provokes, but also in the access it offers viewers to the process of representation itself" (1989a: 71). Fiske's comments prove even more accurate post-expansion, for given what we have said of television entertainment's affective qualities and pleasures, creating one's own flow, and gaining more control over one's viewing experience promise yet more space for play and identification. Dan Fleming's (1996) work on children's play with spinoff toys is illustrative here, for Fleming explains

that much can happen in the toy-playing world for which television is not responsible. When one or more children have a set of television toys, they will, Fleming
notes, usually have a sense of what is appropriate play, and an idea of what they
should do with the toys, but ultimately they are free to write their own stories, and
to identify with toys often in unexpected ways. Toys are fundamentally "open," he
writes, hence part of their attraction to children, as opposed to their televisual or
filmic equivalents that must always "end" (1996: 102). Children can therefore feel
somewhat liberated to explore the stories between the stories (what happened
when the characters were *not* on-screen), and when they do so, the stories may
veer off in different directions. Characters' televisual codings can be flipped, or can
simply be better fleshed out. For instance, Fleming notes of *Star Trek* toys that, "The
child who carries around a little plastic Borg as an object of totemistic attachment
is identifying with the monster, the 'inhuman,' in a way that is never explicitly
allowed by the conventions of the TV series" (1996: 201).

Toys may be an exaggerated example of "open" television overflow, for in actual-
ity, many instances of overflow will limit their prospective uses. In the *Alias*
videogame, for instance, one cannot just take Syd to start a new life as a falafel
cook. Also, as Tim Anderson (2006) states, we may well be in the world of television "end users" editing and playing with content in various ways, but the second
this play stands to earn one money, one can find the full force of a multinational's
legal department ending such play. However, overflow still offers considerable
scope for play and identification, allowing many venues for added involvement and
engagement with favorite narratives. Online fan sites open up vast realms for the
construction of community. Videogames, too, allow an interaction with the imaginative world of the show that may prove as fun to many viewers over time, especially if the quality of the "primary" text has been seen to wane: there is something
quite titillating for a *Simpsons* fan like myself, for instance, to be able to drive
through Springfield, and walk through Springfield Elementary in *The Simpsons Hit
and Run* videogame, or to make myself into a *Simpsons* character, as a "Simpsonizer"
attached to the official *Simpsons* movie website allowed one to do. All overflow
amplifies the affective possibilities and potential of television, for fans, non-fans,
and anti-fans. Moreover, since some of these instances of overflow will prove independently rewarding as media consumption activities, for some viewers, the main
program will become less "primary" or central, as their affective investment is
placed in the overflow, hence producing a rather odd situation whereby the
"primary" text can fail but its transmedia context can still succeed.

Despite the increased prospects for play and identification, though, overflow
offers no automatic promise to improve our experience of television. Overflow
can be a fountain of riches, or it can be the result of a backed-up sewage system.
With such rampant televisual expansion, much of what is good and much of what
we might wish to watch may float by us submerged, as there are simply too many

programs and too much overflow to keep track of. In what has proven a seminal essay in television studies, Horace Newcomb and Paul Hirsch argued in 1984 that television is a "cultural forum," by which they meant that television brings competing logics, arguments, and ideas together, into a central zone in which they do battle, not only with each other, but with viewers playing their own role as the ultimate negotiators of sense. But if television has been our cultural forum (regardless of how complete or incomplete it has been), what happens when the forum expands as has contemporary television? Somewhere in this forum, a wonderful, smart, engaging program might be talking directly to us, but we may not know it exists, and we may not hear it over the clattering cacophony of voices. Hence expansion poses as much of a challenge to us as it does potential, demanding that both as consumers and, as we will examine further in Chapter 5, as citizens, we learn coping strategies. We must learn to listen through the din of a thousand voices.

From broadcasting to egocasting?

When television as a cultural forum has become so heavily populated, we must also ask if the forum still holds, or whether it has become too large, divided now into smaller forums, fiefdoms, and sites of discussion. In other words, is *broad*casting dead? Advertising rhetoric for all manner of new technologies for television is fond of announcing that the technologies offer television "for *you*," "as *you* like it," "*your* style," and so forth; and despite the rank hyperbole, behind this rhetoric lies some truth, for expanded television frequently does offer opportunities for creative cultural appropriation and personalization. But perhaps the "old days" of broadcasting did more than simply deny us choice and freedom, as such ad rhetoric would have it. Rather, to use the metaphor of the cultural forum, the era of expansion and overflow may be losing us a common space to come together. Jostein Gripsrud (2004) in particular looks to broadcasting as a vital institution that is now under threat. Writing with the tradition of European public broadcasting in mind, Gripsrud looks to most national broadcasters' central remit – to offer programming that will cultivate, inform, and in some way bring together national citizens. As Paddy Scannell (1989), David Morley (2000), and others have illustrated, national broadcasting has played a constitutive role in forming the very ideas of nationality that become key identity markers in the lives of many citizens of many countries. Morley has also shown how exclusionary a process this can be, as he writes back against more glowing accounts of national broadcasting, explaining that broadcasters have often underrepresented, misrepresented, or not represented many minority groups; nevertheless, we should not, as a result of such exclusions, give up so quickly on the *ideal* of a broadcaster that speaks to the people of a nation as a nation. An age of hundreds of channels, websites, time-shifted programs, etc., threatens the fate of broadcasting in a very real sense, however.

The ultimate threat may lie in cocooning, and in what Christine Rosen dubs "egocasting" (see Pearce 2006: F8). Watercooler talk becomes hard on a Thursday morning coffee break when some of one's colleagues TiVo'd last night's programs and have not yet watched them, while other colleagues were dispersed over multiple channels. Rosen's particular fear is that we will all become such careful and thoughtful programmers of our own media menus that we will not encounter difference. This world would be a deeply narcissistic one. Niche marketing has also been a driving force here, as, beginning in the 1980s, advertisers have worked alongside media producers to variously create or chart different societal groups or "mindsets" and to isolate them for personalized, directed advertising pitches (see Turow 2006). Thus, whereas in a three-channel system, for instance, one channel's choice to include a gay character might force some homophobic viewers (those who would still rather watch this show than the other two channels or simply turn off, that is) to encounter homosexuality on terms other than their own, when these same viewers have one hundred channels, some catering to their specific desires, their likelihood of changing channels becomes all the more real. As in such instances, then, sometimes lack of choice might be something that we want for society. Beyond the politics of representation, though (to which we will return in the next chapter), remains the concern that viewers will retreat to their own personalized media cocoons.

That said, as Gripsrud points out, broadcasting – or at least something similar – is not totally dead. Rather, rumors of its demise have been exaggerated. After all, who would really want to live in an egocasted world, and who among us is so totally knowable and conformist as to never consume, think, or speak out of their assigned niche demographic? Currently, a great deal of what we talk about with others is media related, and unless egocasting accompanied an exerted attempt to segregate physically oneself and one's like-minded companions from the rest of the world, if viewers "want to take part in tomorrow's conversations at work or in the local bar, they need to concentrate on what goes on in the handful of central broadcast channels" (218). Hence, he predicts the continuing importance of several hub channels, arguing that "the greater the number of channels, the more valuable to viewers are those channels that experience has taught them can largely be trusted as suppliers of reliable information and genuinely high-quality engaging, relevant, and entertaining material" (220). Research suggests that even in the US' multichannel environment, at any given time, 90 per cent of the audience are tuned to one of the networks or the top-ten cable channels (*Economist* 2002: 9). As Chris Anderson (2006) argues, the "long tail" needs the body of the beast itself to survive. Companies hawking their latest gadget or content will no doubt continue to frame their pitch along the lines of what television can do for *you*, but the reality is that television is, has always been, and shows every sign of continuing to be, intensely social and communal. We may enjoy our slides down the long tail every now and then, but we will always return to something approximating broadcasting at some point.

Digital divides: where the flow runs dry

The "we" in my previous sentence, however, needs interrogation. Let me come clean and admit what my own experience of television expansion includes: approximately one hundred channels, (sometimes) HBO, Showtime, and (importantly, for me) their On Demand channels, a VCR, a DVD player with a small collection of DVDs at home, and a larger (departmental) collection at work, and broadband Internet at work and at home, used occasionally to surf Youtube.com and IFilm.com, to watch streaming content, to visit TelevisionWithoutPity.com, and to sample amusing and innovative show websites. Undoubtedly, many of my readers "beat" me, with video iPods, DVRs, BitTorrent downloads and the like. But billions of people have nothing close to the expansion and overflow access that I enjoy. Many options, technologies, and platforms exist for those few of us worldwide who have access, but in truth, many have no or strictly limited access. Television, I have argued in this chapter, has exploded in recent years into multiple technologies and platforms, and many books trying to make sense of our current age agree that we are entering a postmodern space, leaving time and space behind us, with the bold new world of mediated existence and movement ahead of us. Particularly quotable has been Mackenzie Wark's dictums that, as today's postmodern citizens, "we no longer have roots, we have aerials," and "we no longer have origins, we have terminals" (1994: x). Behind such fantasies of transcending time and space, though, we must ask exactly to whom Wark's "we" refers. Even for many of the globally privileged, overflow and expansion have their limit points, as anyone who has struggled to find an Internet café or wireless hotspot knows, and thus access to a world without roots and with infinite televisual possibilities is by no means enjoyed 24/7 by even the wealthy. Indeed, Brooker (2001) coined the term "overflow" in an article that examined how relatively few British *Dawson's Creek* fans bought the show's merchandise, played with its official website, and so forth.

Beyond those who have access to overflow and do not use it, though, are the billions on the planet who outright have no access. Statistics on what has been called the "digital divide" between the technology haves and have-nots are shocking. Lest we forget, large parts of the world do not even have electricity, let alone TiVo. But even in areas with television, not all the bells and whistles accompany the box itself, nor will much of the overflow. Thus, for example, websites and online ARGs mean little to those without Internet access: an estimated 5 billion people worldwide, and well over 85 per cent of many countries' populations, including Brazil, China, Cuba, Egypt, and India. Even in the USA and UK, supposedly more "connected" countries, less than one half of the population go online at least once a month (Clickz.com 2007). Many other forms of overflow require a budget well above many in the world's reach. Obviously, then, this has ramifications for individual viewers and communities, since overflow exacerbates an already huge digital divide. For *consumers* in a burgeoning information economy, this divide is considerably more important with informational media (see van Dijk 2005). For television entertainment, the "loss" is largely relative: to offer an exaggerated example, we should hardly expect farmers in Malawi to be cursing their inability to use an online "Simpsonizer" to create their *Simpsons* avatar. As *citizens*, though, this digital divide could be felt at the level of their local broadcasters' (in)ability to compete with American content. A key reason why synergy has proven a shrewd business strategy is that few companies in the world are rich enough to follow the likes of CBS, Disney, NBC Universal, News Corporation, Time Warner, and Viacom into the world of cross-marketing and multiplatforming. Synergy and overflow can cost a great deal, and while some platforms are relatively cheap, most involve prohibitive costs. Even wealthy public broadcasters, such as the Australian Broadcasting Corporation (ABC) in Australia, BBC in the UK, or Canadian Broadcasting Corporation (CBC) in Canada, can rarely deliver the same level of expansion as their American or local commercial counterparts. In an open market, then, what we might call "overflow rich" content will have significant business advantages over "overflow poor" content, making it yet harder for local broadcasters – whether public or commercial – to compete. Certainly, another key form of televisual expansion is global, as content is moving between borders as never before.

Global expansion, or *Friends* to the world

The globalization of television is important for a consideration of how television creates, networks, and enunciates power, and thus we will return to the topic in Chapter 6. Nevertheless, the globalization of television also represents yet another form of expansion, as ownership, production, programs, formats, and style are all surpassing national boundaries, as we will now examine. Television has rarely if ever been solely national, but with developments in technology and with the business restructuring, mergers, and takeovers of recent years, its global expansion is becoming all the more evident and commonplace.

Ownership

As was discussed earlier, much of the US' mainstream media is in the hands of a few companies. As these companies expand their holdings within the US, though, they are also active in pursuing overseas expansion. Thus all six of the major televisual powerhouses in the US own at the very least a few cable channels overseas.

Time Warner, for instance, owns CNN International, and owns TNT Latin America. NBC Universal has NBC Europe, as well as multiple international cable channels. Viacom's Nickelodeon can be found in many countries, and Viacom also boasts one of world television's most omnipresent names, MTV, with channels from New Zealand to India to Italy. Disney's own omnipresence comes through children's programming and ESPN (with local channels in Africa, Australia, Brazil, Israel, Latin America, Asia (through ESPN Star Sports), and the Pacific Rim). And News Corporation has considerable holdings worldwide, as Rupert Murdoch has gobbled up satellite services around the globe, from Star TV throughout Asia, to FoxTel in Australia, to BSkyB in the UK, to DirectTV Latin America. These multi-nationals have all realized the profitability of sports, children's, news, and youth programming in particular. Murdoch has dubbed sports his "battering ram" into foreign markets (quoted in Herman and McChesney 1997: 75), as he has actively sought coverage deals for many of the world's premier sporting leagues or events, including the Super Bowl and English Premiership Football. Jeannette Steemers notes too that 60 per cent of the world's dedicated children's channels belong to Disney, Time Warner, or Viacom alone (2004: 134). The US' multinationals rule the roost, but they are not alone, and several Western European and East Asian multinationals such as Bertelsmann and Sony join them in owning huge swathes of the world's commercial media.

Production

Television production is also on the move. *Lost*, for instance, is notable for being filmed outside the contiguous 48 states, in Hawaii. Vancouver, Canada stands in weekly for Smallville, Kansas; and has stood in for the various real and fantasy worlds of *The X-Files*, *The L-Word*, *Stargate SG-1*, *Battlestar Galactica*, *Smallville*, and countless television movies in particular. In 1999, Canada boasted 696 weeks of television film "runaway" production, as opposed to California's 152, and before movies of the week fell from fashion, Canada had increased its production of television movies from thirty in 1990 to 139 in 1998 (Miller *et al.* 2005: 141). By a process of what Toby Miller *et al.* dub "The New International Division of Cultural Labor" (The NICL), Hollywood is proving keen to move production to the lowest bidder. Canadian workers come cheaper, are less unionized, and the Governments of Canada, and of British Columbia and Ontario in particular, have offered numerous financial incentives to Hollywood studios, from lower tax rates, exemptions, or refunds, to smoother bureaucracy (see Miller *et al.* 2005, Tinic 2005). Thus, for instance, *Due South* was said to have saved 40 per cent by filming in Toronto, rather than in its natural setting of Chicago (Miller *et al.* 2005: 141). Similarly, animation and other post-production technical work is increasingly going through South Korea, where, once more, lower rates and taxes have encouraged a penny-pinching Hollywood to abandon its local workers. Prominently, *The Simpsons'* key animators work in California, but cell work is then completed in South Korea.

Or, in another form of international expansion, co-production deals are slowly becoming more common worldwide. For instance, many of Discovery Channel's documentary adventure programs are co-produced with the BBC, CBC, or NHK (Japan Broadcasting Corporation), while many reality shows are co-produced by a local company and the foreign format rights holder (see below on formats). In the European Union, moreover, co-productions among constituent nations' broadcasters have been encouraged as a means to create a sense of European identity, and with the hope of challenging Hollywood's dominance in the television export market (see Miller *et al.* 2005). Co-production arrangements often offer partners the abilities to consolidate skill-sets, capital, and television markets, to bypass quota limits on the importation of foreign television, and to qualify for subsidies and tax reductions offered to "local" production. Inevitably, co-production risks flattening cultural specificity in favor of "universally" interesting narratives, and hence, as with runaway production, can diminish a local sense of place in the ensuing programs. Linguistic barriers between nations also place strict limitations on what sort of co-production is possible. But co-production and runaway production can also help to nurse a nascent or underfunded production company with greater capital and production experience, so that future endeavors are better funded and more technically proficient (see Tinic 2005).

Programs

The most overtly visible form of global expansion, though, is that of programs. Certainly, many of this book's case studies and examples will be familiar to non-American viewers due only to the mass export of American programs. The United States accounts for an astounding three quarters of all TV trade by value (Steemers 2004: 4), and was responsible in 1999 for 85 per cent of sales in children's programming sales and 81 per cent in television movie sales (Miller *et al.* 2005: 22). In 2001, the six major studios earned more money from television program and format sales than did the rest of the world combined (Waisbord 2004: 362). The reasons for such expansion are many. In particular, the US television market is by far the world's richest, and thus US companies can frequently turn an immense profit before even looking outside their borders. Not only does this inject the system with yet more cash, allowing higher production values than poorer international competition can muster, but it also means that US multinationals can price their programs well below international competitors. Miller *et al.* reveal that an average hour-long American drama will sell to Australia for $10,000 per hour, to Canada for $50,000, to the Czech Republic for $3,000, and to Mexico for $8,000.

A children's program will sell for $3,000, $25,000, $500, and $2,000 respectively (2005: 24), frequently at a loss because many are loss-leaders for their associated merchandise (Steemers 2004: 136). Clearly, then, such prices for shows with high production values, and often with considerable Internet and pop-culture buzz already in place from their American existence, offer an unbeatable deal for many broadcasters worldwide. By comparison, for instance, Steemers notes that while an American hour-long drama will sell in the UK for $20,000 to $100,000 per hour, in 2001 the average cost of producing a home-grown hour-long drama for the UK's five terrestrial channels was £344,000, or just under $700,000 (2004: 23). Especially with channel proliferation, many channels worldwide face low budgets (due to relatively small markets) and 168 hours/week to program, and hence their choice to fill in many gaps with Hollywood fare is often a foregone conclusion. Meanwhile, of course, many of these channels populating the international televisual landscape are owned by Hollywood, hence further opening up the lines for exported American programs. Hollywood is fond of attributing its international success to aesthetic superiority, and certainly its better programs represent a tour de force of televisual art; but its success should also be attributed to structural factors and outright structural *control*, leading some (as we will study in Chapter 6) to observe a US "culture blockade" (Miller *et al.* 2005: 95).

Other countries' producers have had some limited success on the international market, too, though. Thus, each region has its televisual powerhouses, who enjoy their own degrees of market control: in East and South East Asia, Japan and Korea dominate, in Latin America, it is Mexico and Brazil, in South Asia, India, in Europe, the UK, France, and Germany, and in Africa, South Africa and the former colonial powers. The UK has also had some success on the world market with its signature lavish period dramas, for instance, and Brazilian and Mexican telenovelas have traveled from Tallinn to Cairo. Of particular note, though, for all its export dominance, the US has proven remarkably resistant to importing television. Thus the international flow of programs is uneven, not a general cultural sharing. Global televisual flow may allow for greater connections and shared visual resources between citizens of different countries (hence further challenging fears of an egocasted future), and Homer Simpson, Carrie Bradshaw, Ross and Rachel, and Gil Grissom might now be part of an international vocabulary, but the dams and desserts that meet the flow force us to be cautious in how we discuss the cultural ramifications of flow and expansion.

Formats

A fourth form of global expansion, related to programs, is that of formats. A format is not so much a program as a blueprint for one. With the rise of reality programming, format sales have blossomed in recent years, as, for instance, versions of *Who Wants to be a Millionaire?*, *Big Brother*, *Survivor*, and *Pop / American Idol* have traversed the globe. Purchase of a reality format usually entails access to the program's "playbook" or "production bible," which gives information ranging from marketing techniques, to host selection tips, to lighting and sound requirements. Here, the US has proven a viable importer, as its hits *American Idol* and *Survivor* both originated overseas, and as some of its more notable comedies over the years have been imported formats from the UK, including *All in the Family*, *Sanford and Son*, *Three's Company*, and more recently, *The Office*. On one level, format sales have allowed multinationals continued success, since formats become "localized," and hence do not violate some countries' stringent cultural import quotas (see Waisbord 2004: 363): they are a way to expand into otherwise hostile markets. And as with programs, a select few countries and corporations have profited from the sale of formats, with many based in the US or Europe, including the runaway successes of Holland's Endemol, holder of *Big Brother*, *Who Wants to Be a Millionaire?*, and *Deal or No Deal*, and of Simon Cowell's many reality competitions. On another level, though, they have helped some local broadcasters to get a foot up. Formats are popular, because they are even cheaper than buying a program outright, and yet local broadcasters can then fill them with local talent. Much research has suggested that audiences frequently prefer local programming if given the choice (see Waisbord 2004: 369), and thus formats save a broadcaster costly production costs while offering them the prospect of a bona fide "local" hit. Reality formats in particular have proven rich with overflow possibilities, hence allowing local broadcasters considerable branding opportunities via associated websites, telephone polling, etc. (Waisbord 2004: 366). Hence, beyond overt program expansion is the shadow expansion of formats.

Style

Finally, with the considerable success of American programs (and sometimes Americanized formats), the very style of American television is also on the move. Steemers observes that British programming has often suffered in an international market because it has appeared too British (2004), and because it has been thought "too dark; too slow; unattractive; [and/or] too gritty or socio-political" (Graham 1999: 24). Perhaps, then, the global expansion of American television (and films and music) has engendered a familiarity and attachment to such programs, and hence an expectation of similar programs. To some, in other words, American television may appear to be "how television should be," and thus the mimicking of American shows and style is pronounced worldwide, even beyond direct sales. The imitation is not totalizing, as many nations and programs have succeeded in spite or because of their difference from American fare, as sometimes rivaling a love of American style is an intense dislike of the same said style – obvious in the UK, for instance, when Channel 5 began in 1997, looking very American, and provoking substantial criticism as a result. However, for all the concern regarding globalization of programs, it is the at-times flattening of style, and, importantly, the concurrent trend towards the American style of *structuring* television as an ad-driven industry not a public utility, that may be leading to the more profound transformation of global television.

Finding the TV in TV studies

What does all this global flow *mean* though, where is an overflowing television taking us, and why are television's multiple expansions important? To answer, let us examine what overflow, expansion, and synergy do to television studies itself. Overflow, expansion, and synergy pose a particular challenge to two types of viewer, namely those who are reading this book – media analysts and students. *The more overflow, expansion, and synergy that exist, the harder it is to pin down exactly what and where the program we are studying is.* If Amit and Kellie both watch *Lost*, but Amit watches it in the UK, reads spoilers for it, plays the videogame, and owns the toys, whereas Kellie watches it months later in Australia, avidly reads cast news and interviews, owns the DVD, and regularly visits the *Lost* official and related websites, how can we determine exactly what *Lost* is, if we want to make sense of it as a program that both viewers consume? Television has truly overflowed, expanding and diversifying to a point where even a single show such as *Lost* has become different entities to different viewers, perhaps better defined for some viewers as an "experience" rather than a "show." Following Lee Harrington and Denise Bielby, we might also note that international movements of programs create different programs: not only will different cultures react differently to *Lost*, for instance, but it may be sold differently, marketed differently, and hence *framed* differently (2005: 910). In many senses, to shift metaphors from overflow to roots, televisual expansion produces what Gilles Deleuze and Felix Guattari (1988) call a "rhizomatic text": it has multiple entry-points, no set beginning or end, and no determined path through it. Each viewer's experience of a show can vary markedly from the next's, meaning that the show's ontology (what it is) is forever its phenomenology (how it happens/becomes). While in this chapter, I have been able to distinguish between "the main program" and the overflow, some viewers may not draw such a distinction, seeing them as one and the same. Amit and Kellie will both claim to watch *Lost*, and both will marshal information gleaned from the various instances of overflow in discussing it, often without discrimination.

Brooker's work with fans uncovers that viewers do develop "canons" or hierarchies of texts that are variously accepted or contested (see 2002), but as analysts, what this suggests is that if we go in search of the text or program, we are likely to find it only reflected off the audiences who consume it, and off its various instances of overflow. The comfortable era of understanding a program by studying its production and/or its internal codes alone is over, and a more complex era lies ahead, where we as analysts must also learn to overflow our binaries. As Etienne Balibar and Pierre Macherey note, "Works of art are processes and not objects, for they are never produced once and for all, but are continually susceptible to 'reproduction': in fact, they only find an identity and a content in this continual process of transformation" (cited in Bennett 1979: 68). Thus, if we wish to study a program's effects, its power, its viewers' identification with it, and even its creativity, we must always be prepared to update our understanding of it by examining its various reproductions, interpretations, uses, and forms. Likewise, we must find better ways to account for the conflicting reproductions undertaken by various fans (or even entire cultures), and a closer analysis of overflow, and its subtle or overt acts of reconfiguring a program, will be a particularly helpful tool for the future study of television and its place in society.

Chapter 4

Keeping it real: reality and representation

even the most sophisticated among us can find many components of our "knowledge" that derive wholly or in part from fictional representations. How many of us have ever been in an operating room – awake – or in a court-room during a murder trial? How many of us have been in jail or a corporate boardroom? Yet we all possess images of and information about such places that is patched together from our experiences with dramatic and news media.

Larry Gross (2001: 10–11)

there is never a point . . . at which real-world characters, conflicts and settings find their way directly onto the screen. There are always genres. There are always aesthetic forms. And they always possess their own logic.

Stephen Neale (2000: 213)

Popular cultural texts and practices are important because they provide much of the wool from which the social tapestry is knit.

Joke Hermes (2005: 11)

We all live in and belong to multiple communities that we will never meet in real life. No American will ever sit down with his or her fellow 300 million nationals, a Londoner will never have a conference call with the city's other 8 million inhabitants, nor will a middle-class Latina ever have the chance to meet all other middle-class Latinas. Thus, as Benedict Anderson (1983: 15) notes of the nation, many of the communities and social groupings to which we belong are "imagined" – not imaginary, but never wholly present, always constituted in the mind. True of our own communities, this is even moreso with our knowledge of communities to which we do not belong, and of people and places unfamiliar to us. As Larry Gross suggests, much of our knowledge of the world, and of the places and people that populate it, must come from indirect experience. Multiple sources inform this experience, of course, but given its wide viewership and its often mundane and everyday feel, television entertainment can play a significant and determinative role in telling us of the people, places, and communities of the world. Many of us make the distinction between "the real world" and TV at an analytic, abstract level, but in the trenches of everyday decisions and thoughts, the two merge. We often judge people and places based on televisual depictions, make decisions about everything from dating to job aspirations with "information" learned from sitcoms and dramas, and select many of our heroes or villains from the characters we encounter on television.

Reality and the televised version of reality have thus become profoundly inter-twined. Philosopher Jean Baudrillard (1983b) famously writes of our world as "hyperreal," and he borrows from a story by Borges to illustrate our predicament. A king of a mythical land commissions a group of cartographers to make a national map. They do so, but he is dissatisfied with its poor level of detail, and thus orders them to produce another map, which again displeases him, forcing them to render yet another map. This process continues until finally the king has a map that is so large that it covers the entire kingdom. This map, to Baudrillard, is the world on which we live, as the media has fashioned an alternate reality, and Baudrillard suggests not that this map hides the real world below, but that the real world has vanished, leaving us only with a mediated existence, and a reality more real than reality: hyperreality. Such a tale provocatively insists that that which we call "reality" relies and is based on infinite levels of mediation. If, for instance, we hear a young woman summing up her boyfriend's behavior by stating that, "all men are like that," how can we separate reality and depiction here? Most likely, her construct of "all men" relies on a pool that includes televisual (and filmic) men; it will also include her own "real-life" experiences, and yet we might ask to what degree both her own behavior and that of the "real-life" men in that pool has been determined, colored, inspired, or taught by media depictions of masculin-ity. But, of course, those depictions will have been based in part on the writers' "real-life" experiences, and in part on generic conventions from the media world. And so on. Where the TV world stops and the real world begins is not at all easy to compute.

As Stephen Neale observes, *nothing* we see on screen is actual – it is all depic-tion, and it all relies on aesthetic frames. If on *24*, Jack Bauer punches someone, no *actual* violence has been committed, and even if a character on *The Real World* punches someone, whatever violence has occurred transpired long before the particular episode aired on television, and is therefore not "reality" at the moment of screening, but a re-presentation of it. Since by watching at home we do not have access to the full context in which the punch occurred, the actual character and nature of the punch may well have changed from real world to *Real World*. Art is a signification and representation of reality, not a reflection of it, since everything that happens in a work of art is symbolic. A punch, then, is not just a punch. Jack Bauer's punch may signify his rugged masculinity, heroic desperation and resolve, and love of nation, for instance, whereas our *Real World* cast member's punch may signify his intoxication, rage, and inability to control himself. However, while one could conclude from this, and from Neale's observation, that television is patently unreal, and while one would be correct in doing so, the more challenging task lies in asking how television entertainment's representations and significations of reality nevertheless talk about the real. What does television tell us about reality, and how does it allow us to better understand the reality of the world's many places, people, and institutions? After all, fiction and depiction may not *be* reality, but they often concern themselves with it. As Joke Hermes suggests, since so much reality (our "social tapestry") is constructed – map like – from the programs that entertain us, and since so much of our knowledge and experience of the world relies on television's depictions of reality, a vital component of any analysis of television entertainment must be the interrogation of its capacities and strategies for representing and creating reality. John Hartley writes of television's potential powers to make democracy a reality by offering a space for "cross-demographic communication" (1999: 31), whereby one individual or group can talk to and represent his, her, or their interests to others, but if this is television's great promise and a key reason why so many care so deeply about the nature and variety of its messages, we must examine how it does or does not live up to this promise.

This chapter will begin with an examination of how television entertainment introduces us not only to the unknown but to the known, and I will focus particularly on the many risks inherent – especially to minority groups – when television is allowed the power to create the world around us. However, I will then analyze how the clearly unreal might allow us to understand the real better, offering cross-demographic communication even in an unreal space. Then, as we continue to navigate the territory between real and unreal, I will discuss the industrial and institutional pressures exerted on much television entertainment to produce certain images of the real, in particular the dreamworlds of happy, middle-class, white urbanites with which many television programs are populated. Ultimately, our interests in any representation – real, hyperrreal, unreal, silly, serious, animated, live, rerun, or otherwise – should lie in *what the representation says or does*, and in *how audiences can use this representation*, and thus this chapter will focus on these two key issues. It is a common trope to ask, "What would a Martian think of our world if it only had television to learn from?" but unlike Martians, we are of this world, and hence we all have an understanding that television entertainment is depiction, play, and art. The more interesting question, then, is, how do *we* learn from television, and how do we use television to inform our interactions with the world and our creation of reality?

Mapping the world

As was discussed briefly in Chapter 2, one of television entertainment's greatest abilities is to transport its viewers to another place. Similarly, it can introduce us to all sorts of people and ideas that our lived environment may not provide. If one has never been to Harlem, met an accountant, observed the process of forensic investigation, or seen how movie stars spend their time and money, television can seemingly fill in such knowledge gaps. However, with this considerable power comes considerable responsibility to get it right, and thus while *seemingly* television entertainment can transport us and educate us, often it merely tricks us into thinking it has done so. Borges' tale of the cartographers implies that their map was accurate, but in truth, television's own cartographers often prove woefully inept. Frequently television's writers and artists see themselves as creating a singular story or character, not a part of a map, yet precisely because many of these stories and characters provide us some of our only interactions with foreign places, people, and ideas, the singular story or character easily risks becoming a representation of a larger group. As John Corner notes, "The capacity of television to combine the shown particular with the implied general is the source both of its discursive power and its controversiality" (1995: 31). For instance, any number of *Law and Order* episodes in which an African-American man in Harlem attacks a white character, come heavily loaded, implying inherent criminality in both Harlem and the African-American population, and positing whiteness as under threat from blackness. Given television's unique abilities to network large portions of society, Hartley is correct to diagnose that television *must* play a vital role in bringing society together; but television also risks basing cross-demographic communication on faulty, ill-informed assumptions and on stereotypes.

These risks are especially prominent when one is faced with the unknown. For instance, a great privilege of being rich is that one can live far away from prying eyes, behind multiple gates, golf courses, and gazebos. Similarly, many of the poorest people in the world live out of site, washing dishes in the back of a restaurant, or scrubbing Wal-Mart floors at 3 a.m. The very rich and the very poor, then, are out of sight, meaning that for many privileged members of society, interaction with them may come through the television, and thus the question, "what is it like to be very rich/poor?", will likely be answered by television. Meanwhile, many communities are racially segregated, with black and white areas of town, schools for the middle class and schools for the lower class, and so forth. Hence, barring exerted efforts by us to see others with whom we share a city, television is more likely to be forthcoming in answering questions we might have about who lives "over there" and what they're like. In this respect, for instance, *The Cosby Show* may well have "introduced" more white Americans to African-American life and culture than several decades of court-mandated bussing programs . . . therefore explaining why the show remains one of the most heavily analyzed programs in television history, because so much was at stake in the nature of its depiction.

Rather than simply move us through space, though, television can also move us through time, for as we will discuss in greater detail later in this chapter, television entertainment has become many people's historian of choice. Much of television's history, of course, comes daily from the news, but in the realm of entertainment, sitcoms especially have played a key role in constructing images of times gone by. Kompare (2005) observes that television's move towards a syndication-reliant economy led to reruns becoming our televisual heritage. Thus, Lynn Spigel (1995) notes that many of her students know the 1950s, and the place of women in the 1950s, through *I Love Lucy* and other reruns. Actual census data regarding women in the workforce and family structure in the 1950s clashes with what *Leave It To Beaver* and *Ozzie and Harriet* reruns have suggested of the white nuclear family with mum dutifully baking cookies at home while dad works at the office, and little Jimmy and Susie play at school (Coontz 1998). Even 1950s sitcoms that featured ethnic and immigrant families, such as *The Goldbergs* or *I Remember Mama*, have disappeared from television. Since history does not merely sit quietly, but is instead activated to produce scripts of what the world could look like, "the way we used to be" golden age myths, and narratives of national belonging and exclusion (see Morley 2000), when we allow the remaining sitcoms, *The Waltons*, and so forth to tell us what, in this case, the US used to be like, we automatically favor or disfavor certain scripts for what the US is or should be like now. Family structures that were quite common become displaced and labeled as "alternative," the utter whiteness of many American suburbs seems normal or even preferable, and women's historical presence in the workforce is reduced to a footnote or a particularly amusing *Lucy* episode. Since history is what we build the present on and with, when television gets that history wrong, our building blocks for the present are changed, as if our cartographer started to draw a lake where there was a stream, or a mountain where there was a valley.

Over time, too, television's various cartographers have learned bad habits from previous shows and writers, and thus many stereotypes and regressive depictions have become archetypes. A stereotype is a fixed, reductionary image of a particular type of person (such as the belief that Latinos are good dancers, "hot" lovers, and prone to a bad temper), whereas an archetype is a stock character of the story-world, used to save a writer time in establishing motivation and psychology (such as the character of the buffoon, seen in *Married . . . with Children*'s Al Bundy, or *The Simpsons*' Homer, among many other shows, or the bawdy woman, as represented by, for example, *The Golden Girls*' Blanche or *Ally McBeal*'s Elaine). When archetypes take on stereotypical overtones, the storyworld becomes invaded by prejudicial and demeaning images. Sadly, though, television has developed numerous archetypal characters with worrying depictive potential. Thus, we have all become familiar with the sad young gay man (see Gross 2001: 169), the "white trash" poor Southerner, the slimy Frenchman, the effeminate (or, by wild contrast, kungfu expert) Asian man, and the pimp daddy black man, for instance, or the wholesome white soccer mom and the ruggedly handsome, debonair white man. In 2007, the premiere of ABC's *Knights of Prosperity* introduced us to a cast of characters seemingly pulled from Chapter 1 of *How To Write an Offensive Stereotype* (see Figure 4.1), and thus perhaps contributing to the show's rapid cancellation. While such characters serve an archetypal role within the given program, reflected out to reality, they serve a stereotypical role.

However, it would be an open trap to see television's representational power as limited to depicting the unknown and unfamiliar. Rather, television also adds thousands of examples of seemingly known and familiar quantities. Thus, when the Glasgow Media Group examined audience reaction to television depictions of the mentally ill, they found that even nurses who had worked with multiple schizophrenic patients over many years were still prone to discount their own experiences as exceptional, when compared to television's overwhelming depiction of schizophrenics as dangerously violent. One nurse, for instance, stated:

Figure 4.1 The cast of the short-lived *Knights of Prosperity*, including multiple stereotypes: two slobbish white working-class men, an effeminate college nerd, an irate South-Asian taxi driver, the "saucy" Latina, and the heavy-set cigar-chompin' African-American

> The actual people I met weren't violent – that I think they are violent, that comes from television, from plays and things. That's the strange thing . . . it wasn't the people you hear of on television . . . None of them were violent but I remember being scared of them . . . the people I met weren't like that, but that is what I associated them with.
>
> (Philo 1999: 56)

Or more familiar still, television entertainment allows us to compare our own family members to, and even rate them against, thousands of televisual equivalents. So too with places: one might experience one's city as safe and welcoming, yet start to doubt the validity and representativeness of such experience should numerous cop shows, for instance, show the city as home to a dark, sinister criminal element. Media depictions even hold the power to dictate one's own background, genetics, and heritage, as illustrated in Frantz Fanon's pained discussion of the legacy of European colonialism's systematic campaign in literature and science to code the African as an inferior being. *Black Skin, White Masks* (1968) remains a seminal examination of the considerable psychological scarring inflicted on generations of young Africans and black Europeans and Americans who were taught to hate their culture, and yet it is by no means alone, for we could place it alongside, for instance, tell-alls by anorexics who were being told by the media to slim down always more, or tales from gays and lesbians who feared and despised their own sexuality due to an avalanche of homophobic media depictions. In these and countless other ways, television's narratives and characters can, as will be discussed further in Chapter 6, "normalize" ideas and ways of being, shaping the way we think about ourselves, our immediate environment, and our place in that environment.

This process of defamiliarizing that which is familiar and giving it new meaning will by no means always be a damaging one. As was argued in Chapter 1, a key power of art is precisely this ability to defamiliarize, to create a contemplative space in which one can rethink life, self, and everything else. Television provides destructive ways to engage in defamiliarization, but also wholly helpful and creative ways too. By watching another family deal with a problem familiar to one's own family, one may learn new coping mechanisms, or by watching a particularly positive depiction of, say, an Asian man (as, for instance, when the buff, personable, and crafty Korean-American Yul Kwon won *Survivor 13* in the US, breaking numerous stereotypes along the way), one might reconsider pre-existing stereotypes of Asian men, and so forth. To be excluded is to be removed from the map altogether, to be mis-characterized or stereotyped is to have one's place in the social landscape limited, and yet occasionally, one's place on the map can be etched with considerable detail, care, and attention, hence providing the basis for meaningful cross-demographic communication.

The weight of representation: from *The Cosby Show* to *The Wire*

How does one "weigh" or "measure" a depiction or representation, though? People commonly talk of "positive" or "negative"/"good" or "bad" depictions, but what do these terms really mean? What does a "good" depiction look like, or how do we recognize a "bad" representation? Who gets to decide what is "good" or "bad," and thus what is real or not?

Our first urge may be to link such terms to accuracy. Some analysts, for instance, have turned to content analysis and numbers. For several years, the Gay and Lesbian Alliance Against Defamation (GLAAD) has counted representation of varying sexualities, gender, and race/ethnicity on American television each year. Some of the numbers are telling. In the 2006–07 season, in scripted primetime network programming:

- 57 per cent of regular characters were male, with only 43 per cent female, though currently 50.9 per cent of the American population are women;
- lesbian, gay, bisexual, and transgender characters accounted for a mere 1.3 per cent of regulars, featuring in only eight programs (two of which were eventually cancelled), though all reputable numeric estimates of the LGBT population are considerably higher;
- only 14 per cent of FOX's regular characters were non-white, though 30.9 per cent of the American population are minorities.[1]

Yet, as with all statistics, many truths are hidden behind or beneath them. For instance, the UCLA Chicano Studies Research Center noted that measuring proportional representation of ethnic minorities on primetime against the national population is deceptive, since one should look instead at proportional representation relative to the program's setting (Hoffman and Noriega 2004). Except for suggesting overrepresentation of whites and underrepresentation of Latino/as, GLAAD's 2006–07 figures for regular characters on primetime television – 75 per cent white, 12 per cent African-American, 7 per cent Latina/os, 3 per cent Asian Pacific Islanders, 1 per cent Middle-Eastern, and 2 per cent multiracial – do not stray too far from Census 2000 figures for the population *as a whole*,[2] but the Center counted primetime characters in shows set in the Los Angeles, New York, and Miami areas, and found large disparities between real life and reel life. For instance, while Latino representation as regular characters on primetime network television (4 per cent of characters in the 2004–05 season) equated to less than one-third of the Latino presence in the American population, the representational gap only increased when examining shows set in these three areas (see Table 4.1).

Table 4.1 LA, New York, and Miami's racial makeup: real world vs. TV world

Place	Real world	TV world (2004–05)
Los Angeles County (8 shows)	31.1% white	47.6% white
	44.6% Latino	14.3% Latino
	9.8% African-American	38% African-American
	12.2% Asian American	0% Asian American
New York City (16 shows)	35% white	78% white
	27% Latino	8% Latino
	24.5% African-American	13% African-American
	9.8% Asian American	1% Asian American
Miami/Dade County (2 shows)	20.7% white	27% white
	57.3% Latino	27% Latino
	20.3% African-American	45% African-American
	1.4% Asian American	0% Asian American

Source: Hoffman and Noriega (2004)

Meanwhile, from watching *The OC*, *Laguna Beach*, and *The Real Housewives of Orange County*, one might imagine that Orange County, California is white not Orange, and yet statistically, only one-third of the population is non-Hispanic white.

Such numbers are eye-opening, pointing to the statistical overrepresentation of whites and occasionally African-Americans, and to the significant underrepresentation of other racial or ethnic groups. But they also leave open the question of what *sort* of representation is taking place. Racial minorities have often served solely as sidekicks or backdrop for the more nuanced, carefully written white leads, for instance, hence holding little importance to the onscreen action (see Kim 2008). Or turning to depictions of women, Martha Lauzen (2005) has found that a large number of television's women are younger, a finding that suggests the industry's preference for women as "eye candy." Beyond issues of proportionality, as we observed earlier, depictions often have two levels – the shown particular and the implied general. Accuracy on the particular level may be woefully inaccurate on the general level. There are, no doubt, black drug dealers, Latino wife-beaters, and Chinese people who are good at math, so as characters, none would be "inaccurate" on the level of the shown particular, but all risk implying something general about the respective races or ethnicities.

Beyond accuracy, then, another criterion for evaluation might be flattery, whereby a "positive" depiction would be one that flatters an individual, group, or place, whereas a "negative" depiction is unflattering and critical. However, flattery quickly runs into the brick wall of believability, as, for example, with the case of the Cosbys, who to many viewers were too perfect. Thus, flattery can be as reductive and crude a method of depiction as can outright insult. Flattery also creates impossible expectations – surely, few if any African-American mothers could live up to Clair Huxtable, the funny, caring lawyer, who was supermother to five and super-grandmother to one, and thus Clair casts a formidable shadow over real-life African-American mothers (and all mothers in general). Television's early forays into depicting any group often swing violently between the two poles of vilification and heroization, leaving little ground for "real," believable characters in between. The "special episode" that introduces us to a young gay man often makes him either sad and pathological, or a football star at his university, everybody's friend, and an all-A student. Or, this trend is arguably most evident in media depictions of those with disabilities, who too often become the objects of countless demeaning jokes, or the philosopher kings whose mere presence makes everyone a better, more caring person. As in such cases, then, flattery can still produce stereotypes, as, for instance, with images of the naturally gifted black athlete, the Asian genius, or the wholesome white soccer mom. Any and all forms of stereotypes attempt to essentialize a group of people, attributing successes and failures to genetics, naturalizing difference, and denying inherent complexity in favor of oversimplified caricatures.

How then to navigate between these two intersecting spectra of depiction: accuracy and flattery? Ultimately, we can only truly evaluate depictions relatively, by comparing them to other depictions within the same program, and *intertextually*, to other depictions in other programs. Returning to *Knights of Prosperity*, for instance, since American television has so few other South Asian characters to balance, qualify, or dispute the messages sent by his depiction, the irate taxi-driving stereotype held all the more representational power. It was down to him, *The Simpsons*' Apu, *Heroes*' Mohinder, and *ER*'s Dr Neela Rasgotra! In cases such as his, where television provides so little representation, those few characters that do exist become densely loaded with expectation and representational weight. Should the show make it to the UK, however, the greater (though still insufficient) representation of South Asians there would likely take some of the representational sting out of his tail. Or, back in the US, HBO's *The Wire* has more African-American regular or recurring characters than most network programs combined, and thus although many of these characters are (potentially stereotypical) drug dealers, thugs, killers, and angry young men, the show also offers us African-American beat cops, police upper brass, politicians, longshoremen, teachers, clergy, and regular citizens. In doing so, *The Wire* shifts the weight of representation across more than one hundred characters. For this reason, *The Wire* stands out as an excellent if rare example of how multiple representation might provide the widest scope for varied images of, here, African-American life. Though, admittedly, *The Wire* is another show with a plethora of African-American villains, no one token character carries the burden of representing "African-Americanness" and hence "African-Americanness" on *The Wire* is significantly more varied and complex, and is less encumbered by the tendency towards poor, hurried representation that characterizes many of television's encounters with minorities.

Rarely is the process of representation cut and dry, however. Looking closer at *The Cosby Show*, for instance, we find a representational puzzle. Intertextually, even moreso than *The Wire*, the program came at a time when an overwhelming number of television's depictions of African-Americans (both in entertainment and on the news) were limited to poor drug dealers, muggers, or breakdancing basketball stars. Given this environment, *The Cosby Show* offered something new and different, and though it turned the Cosbys into the super-family (see Figure 4.2), such amplification was perhaps necessary to be heard among the many family sitcoms that suggested white suburbanites had a monopoly on healthy relationships, and among the many crime dramas and news reports that depicted blacks as dangerous and antisocial. In this respect, we can judge the show a wonderful success. Except, as Sut Jhally and Justin Lewis' interviews with *Cosby Show* viewers revealed, many white viewers took the (intertextually strategic) depiction of the wealthy Cosbys as "proof" that institutional racism against blacks

Figure 4.2 The upper-middle-class Cosby family joke their way through another minor misunderstanding

was all in the past. Similarly, shifting the focus from race to class, Jhally and Lewis (1992) observe that *The Cosby Show* perpetuated the family sitcom's (and other genres') longtime normalization of the middle class (see Jones 1992, Marc 1989, Tueth 2005). Then, mixing race and class as registers, they note the danger of *The Cosby Show* implying that those African-Americans *not* in the middle class had somehow failed: since *The Cosby Show* refused to discuss institutional racism, instead suggesting that the Cosbys had a clear path to the American dream, the program sent a message to some viewers that those African-Americans *not* in the middle class were there wholly due to their own personal failure. Thus, an analysis of *The Cosby Show* shows how conflicted and complex the process of evaluating representation proves, making it hard to pin down "positive" or "negative" depictions, since the same depiction might be both.

Jhally and Lewis' study also shows how various identities often collide. After all, *The Cosby Show* did not just depict African-Americans; as their research showed, it also depicted *upper middle-class* African-Americans (and hence also upper middle classness), and, we could add, upper middle-class African-American *men*, *women*, and *youth* (and hence also gendered and generational representations). Identity can rarely if ever be mapped onto a singular dimension, as instead it is always an intersection of varying other identities. Television images are thus important not only for how they depict singular identities, but also for the ways in which they pose various intersectionalities (as with, for instance, the news and popular entertainment's normalization of white upper middle classness, or of black male violent criminality), and for the ways in which they combat dominant notions of how various identities intersect (as *The Cosby Show* attempted to do with its depiction of Bill Cosby as the upstanding citizen, gentle, loveable funnyman, and established member of the professional class). In addition, though, we must also examine how progressive movement along one or more dimensions of identity often unfortunately relies upon stereotypical notions of another dimension. For example, Jhally and Lewis show how *The Cosby Show*'s reconfiguration of "African-Americanness" and, through Cliff and Theo Huxtable, of African-American masculinity relied upon a problematic notion of upper middle classness as morally superior. In doing so, *The Cosby Show* risked limiting its "new" depiction of African-Americanness and African-American masculinity to the upper middle class alone, without acknowledging any of the structural barriers that make it difficult for many African-Americans to move into this socioeconomic class, and thereby illustrating how the intersectionalities of various identities can heavily impact upon a show's attempts to reconfigure any individual dimension. Just as we must evaluate images across programs – intertextually – therefore, we must also evaluate them across identities and intersectionalities.

Moreover, though, to compare representation to reality assumes, optimistically, that reality is easy to access. As *The Cosby Show*'s varied interpretations also illustrated, however, different viewers see different realities. The "real" as discursive category can change according to who is defining it, as evidenced by television programs (or particularly special effects) that were seen as realistic in their day, yet now appear contrived. What is "real" or not can also depend upon the viewer's different lived experiences, or upon varied realities. For instance, comedian Dave Chappelle rocketed to fame in 2003 with *Chappelle's Show* on Comedy Central, a sketch show that became known for its edgy racial humor that frequently relied upon playing with African-American stereotypes, such as the poor black crack addict or the black minstrel or "pixie" from the slave era. However, two years later, Chappelle abandoned his program in part because he felt that while some audiences had sufficient access to African-American realities to understand his caricatures of black stereotypes to be exaggerated and satirically unrealistic, other audiences were laughing at the wrong things, seeing his comedy to be poking fun at *real* "black" characteristics (see Haggins 2007: 229). Meanwhile, of course, there is no one African-American reality experienced equally by all 40 million African-Americans. Thus different audiences not only have access to differentiated experiences of reality, but some also often fail to recognize the multiple possible realities that make up, here, the experience and feeling of being African-American. To some, this slippage between varying realities may inspire a relativist stance whereby any and all representations become equally valid, lest they otherwise all be trapped in a politically correct void in which everything will offend someone. However, such a response abdicates responsibility to call for better depictions; instead, then, the existence of multiple realities demands that television, both across and within programs, should strive to depict *multiple* realities, and to encourage viewers to appreciate the complexity of social groups.

The Cosby Show and *The Chappelle Show* also illustrate how important *use* can be, for precisely because the programs' depictions and uses of African-Americans had both admirers and dislikers, and because they provoked debates over African-American realities, both shows succeeded at inspiring discussion. The plight of African-Americans and the nature of institutional racism are hardly light conversational fare, and thus as Nina Eliasoph (1998) notes of many political issues, in and of themselves, they are likely to remain taboo and undiscussed by many. However, television entertainment can at times provide an "alibi" for discussion of such loaded topics, or at least a way to start the conversation. Marie Gillespie, for instance, found that talking about soap operas allowed Punjabi teens growing up in London "a crucial forum for experimentation with identities. It is possible to say things in TV talk which would be otherwise difficult or embarrassing if not unsayable" (1995: 25). Hence beyond (and because of) questions regarding whether *The Cosby Show* dealt honestly with race and racism, or whether *The Chappelle Show* fought or engendered racism, the *discussion* of both programs opened up considerable ground for the analysis of race, racism, and reality. In this way, the weight of representation lies not only on any given television program, but also in the uses and discussion of that program.

Telling the truth by lying: affective representation and fictive reality

To talk of the uses of programs is to open up another key way of evaluating representations: by the amount of affect they inspire. *The Wire*, for instance, succeeds not only because of its range of characters, but also because of its *depths* of characterization. Here, it illustrates how television's representational and affective powers can be harnessed and combined for a positive social purpose. The program began ostensibly by following a police unit's surveillance of a major drug-dealing operation in West Baltimore. Season 2 then took us to the ports, adding another layer to the picture of drug-dealing, criminality, and policework. Season 3 added the political picture, by focusing in part on the city's mayoral election and civic politics, Season 4 took us to West Baltimore's schools, and Season 5 focused on the media. All the while, the program kept many of its characters. Thus, rather than provide viewers with short episodic snapshots of criminality, as do many of the procedural shows such as *Law and Order* or *CSI*, or as do reality shows like *Cops* and *America's Most Wanted*, *The Wire* both focused on the institutions – politics, policing, neighborhood, foster care, schooling, the media – that surround, precede, and determine this criminality, and it traced many characters across numerous events and experiences. As a result of the latter, when a character kills another, for instance, often we know both the killer and victim well. Episodic procedurals offer little information about their criminals or victims, and *Cops* offers us no more than the featured officer's fifth-rate psychoanalysis of the perp-of-the-minute, and hence such shows frequently pull criminality out of its natural context. By contrast, *The Wire* is at pains to explore and provide this context, as it uses its viewers' emotional involvement with the characters to render acts of its predominantly African-American criminals with more context, care, and thus more meaning. *The Wire* challenges television's longstanding association of blackness with criminality not by populating the show with non-black criminals, but by depicting causative factors behind criminality that emanate from institutional issues, not genetics. And since I *care* about many of these characters, their actions, their deaths, and their institutional predicament live with me long after each episode, as I think and talk them through. Representation, then, is enabled and extended by affect.

Here we reach a peculiarity of how representation works, though, for *The Wire* is fiction, its characters and plotline creations of a writing team. How, then, can one say it does a better job of representing reality than another program, such as *Law and Order*, when both are fictional, or of a "reality television" show such as *Cops*?

Similarly, when Christopher Campbell (1995) can state that fiction often does a better job of representing the realities of race in the US than does the news, or when interviewees with whom I was discussing *The Simpsons* talked of the show's yellow, four-fingered, animated characters as more real than most programs on television, how can we understand such comments?

Ang asked the same question, in 1985, of *Dallas*, for many of her respondents saw the program as "realistic," and, as both she and others (see, for instance, Lembo 2000: 196) found, many viewers need to see a show as genuine and "realistic" before they can enjoy it in the first place. Dislike a show, and likely one of your first complaints will be that it is unrealistic. In a culture in which "real" has become synonymous with worth (as in the direction to "keep it real"), the label of "real" is likely to follow any beloved show, yet be withheld from disliked shows. Yet, as we began the chapter by noting, *all* programs, and all representations are unreal – they are representations, not reality. Ang argued, though, that many different forms of realism exist; of *Dallas*, she notes, the realism "is produced by the construction of a *psychological* reality, and it is not related to its (illusory) fit to an externally perceptible (social) reality" (1985: 47). In other words, *Dallas'* set-up, characters, and plotline may all be larger than life, yet Ang's respondents felt that the choices those characters made, and the interplay between them, was reasonably reflective of reality. Countless other examples present themselves from today's television, so that, for instance, we can play a game of finding a fictional program more real than reality television quite easily. *Survivor* maroons its characters on a desert island, but it is the fictional *Lost* that frequently offers a more emotionally and psychologically realistic image of the experience of being marooned. *The Bachelor* is a popular reality dating show, and yet *Sex and the City* often captures more salient truths of dating life. And both *Big Brother* and *The Real World* have proven hugely successful reality show examinations of the dynamics of urban living and of coping with one's roommates, yet so too did *Friends*. The point is not that *Lost*, *Sex and the City*, and *Friends* all provide images of reality whereas their reality-television counterparts fail. Rather, all of the programs have proven successful, and a quick browse through their respective fan sites will confirm that all have audiences who consider them to be realistic. The reality shows' elimination theatrics, *Lost*'s smoke monsters and cursed number sequence, *Sex and the City*'s laughably high salary for its lead character, *Friends'* impossibly low Greenwich Village rents, and all of these shows' beauty pageant casting and social engineering smack of a complete lack of reality . . . yet all in their own ways have regularly captured an emotional, psychological reality that has proven poignant and profound for their audiences. Perhaps an unreal show can nevertheless keep it real.

Illustrating a notable extreme of representation and reality, Jeffrey Sconce has written of FOX's *Celebrity Boxing* bouts as excessive, absurd, and seemingly all play, and yet also uncannily commenting on reality with style and skill. One of these bouts, for instance, saw early 1990s white suburban rapper Vanilla Ice take on *Diff'rent Strokes* star gone wrong, Todd Bridges. As Sconce notes, while "Reality TV may look no better than the spectacle of Christians being thrown to the lions, . . . in point of fact, the genre takes great care in pairing specific Christians and hand-picked lions" (2004a: 258). Vanilla and Bridges:

> brought much more with them than simply two rather undistinguished celebrity pedigrees. Bridges's trouncing of Vanilla provided another strange chapter in the story of a middle-class black kid cast to play a ghetto refugee who then descended into an actual life of street crime. On the other side stood the middle-class white kid who played at life in the hood, blew his own cover, and then spent the rest of his days claiming that others had "forced" him into "selling out." The mind reels in considering the implications of race, represen-tation, and "reality" at work here – a testament to the pop-cult savvy of the fight's "promoters." This was truly a fight where nothing and *everything* was at stake at the same time.
>
> (Sconce 2004a: 259)

Sconce makes sense of celebrity boxing within a postmodern framework, noting that "reality TV celebrates the exhilaration of occupying a world where true and untrue, reality and artifice, event and gesture, premediated and postmediated have lost their meaning" (2004a: 265). However, while this silly and absurd spectacle's ability to comment nevertheless on the realities of race certainly points to the degree to which television entertainment can challenge the firm line between arti-fice and reality, it does not erase the distinction altogether. Rather, celebrity boxing shows the degree to which artifice and play need not be *only* about artifice and play: they can also make provocative implications about important social reali-ties. Kevin Glynn (2000) similarly studies tabloid television, from *Jerry Springer* to gossip shows, and finds yet more evidence that in among the carnival of alien autopsies and grandmas stealing boyfriends, such shows can offer important commentary on the nature of class, gender, and race relations, as will be discussed further in Chapter 6.

Laughing at reality

Comedy such as celebrity boxing has long been discounted as "just entertainment" and as mindless diversion, but a closer look at how comedy works reveals a genre with considerable potential and power to speak quite seriously of the real. We have already established that art defamiliarizes, but so too can good comedy. As Simon Critchley states, "jokes are further descriptions of phenomena that show them in a new light. They are acts of 'everyday anamnesis' [a recalling to mind] that remind us what we already know in a new way" (2002: 86). Much humor relies pre-eminently on a firm knowledge of social rules and conventions, with those rules and conventions becoming the object of laughter, and our laughter evidence that the comedian has helped us to step back from the rules or conventions and see them in a different light. For this reason, Critchley writes that humor offers "anti-rites" (2002: 5): humor draws us back from the logic of the world, creating room to contemplate and reflect upon – even if only fleetingly – the social rites that form the basis of the comedy. In Mikhail Bakhtin's (1984) words, humor can be "carnivalesque," and just as carnivals provide a zone outside regular lived reality for play with, mockery of, and release from that reality, so too can comedy create a zone that, while outside the logic and norms of everyday life, allows us a space of reflection upon that life. In doing so, good humor can invite us "to become philo-sophical spectators upon our own lives" (Critchley 2002: 18). Yet it frequently does so by bending the logic of the world, working instead with "the logic of the absurd" (Palmer 1987), and engaging in all manner of patently odd behavior.

> The comedian [or comedy itself] behaves like a visitor from another planet . . . But we watch the comic from a this-worldly perspective, like Sancho Panza, enjoying the delusory *epoche* from a certain distance, where we can suspend reality, and yet still engage in reality testing. The comedian is psychotic, whereas his audience are simply healthy neurotics.
>
> (Critchley 2002: 88)

Take, for instance, Jerry Seinfeld's famed proclivity, on *Seinfeld*, to break up with girlfriends for trivial reasons, such as the "mannishness" of their hands or their use of his toothbrush. Such behavior is excessive, absurd, and (we would hope) unreal-istic. But the humor, the "anti-rite," lies in *Seinfeld*'s ability to point out how trivial many reasons for breaking up might be, and in its play with the expectations for the perfect woman. Thus, while absurd, the joke holds significant potential to repre-sent and to comment upon reality.

Humor and comedy, then, can often present instances when what is on-screen is illogical, nonsensical, and surreal, yet the message being conveyed is wholly logical, sensible, and intimately concerned with reality. Arguably the clearest examples of such humor are satire and parody. We will have more to say of satire in the next chapter, since satire is often deeply political. Closely related, though, is parody – the mockery of the form, rules, and conventions of other forms of art. For instance, in one episode of medical sitcom *Scrubs*, lead character and narrator J. D. wonders what hospital life would be like if it resembled a traditional three-camera sitcom; then, following a commercial break, we return with live studio audience and three-camera style. All of a sudden, the lights are brighter, the nurses' outfits are more revealing, everyone's smiles are wider and laughs longer, the plotline is more predictable and schmaltzy, and the jokes cheesier. Before the break in style, J. D. struggles with how to tell a patient he is dying, yet after the break, he breaks the news, only to have the man quip, "Oh well, at least I won't have to worry about eating my wife's cooking anymore!" And whereas before the break, Dr Cox is forced to lay off a worker, following the break, there is now a talent contest with a generous sum of prize money that the worker (played by *American Idol* runner-up Clay Aiken) wins, making everything (even Aiken's own loss?) alright. The entire three-camera segment is framed as one of J. D's daydreams, and is appropriately oddball, unrealistic, and off-the-wall. Yet our laughter is elicited by *Scrubs'* defamiliarizing of the traditional three-camera sitcom format, along with its many rules and conventions (live studio audience, bright lights, stock characters, watered-down and obvious jokes, happy endings, plenty of deus ex machina, etc.), and thus acts as an extended "anti-rite" that allows us to analyze traditional three-camera format. The absurdity has much to say about reality, and about how many sitcoms depict and augment reality.

Our current era of television is rich with parody and parodic edge (see Gray 2006), from *The Simpsons* to *South Park*, *The Daily Show with Jon Stewart* and *The Colbert Report* to *Saturday Night Live* and *Family Guy*, or to parodic sequences on many other shows. Much of the fan base for such shows lies in the thirty-something and younger crowd, those who have grown up with a television-saturated existence, and hence whose lived environment from early childhood to present has involved many of the shows, genres, and characters that contemporary parody attacks. Those of us in these generations have been encouraged to see the world through the eyes of television, and much of our constructions, past and present, of the world around us, come to us de facto from television news, ads, and entertainment; therefore, parody's undercutting and defamiliarization of these shows, genres, characters, and conventions might allow us moments of distance from the current of our televisualized environment, as if pulling us out of the water for air. Sometimes, the substance of such parody will involve talking fecal matter, as in *South Park*, habañero chili-induced trippy nightmares, as in *The Simpsons*, or flashy ads for funeral services, as in the premier episode of *Six Feet Under*, and so absurdity is at a premium. Much contemporary parody is animated, too, and is thus visually "unreal." But the commentary on society and the firm, albeit refracted, attachment to reality is rarely far behind.

History, affect, and experiential realities

As with the cases of *The Wire*, *Celebrity Boxing*, or *The Simpsons*, fiction or stylized "reality" can tell truths by lying, and thus can become a powerful vehicle for relaying history and other social realities. Critics have often looked first and/or only to the news and/or documentaries to provide us with a window into such realities, but "pure entertainment" can often be highly informative, and an equally if not more powerful instrument for educating viewers about the diverse world. Thus, while historians and social critics alike have often grimaced (and frequently with due cause) at the representational damage done to history and social realities by entertainment, we should not be so quick to excuse all television entertainment as being able to discuss and depict the world just because much of it is inaccurate.

Arguably American television's most famous "social issue" television program was *Roots*, an ABC mini-series following Alex Haley's novel of the same name. *Roots* charted an African-American family's history from Africa to the US, slavery to modern day. As Glen Creeber points out, though, the show's translation of real-life slavery to screen occurred not without its problems. Namely, in broadcasting this story for an audience that would likely include many whites, ABC painted Gambian village life at the beginning of the story with very Anglo-European brush strokes, providing little sense of cultural difference, and struggling instead to make them seem very white American in culture. *Roots* reduced the African-American struggle to an immigrant's tale, folding in the black experience in the US with that of any other immigrant group; and Creeber notes that *Roots* ends with the suggestion that racism is over, and that the US has "atone[d] for its sins and accept[ed] Kunta Kinte's ancestors into its seemingly tolerant and multicultural bosom" (2004: 26). From both a historian's and a sociologist's perspective, then, *Roots* is deeply problematic to say the least. However, as did Ang with her *Dallas* viewers, Creeber argues that *Roots'* power lies in its emotional reality, and in its affective powers. "For a rare moment in American television history," he notes, "a national audience was actively made to identify with black characters and black history, an event that arguably forced viewers to re-evaluate the issue of racial discrimination from within both a contemporary and historical perspective" (2004: 23–4). Whereas black history and the experience of slavery may have long been seen as foreign by white Americans, *Roots* may have offered viewers an affective passport into that history. Warts, historical inaccuracies, and contrived happy ending notwithstanding, then, *Roots* offered a window into the *experience* of history, less so than an accurate *factual* retelling of that history. And from this perspective, for instance, Creeber notes that the Disneyesque depiction of Gambia in the first episode, while historically suspect, was a "device that brutally brings home the sheer unadulterated misery of being torn from everything you know of and understand as home" (2004: 28): precisely by depicting Gambian life as middle-class white American, *Roots* brought home the horror of being dragged away from that life to viewers whose prior televisual and filmic knowledge of Africa was likely as uncivilized, barbaric, and hence somewhere one might *want* to leave.

As Robert Rosenstone has noted of history on film, images can tell some things that words cannot (1995: 5), for screened entertainment and narratives can hold remarkable affective power. Creeber's argument regarding *Roots*, then, can be applied to many other programs that may have bent and augmented the historical record in their telling – and that should therefore be criticized for this – but that also offer viewers an experiential history, asking them to imagine themselves as another. We can also apply his argument to shows that have tackled other social issues. For instance, soap operas have often been at the forefront of television in dealing with various domestic, lifestyle, and health issues. When *The Guiding Light* gave one of its characters uterine cancer, health officials reported high numbers both of women going in to get checked out, and of women being diagnosed early enough for aggressive treatment (Kubey 2004: 73). Or, when Ryan Phillippe's Billy Douglas became one of television's first regular gay characters on *One Life to Live*, Phillippe reported receiving hundreds of letters from gay viewers and family or friends of gays or lesbians, thanking him for humanizing homosexuality (Gross 2001: 216). Taking yet another approach to humanizing homosexuality, when *All My Children*'s longtime character Bianca Montgomery came out as a lesbian, viewers all of a sudden had a fully developed character who happened to be a lesbian, rather than the more common "special episode" with a lesbian who is introduced as a lesbian and little else (Gross 2001: 220). In these and other ways, television entertainment can use its affective powers to encourage identification with those who we might otherwise be inclined or encouraged to view as odd, other, and pre-eminently "different."

In this regard, we might distinguish between depictions that, accurate or not: (a) encourage us to experience or contemplate difference and reality; or (b) merely reinforce otherness and close down paths to identification with other people. Sadly, television has provided many of the latter. Often, then, television's depictions and televised versions of history have constructed others that exist solely to make us feel better about ourselves – crazy, barbaric others with no regard for law, logic, or order, whose dramatic purpose seems to be little more than to convince us that we at home are smarter, more civilized, more enlightened than the irrational, unexplainable masses. Racial stereotypes, for instance, tell us that "our" race is normal, caricatures of the other gender make them seem weird and incorrectly wired, and so forth. The very process of othering is a means of identity creation, whereby we fill an other category with all that we do not want to be (see Said 1979), thereby constructing a normal mainstream at the expense of creating crude two-dimensional fictive caricatures of minorities. Anything on television can frame and represent reality, and hence is open to bastardizing that reality, but a key question for analysis should be: does this program encourage me to seek out reality, or does it encourage me to replace reality with fiction and untruths, and to produce yet more "thems" that can be contrasted to "us"?

Constructing dreamworlds

To many readers, though, shows that move us away from reality may seem favorable to those that bring us closer to it: after all, television's "escapive" qualities are some of its most admired. After a long day of work, many of us turn to programs that are patently unreal precisely to take a break from the hard slog of reality. As such, by encouraging us to hold shows accountable for the degree to which they push or pull us closer or further from reality, I do not mean to endorse a television entertainment that is wholly educational, informative, and lobotomized of fun, spectacle, and fantasy. "Escape television" is often a healthy coping mechanism, an important source of play, and a rich zone for aesthetic appreciation. But as was discussed in Chapter 2, even escape television has moments at which it either directly comments upon the real, or at which it uses or implies facets of reality in order to establish its creative, escapive difference. What a program says of the real *at those moments* is important, since they set the parameters of the escape. Television entertainment creates dreamworlds and fantasy-scapes into which we can step, but we must nevertheless remember that dreams and fantasies tell us about the real, setting up hierarchies of the mundane and the magical that hold significant potential both to represent real people, places, and things, and to set ideals against which we measure real people, places, and things. Thus, just as one might analyze one's dreams in order to interpret one's inner thoughts, so too can we analyze television's dreamworlds in order to see what they say about reality.

The interpretation of individual dreamworlds is an exhaustive task, and a driving force behind much of television studies, but here I wish to discuss common trends across television entertainment. In other words, does television entertainment have any recurring dreams? In general, a combination of industrial constraints, a widespread broadcaster preference for least-objectionable programming, and the belief that audiences dream upscale work together to produce a sanitized world, especially in most programming intended for youth.

As discussed in Chapter 1, a commercial television industry is guided first and foremost by the desire to sell all manner of consumer goods and services. Given that advertisers pay for this system, they exert pressure – whether direct or indirect – to ensure that television not only exhibits ads, but produces an environment conducive to those ads' messages. In other words, advertisers want television to romanticize consumption and consumerism. Aware that his frequently anti-corporate consumerism television show, *The Awful Truth*, was likely to detract potential advertisers, Michael Moore (funded in part by the BBC's public broadcasting money) began one episode announcing tongue-in-cheek that he would henceforth honor advertisers appropriately. To "prove" his conversion, he cut to numerous testimonials from supposedly convicted criminals declaring their favorite toothpaste, soda, or so forth. An amusing gag, the testimonials pointed to how much advertisers care about the content of a program as a vehicle for their ads, and they jarred with our experience of television precisely because most shows have effectively internalized worship of consumerism. As Richard Simon reminds us, television advertising's own version of reality is a remarkably odd one:

> Poverty, suffering, and hate do not exist, and although few people work, there are more than enough goods and services to satisfy their needs – everything from breakfast cereals and deodorant to long-distance telephone service and beer. People consume these products constantly and compulsively, and if they sometimes also swallow pain killers and digestive aids along the way, this seems a small price to pay for so much good fortune. They are self-centered and indulgent, and materialistic beyond measure, and yet the world in which they live seems better than ours; as if their selfishness has turned out to be a kind of virtue . . . No one is homeless, or seriously ill, or discriminated against, and the only real problem ever faced by African Americans is diarrhea.
>
> (1999: 77, 80)

With such a vision or version of reality behind commercial television, it is no wonder, then, why relatively little commercial television deals openly and actively with working-class life or issues, since such issues are assumed to be depressing and hence not conducive to a selling atmosphere, since they frequently point to or imply corporate complicity with, for instance, laid off workers, no healthcare benefits, or poor living conditions, and simply because shows set in the middle or upper classes allow so many more prospects for conspicuous consumption and the celebration of a consumer society. We can also understand why television rarely deals with institutions, instead focusing on the individual, since the individual is the centerpiece of consumerism, and advertisers commonly make their pitches to individual not community desires. Meanwhile, many advertisers want to avoid controversy, and to maintain a spotless corporate image, and thus few advertisers will support shows that run counter to the mainstream, or that seriously challenge widely held beliefs.[3]

Rocking a few boats and risking offending some (mainstream) viewers is restricted mostly to advertisers and channels intent on wooing a young, cool audience. Or, beyond issues of corporate or public pressure, art has long been obsessed with the exploits of the wealthy and the middle class, caring little about the poor, and despite evidence to the contrary from the success of shows such as *The Wire*, *Roseanne*, or *EastEnders*, many artists and producers assume quite simply that "escape" television must entail an escape into wealth. Together, these various pressures set firm parameters for many of television entertainment's dreamworlds.

Most notably, many television genres have specialized in providing a happy world of happy people with few real problems. Of the traditional American domestic sitcom, for instance, David Marc notes that all real-world problems stopped at the community's borders, producing the particular oddity of 1960s' sitcoms which:

> remained aloof from the battles outside that were raging. Drugs, sexual deviance, poverty, violent criminality, and the denial of constitutionally guaranteed rights could be shown on the mean city streets of Los Angeles or New York or Birmingham in crime shows, in movies, or in The News, but such things were not to cross the family threshold of situation comedy.
>
> (1989: 127)

Or, writing of *The Cosby Show*, Jhally and Lewis realize that its failure to deal with institutional racism was to be expected, since a more incisive look at the realities of racism might prove commercial suicide for a primetime network sitcom (1992: 4). A spate of programs in the late 1980s and early 1990s began to challenge this version of sitcom suburbia, but as the sitcom subsequently headed to the cities, it kept the magical fairytale aura, with the characters of *Friends*, *Seinfeld*, *Mad About You*, *Frasier*, *Sex and the City*, *Spin City*, *Just Shoot Me*, and so forth moving instead to a controversy-free adult "playground" (Tueth 2005: 141). Families, meanwhile, headed out of the sitcom, and into the nostalgic warmth of hour-long small-town family dramas such as *7th Heaven*, where racism might exist, but only for one episode, and nothing that a town carwash couldn't clean up, as in the episode "Got MLK?".

The whitewashing of sitcoms, family dramas, and much television entertainment may be understandable from an industrial perspective, for any of the reasons listed above: to keep advertisers happy, to keep mainstream and majority viewers happy, or to provide a relaxing escape from real-life problems. And certainly, some of these shows are excellent. Nor would it be fair or rational to judge each and every show as problematic simply because it did not deal with all (or even any) real-world problems. We should be able to celebrate *Seinfeld*'s comic mastery, for instance, without requiring that it include careful analysis of race or class in the US. However, and importantly, *when multiple shows start to exhibit the same blind spots, this causes a major problem for the depiction of reality*. Therefore, while we might understand why *The Cosby Show* didn't discuss institutional racism, the result of its and many other programs' failure to address such an issue is an impoverished televisual account of the realities of race in the US.

Here, then, we must pause, and shift to another definition of the term "representation" in order to ask who does television tell its stories for and on behalf of? For when it avoids controversial issues regarding race, class, gender, or any other societal problem, it asks that racial minorities, women, the working class, gays and lesbians, and any other group or community not in the power bloc or in mainstream society pay the price for its fantasies for the mainstream. Morley writes of how several British and Australian soaps, such as *Coronation Street* and *Neighbours* create a nostalgic portrayal of life without immigrants, offering a form of "white memory" (2000: 38), and Jhally and Lewis note their white respondents' appreciation of how *The Cosby Show* never held them to task, effectively allowing them to ignore racial inequality (1992: 72), both suggesting that British, Australian, and American television have often directed their fantasies at a white population. Similarly, while *The OC* showed no problem in bending reality to depict a world of affluent abundance, it only invited white characters into this dreamworld, its representation of racial and ethnic minorities largely restricted to the very real-world Southern California depiction of a Latino gardener in the first season. And when television shies away from including non-offensive gay or lesbian characters in its shows, it suggests that its many dreamworlds are there for the straight, not the gay. Or even when real-world problems are depicted, television's love for happy, tidy endings and quick morals can lead to rushed and untidy explanations, as Jon Kraszewski (2004) notes, for instance, of *The RealWorld*'s frequent trope of depicting racism as personal, rural, and Southern, so that its urban, Northern audience can absolve themselves from being implicated in racism's continuation in the US.

Structurally, television entertainment frequently depicts works by the mainstream about the mainstream for the mainstream, or at least by and for the mainstream, about others (Gross 2001). As Meehan's (1990) and Napoli's (2003) discussions of the Nielsens render clear, ratings are concerned with majorities, not minorities, as broadcasters too often conceive of the "public" that they serve as the majority, not the *entire* public. Exacerbating this problem, television executives have often run on the assumption that minorities will inevitably be pulled toward the center. After all, as Gross notes, "Minorities will invariably be culturally bilingual, while members of the dominant majority will have no such burden, or opportunity" (2001: 151), meaning that television executives can often rely on minorities learning to love, or at least begrudgingly accept, mainstream content. Those who are "doubly" marginalized, such as African-American women, may also be required to support shows that challenge only one act of marginalization, as bell hooks (1995) notes of black women who are considered to be betraying racial solidarity if they protest against misogynist images perpetuated by black men. Furthermore, as Napoli observes, the low number of minority audiences exerts a downward pressure on the budgets of media outlets dedicated to serving those minorities (and hence even more downward pressure on doubly marginalized communities), potentially leading to the loss of minority media's appeal to some who are instead drawn to the budget-rich mainstream outlets. Thus, even to minorities, minority media can lose out to mainstream media (2003: 130). At various times in television history, programmers have realized the strategic utility

of appealing to minority audiences, since, as poorly served communities, compara-
tively little attention may well win them over. Thus, when FOX began in the late
eighties, it offered more African-American themed shows than any of the other
networks, and so too did both WB and UPN appeal to African-American audiences
in their early days. However, both FOX's and WB's love affair ended soon, as they
dropped the African-American audience altogether to pursue instead young white
Americans (see Spigel and Olsson 2004: 16), and when WB and UPN merged into
CW, UPN's African-American shows were segregated to one night of the week.
Such moments in television history show how little minority audiences have
mattered to broadcasters, except at rare and solitary moments.

We should not overstate the exclusion of minorities, as some producers,
writers, and executives have proven staunch advocates of inclusive hiring. Thus,
some of today's more beloved programs include numerous minorities, from *Lost*
and *Grey's Anatomy* to *Heroes* and *24*. As Hollywood sets its sights on ever-more
global sales, multiracial casting as in such shows (all successful worldwide) may
even become more common. But if we are to understand television's sloth-like

Figure 4.3 Progress, slow progress, or no progress? *The Grey's Anatomy* cast, Season 1. Gifted
with a multiracial cast offering some performances that transcend type, the show includes
multiple stereotypical characters, including a wiser older African-American man, a short stocky
straight-talking black woman, an overachieving East Asian woman, and an angry young black
man, reserving the roles of romantic leads for the white Meredith and "McDreamy"

pace in offering more inclusive programs, we should look not only to pressures from advertisers or viewers, but also to the personnel and hiring within media industries. Hollywood is still overwhelmingly male, to begin with, from the executive ranks down to producers, directors, and writers. When Lauzen (2005) examined a random episode of every primetime drama, comedy, and reality show on the six networks in 2005, only 25 per cent of the 2419 individuals working behind the scenes were women, with only 13 per cent of the directors being women, 89 per cent of the shows without a female director, and 78 per cent of the shows without a female writer. Racially, Hollywood is very white, as are the top brass in British broadcasting. Of course, being, say, a South-Asian British woman does not ensure that one will write well about South-Asian British women, nor that one will write poorly about other groups, and we might note that despite its racially diverse cast, African-American writer Shonda Rhimes' *Grey's Anatomy* is still centered by the white Barbie and Ken-doll figures of Meredith and "McDreamy" (see Figure 4.3). However, with so few female and/or non-white topflight writers, directors, or producers in the US and UK, the men and the white Americans or Britons holding such positions have all the more barriers in place restricting them from dealing with women's or minority issues with greater sensitivity. As Fiske writes, "Cross-cultural communication which is initiated and directed by the more powerful of . . . two cultures (for power difference is always part of cultural difference) always runs the risk of reducing the weaker to the canvas upon which the stronger represents itself and its power," and therefore, the weaker of the two cultures (the minority group), must "be able to represent itself rather than be the object of representation" (2003: 277). Adequate representation behind the camera is no golden ticket to adequate representation in front of the camera, but the latter must often begin with the former if an inclusive ethos is to work its way through the industrial apparatus to the plots and characters of television entertainment.

Television's ability to offer vivid and lifelike dreamworlds explains much of its cultural appeal. The turn away from reality in order to depict such dreamworlds is in and of itself an unobjectionable act. However, when many of those "unobjectionable acts" start to mimic and echo each other with regards to who or what is in the dreamworld, and who or what is left outside, they may well produce an objectionable act as a combined whole, and it is thus important that we continually interrogate who television is representing and who is paying the price for its dreamworlds.

Life outside the *Big Brother* compound

As was argued in Chapter 2, though, no program holds the magical power to invade all audience member's minds, taking over their thoughts as a computer virus corrupts a hard drive. Thus, as discussed earlier, *use* becomes a vital part of the equation in evaluating representations and depictions. To turn to a particularly notable example, in January of 2007, not only Londoners, but Britons, Indians, and the South-Asian diaspora worldwide were abuzz with discussion of Bollywood star Shilpa Shetty's poor treatment and subjection to racist bullying in the *Celebrity Big Brother* house in the UK. A trio of celebrities in the house made numerous racist comments to Shetty, which in a short time exploded into a fireball of discussion outside the house not only about broadcaster Channel Four's responsibilities to curtail such behavior, but also about the treatment of South-Asian communities in multiple countries. The incident was covered widely by the national and international press, led to numerous protests in Britain and abroad, soured Prime Minister Tony Blair's concurrent official visit to India, and became a lightning rod for debate about racism, the responsibilities of broadcasters in relation to policing racist behavior, the ethics of reality television, and more generally, the politics of national belonging and exclusion. In making sense of this episode of *Celebrity Big Brother* history, we could first pause to ask, as did many in Britain, whether *Celebrity Big Brother* should have shut down shop or made other moves to protect Shetty, and we could analyze the program's own role in its cast members' expressions of racism. But one could also examine how the show opened up the public sphere to active and much-needed discussion of racial tensions that had long bubbled underneath the veneer of British society. Clearly, this was not the producers' *intent*; nevertheless, here, the hazily real show, and its promise to present the real, led to active and vital discussion of real-life issues outside of the mediasphere. As such, what many felt to be a poor and demeaning depiction (or, more accurately, a failure to manage depiction) resulted in meaningful debate and public discourse on race, reality, and the ethics of television. By no means do all poor depictions carry such goods in their wake, and thus I am not foolishly arguing for a celebration of demeaning representations, but occasionally, even the worst renderings of reality lead, through rejection, to much-needed discussions of reality.

Though rarely reported on, multiple similar acts of rejection and discussion occur on a daily basis. Bakhtin (1981) wrote of the novel as a "dialogic" entity, meaning that it placed multiple characters and belief-sets into interaction in a way that rarely allowed a singular voice to emerge – instead, a dialogue between voices occurred. Many of today's television shows are similarly dialogic. Thus, for instance, *The Bachelor* may seem to favor a romantic fairytale myth, but one is free to identify with the rebellious women who act out and reject the patriarchal storyline, or even to identify *against* the women therein, using them as exemplars of how not to be a modern woman (see Gray 2008). Fictional programs, too, offer certain heroes, but we are free to identify with supporting characters or even villains. As did the novel, many television programs succeed precisely because they allow various entrypoints for identification. Of "tabloid television" such as *Cops* or *Jerry Springer*-like talk shows, for example, Kevin Glynn notes that "One consequence of its penchant for conflict, confrontation, and explosively sensational material is that [it] exerts only very loosely constituted discursive controls over its content. This opens it up, on the whole, to a range of competing voices and perspectives" (2000: 32), a comment which could just as easily be applied to any number of reality television shows in particular. Even at a textual level, then, many shows allow and encourage various perspectives on reality, throwing forward questions as much as, if not more than, providing determinate answers. Admittedly, some images alienate viewers and communities, so vigorous discussion of all television's contentious programs and issues is neither guaranteed nor something that should be naively celebrated. Nevertheless, especially in an age of expansion, fan discussion, fan fiction, and simply water-cooler talk can quickly turn representations on their heads.

Crudely conceived depictions of reality can even provide the source of significant entertainment, through the strategy of "camp" reading. Laughter and ridicule can be two of our more powerful weapons, and the camp act of relishing television shows with, for instance, offensive caricatures, saccharine, schmaltzy morals, and poor production values, can allow us to step back from the unreal, render it as spectacle, and in doing so, look to reality through ironic reflection (see Gross 2001, Sontag 1964). The humor of camp frequently arises from the distance between reality and the painfully constructed televisual edifice, and hence, albeit tangentially, when we appreciate a program for its camp value, we are reflecting upon the real.

That said, we must not over-exaggerate the prospects for and incidence of reading against the grain. As was argued in Chapter 2, being an active viewer can be hard work. Moreover, to reject a media depiction often assumes that one has the requisite real-life experience to recognize its lack of reality – a situation that may in some cases prove rare. Or even in cases when we merely sense, cynically, that a program is lying to us, rejection of the unreal in and of itself does not provide the real. As Justin Lewis argues, "For all our self-professed savvy about the 'unreal' nature of the TV world, fictional television provides semiotic resources to draw on for describing the category of real life" (2004: 293), and thus even when we sense that what we are watching is not real, with the lack of more accurate, "real" knowledge or experience, it becomes all too easy to fall back on the unreal. For instance, when S. Elizabeth Bird asked her interview subjects to design a television program with a Native Indian character, although many knew the dominant stereotypes of the in-touch-with-nature, shamanistic Native to be incorrect, they had little real knowledge to fall back on, and hence either replicated this image in their own programs, or simply produced a polar opposite (2003: 99). Thus we see the power of media representations to construct images of the "normal," an issue to which we will return with renewed vigor in Chapter 6. For our purposes here, Jhally and Lewis', and Bird's work should remind us that despite the powers of rejection and of reading against the grain, mere rejection is often not enough.

Ultimately, television entertainment's power to invoke, depict, augment, create anew, and/or criticize reality demands that we constantly study its representations. Some viewers complain that academics in particular should just learn to watch and not criticize, but since television entertainment can provide us with cross-demographic communication, and with much of our knowledge of the world, the nature of its map, how we use this map, and everything that television depicts – from the grand to the mundane – feed into our daily decisions, feelings, beliefs, and attitudes. Thus we could not overlook the evaluation of such information even if we tried: the digestion of televisual renderings of reality informs our experience of everyday life and our understanding of what precisely is real, what is fantasy, what is a lie, and what is glorious fiction.

Chapter 5

Plugging in: politics and citizenship

They identified with television programs, films, and popular music in a way that they would not even consider about politics. These texts unleashed the memories and experiences suppressed by the dominant rhetoric of their private and public lives. Here, hope was still an issue, and happiness was still possible. The gap between dominant political rhetoric and their lived experiences left them with enormous tensions and anxieties with no outlet for expression save in their responses to popular culture texts. Here was a sphere they saw as their own, a presentation of choices about the world that mattered to them, and in discussing these texts, they brought forth the full passion and anger and hope that they repressed elsewhere.

George Lipsitz (1990: xiii–iv)

Popular culture . . . needs to be acknowledged as a relevant resource for political citizenship: a resource that produces comprehension and respect for popular political voices and that allows for more people to perform as citizens; a resource that can make citizenship more pleasurable, more engaging, and more inclusive.

Liesbet van Zoonen (2005: 151)

Popular politics

Given television entertainment's powers to present various depictions of reality, and to inform us – whether correctly or erroneously – of the essence of people, places, and things, it also has considerable power to offer representations of how these people, places, and things do, could, and should interact. Therefore, since politics is precisely about how people and institutions should interact – who runs a country and how, who provides public services and how, the rules governing interactions between individuals and corporations, which individuals have what power over others, and so forth – television entertainment plays a vital role in connecting us to the world of politics. Through fantasy and fiction, television entertainment can offer scripts of a better or a worse world, and it can offer advice on how to achieve or avoid such worlds, but it also tells us about our own world in the here and now, for its representations and images often become key resources with which we evaluate the world around us. Since "the world around us" is never wholly visible, television frequently serves as our eyes, and just as messages from our eyes tell us how to act and react to the world around us, our televisual eyes help us to determine how to make our own imprint upon the political world, and how we see our own role in society. Many of the political units to which we belong, whether city, country, or world, are too vast to offer communal meeting places in the physical world, and hence they must conduct their business virtually, with mass media such as the television playing a constitutive role in networking the political unit. Similarly, therefore, the practice of citizenship, of being an active member of a social, cultural, and/or political unit, must quite often be enacted with significant assistance from television. As such, this chapter turns to politics and citizenship, asking how television entertainment informs, activates, and/or limits our experience of both.

Precisely because many political units are too vast to meet physically, scholars of both media and politics have long looked to mass media such as television to play the role of virtual meeting place. Prominently, for instance, Jürgen Habermas (1989) writes of society's need for a "public sphere," which Peter Dahlgren neatly glosses as "a space – a discursive, institutional, topographical space – where people in their roles as citizens can have access to what can be metaphorically called socie- tal dialogues, which deal with questions of common concern: in other words, with politics in the broadest sense" (1995: 9). In such a public sphere, individuals could not only *listen* to societal dialogues, and hence gain information and ideas, but could also *participate*, sharing information and opinions, or at least feeling enabled to act upon such information and ideas elsewhere: "the public sphere is not just a 'marketplace of ideas' or an 'information exchange depot,' but also a major societal mechanism for the production and circulation of culture, which frames and gives meaning to our identities" (Dahlgren 1995: 23). Hence, a fully functioning public sphere would be one in which individuals become citizens, and are granted the full rights of democratic citizenship, and it would be of equal value to the individuals who are empowered by it, and to the nation or other political unit that would benefit from the results of such open societal dialogues. Scholars have often referred to the Greek agoras, where citizens could meet to discuss the issues of the day free from the power strictures of the private and domestic sphere, the corpo- rate sphere, or the established and institutionalized political sphere, and Habermas himself painted a (heavily romanticized) picture of eighteenth- and nineteenth- century coffee-houses as such spaces too; projecting out from the agora or coffee house, public sphere scholars have long hoped for the media to act similarly, only on a much larger scale.[1]

However, public sphere discourse often turns quickly to the news as the zone proper of politics, citizenship, and societal dialogue. This turn is fuelled in large part by the fact that the news promises to offer current information; thus, priding itself as a genre of information dissemination, and especially given its delivery in real time, the news is a natural genre for the nurturing of a public sphere. At the same time, though, following Habermas, many scholars have exhibited significant suspicion or outright disbelief of entertainment's abilities to contribute to such a project. Habermas regarded the public sphere as by necessity serious and rational, a stipulation that seemingly discounts the logic of art, fiction, and entertainment, all of which frequently rely on the arational, the deeply affective, and the emotional. As was described in this book's introduction, many both in and outside of media studies have long doubted television entertainment's capacity to provide anything more than bread, circuses, nice stories, and the occasional poop joke. Similarly, many audience members have long resisted the notion that television entertainment might be in any way political ("it's *just* TV," we hear them say), since politics itself has become a dirty word.

To highlight the importance of studying the representation of politics and the practices of citizenship outside of the news, though, I turn to the quotes that open this chapter. The "they" to whom George Lipsitz refers are many of the working-class students he has taught over the years, and he describes a truism of our day – that many individuals feel wholly isolated and divorced from the world of "Politics," whether unable or unwilling to participate (see also Bhavnani 1991, Buckingham 2000, Eliasoph 1998). Certainly, to many critics (see, for instance, Cohen 2005, McChesney 2004), the news has failed so miserably to welcome and empower its audience members, and hence is largely responsible for what many observers see as a crisis in citizenship, whereby more people vote in tele-vised reality shows such as *American Idol* or *Big Brother* than in national elections. Yet in describing his students' passion for popular culture, Lipsitz illustrates the degree to which television shows, films, and songs often not only welcome and involve their consumers, but also speak powerfully to and about these students' everyday lives. Popular culture, in other words, succeeds here where official "Politics" does not, discussing issues of dire importance to the students, making them care, and speaking in a language that they understand and to which they can relate. As this book has already discussed, such are the affective powers of good television entertainment. But if popular culture and entertainment can do this, then perhaps they are at least as well equipped as is the news to discuss politics, and to construct public spheres, if not sometimes moreso. Liesbet van Zoonen takes up this argument in her book *Entertaining the Citizen: When Politics and Popular Culture Converge* (2005), writing of the possibilities for entertainment and popular culture to create political public spheres that welcome many of those individuals and communities long since abandoned by our more traditional public spheres, and that make the practices of citizenship a passion and a pleasure, not solely a solemn duty.

Van Zoonen notes the considerable Habermasian concern that politics become trivialized when not wholly rational and serious, but insists that dividing the world into serious politics and non-political fun is foolish. "[T]o set politics apart from the rest of culture," she writes, "is not a feasible option for the maintenance of citizenship: not only will it not survive the competition for spare time, but more importantly it will also be separated, different, and distant from everyday life" (2005: 3). Lipsitz's students had turned away from "Politics," he suggests, because "Politics" felt foreign to them. Thus if we are to encourage deserters from parliamentary/congressional Politics to return to politics with a small "p", and to politics in its broadest definition as being about *the rightful interrelationships of people, power, and institutions*, and hence if television is to play a role in developing citizenship, the connections between politics and everyday life must be made clear. Popular culture and television entertainment, van Zoonen suggests, might therefore have an important role to play in such a struggle. Of course, precisely because it is a struggle, and because many have abandoned "Politics" while television entertainment has been on the scene, we would be silly to imagine television entertainment offering the panacea that makes everything in the political world better, and that makes everyone's citizenship a reality. Much television entertainment fails abysmally at developing citizenship, distracting individuals from important political realities, and/or alienating them from the field of politics altogether. Meanwhile, if we set out with nothing less than lived and active citizenship for all as the only recognizable achievement, even television entertainment's better and more profound programs will be bound to fall short of the mark, as will any single effort. Both the news and various other institutions (namely, the educational and political systems of a country) must play their own part too. Nevertheless, throughout this chapter, I will examine various programs that contribute to this effort, and various textual strategies for engaging with politics.

That said, an important distinction must be made at the outset, between engaging with politics knowingly, perhaps even eagerly, and engaging with politics at all. Later in the chapter, I will examine several programs that discuss the political in explicit and open terms. However, all shows are political in one way or another, and thus whether we like it or not and are consciously aware of the fact or not, all programs, whether from the news, ads, or entertainment, are constantly offering ways to make sense of the world. As Morley notes, "there is, in television, no such thing as an 'innocent' text – no programme which is not worthy of serious attention, no programme which can claim to provide only 'entertainment' rather than messages about society" (1992: 82). Rather, what a program says, what it fails to say, what it takes for granted, what values it celebrates, derides, or ignores, and who it gives what sort of power over others to, all combine to offer political messages. Sometimes these messages will be subtle, marginal, and/or poorly communicated, whereas at other times they will be more pronounced and proficient. But beyond the issue of *whether* a show invites us to consume as citizens, is therefore the issue of *how* it invites us to consume at all, and what understanding of the world around us it provides. If every program in television's public sphere or "cultural forum" (Newcomb and Hirsch 1984) has something to say, though, a fruitful place to begin an examination of politics and television entertainment is by asking whether any particular messages appear to prevail, and whether television has its own politics. Thus, before examining how citizenship can be enabled, first I will examine the general political tenor of the cultural forum.

"It's just common sense": ideology and the status quo

Television programs do not need to be *about* politics to be political. Certainly, one of the more sophisticated understandings of how power, ideology, and politics work comes from Antonio Gramsci (1971), who notes that when any given ideology is in the ascendance, it will function as common sense, not "ideology," to most individuals. Thus, the term "ideological" is commonly used to suggest "politics other than my own," much in the same way that most people believe that their own spoken accent is normal, and everyone else's an accent. Gramsci notes that dominant ideologies become so resilient precisely by avoiding the appearance of being ideologies; their politics work by not seeming political. Hence, for instance, in the more consumer-driven capitalist society of the US, teacher evaluation forms are common in universities, and all universities at least pretend to take them seriously, whereas in the UK, where the vestiges of an aristocratic society live on, teaching evaluations are significantly less common or important; as the UK moves closer to American consumer capitalism, though, teaching evaluations and other consumer-driven evaluation/feedback mechanisms are becoming more common, and are often resisted as counter-productive or welcomed as common sense, often depending upon one's views of American consumer capitalism. A Gramscian view of power and ideology allows us to see how politics become infused in even the most unlikely of places such as teaching evaluations. It also therefore suggests that *all* programs will be political, just as all people speak with accents – it is just a matter of *which* accent, *which* politics. When we do not sense the presence of the political, we are likely experiencing the status quo. That which may seem natural, common sense, or "real" to us is indeed political – as Jean-Louis Comolli and Jean Narboni note, "reality is nothing but an expression of the prevailing ideology" (1993: 46).

To provide an example from television entertainment that has already been discussed in this book, many viewers may have seen the traditional family sitcom that proved immensely popular in the US from the 1950s to at least the early 1990s as a simple reflection of reality – suburban family life in its mundane yet pleasing form. But the messages it offered were deeply political. As was discussed in Chapter 4, sitcoms often created their nostalgic dreamworlds in racially (and heteronormative) homogenous neighborhoods run by men. Family sitcoms privileged and idealized a world without change or complexity. Even in the sixties, when civil and women's rights discourse was blossoming in the US, the American domesticoms of the moment saw *Bewitched*'s Darren forbidding his wife Samantha to use her witch powers (easily interpretable as the powers of women's liberation, as Marc argues (1989: 136)) to do chores, since instead she needed to be a "good little woman" in the old-fashioned way. Domesticoms played an important role in normalizing a patriarchal, racially segregated, conservative culture, as best evidenced by George Bush, Sr.'s and Dan Quayle's heavy use of such shows in speeches promoting their conservative "family values" platform in the early 1990s. Bush and Quayle yearned for a world of *The Waltons* and *The Andy Griffith Show*, but railed against *The Simpsons'* parodic undercutting of "normal" family life, and against *Murphy Brown*'s working single mother, since they saw these as politically problematic. Their liberal opponents, however, complimented *The Simpsons* and *Murphy Brown* for their "realism" and for actually "showing it like it is." Here, then, we see how "realism," "normality," and the taken for granted can all be deeply political. And if a seemingly innocuous genre can be so heavily steeped in politics, clearly we do not have to be consciously seeking out the political for the political to occur within a program. Many or even most shows do not announce their political intentions, and many producers may even be unaware of the politics espoused by their shows' prevailing sense of "realism."

Genre alone can be responsible for much of a show's politics. Genre is, after all, a rule book for proper behavior of and interrelationships between characters and institutions, just as are politics. And since genre rules also work as a set of audience expectations, they become the "common sense" and ideological norm within the generic program. Hence, for instance, the traditional family sitcom holds much of its politics within its structure – most episodes see a kid doing something wrong, only to be corrected by the father, reaffirming patriarchal control, or they depict the family struggling with an external influence, hence suggesting the inherent suspiciousness of outsiders and outside elements. The traditional family sitcom must end exactly where it began, and thus progression and/or change are out of the question: the ideal is posited as that with which the family begins each episode, never as something to which it must aspire. No progression and no need for change equate to a staunch conservatism, especially when the sitcom's proclivity for patriarchal control and xenophobia are considered. David Grote (1983) has charged that this form is wholly antithetical to the entire history of comedy in Western culture, whereby change was always worked towards, making it an inherently progressive genre. That said, some sitcoms have played with the form to show a continuing yet never realized struggle for change. Patricia Mellencamp notes, for instance, that Lucy's never-ending attempt to move beyond husband Ricky's orders and proclamations on *I Love Lucy* arguably ensure that every episode centers on feminist desires for liberation from patriarchy, so that "if Lucy's plots for ambition and fame *narratively* fail . . ., *performatively* they succeeded" in evoking sympathy for her cause (2003: 49). Or, similarly, *The Simpsons* flips the rubric of traditional family sitcoms, beginning with dysfunction, not the ideal, and thus when the episode ends, and all is reset, we experience a Sisyphean return to dysfunction. Therefore, clever artists can play with genre and formula, but genre and formula nevertheless often predetermine politics for many shows.

The world of the Schwarzenegger Republicans

What other political messages are dominant in television? In the US, right-wing pundits and commentators frequently allege that Hollywood is rife with liberalism and filled with "lefty" propagandists, and while Hollywood's beliefs on issues such as abortion, capital punishment, and gay marriage are often decidedly liberal, the right-wing critique conveniently overlooks the fiscal and macro politics of Hollywood, particularly of its owners and shareholders, not just its celebrities and writers, and particularly with television, it also overlooks the politics of advertisers. Once factoring in these political forces, we can see how television entertainment's politics are considerably less clear than crude suppositions based on a few celebrities' political stump speeches might suggest.

First, as was noted in Chapter 1, commercial television is also a business, not simply a bohemian art house. The degree to which Hollywood's own brand of liberalism can actually be equated to explicit left-wing politics is questionable at best, and this link is even less clear in countries where attachments between celebrities and left-wing political parties are less solid. But George Clooney liberals, Arnold Schwarzenegger Republicans, or Mel Gibson Christian Conservatives notwithstanding, we know that actors and writers do not control shows – control also comes from above. Thus, while Chapter 1 inquired into what corporate control means for innovation, here we might note that with megacorporations behind commercial television, and with the system's infusion of money coming from advertisers keen to promote conspicuous consumption, a truly anti-capitalist left-wing politics would be totally incommensurate with the system. Expecting the likes of Viacom, Time Warner, Disney, News Corp, and General Electric – some of the world's most successful capitalists, in other words – to eschew capitalist politics is absurd. As do savvy ads, television may want to *flatter* us by suggesting that we are cool style-leaders, outside of conformist consumer capitalism, but it has an active interest in keeping us neatly within that brand of capitalism, and therefore much of television's citizenship training takes the form of disciplining us as capitalist subjects (Miller 1993). Advertisers want us to buy and buy more, while television wants us to consume and consume more television, and thus much of the medium's politics emanate from these two key desires.

One of commercial television's most adamant critics, Mark Crispin Miller, alleges that corporate politics have rendered the medium a "great boiling cesspool" in which, "[g]uided by its images even while he [sic] thinks he sees through them, the TV-viewer learns only to consume" (1988: 31, 327). Sitcoms, he argues, become showcases for various consumer items, as indeed they were first designed to be, while dramas and anything that seems vaguely political in fact lulls us into a sense of security with the world around us, telling us that everything is fine and nothing really needs changing. American network television, he states, has "gradually purified itself of all antithetical tones and genres," convincing us that the only change that matters is offered by television itself, and ultimately reducing the field of politics to a spectacle, whereby we watch it just as we watch everything, "not bothering to participate, because participation won't be needed. The show, we'll figure numbly, must go on" (10, 88). Miller is a master of overstatement, exhibiting no real faith either in creative personnel as anything more than corporate lackies, or in audiences as intelligent, media-literate beings. However, even if overblown, his criticism points to reasonable fears that many critics have of commercial television: that its bills are paid by advertisers, and thus it will always treat them lovingly. "Consumer therapy" is advocated by most television shows, only the poorest of characters ever seem to wear the same clothes twice, and new cars and electronics abound, especially in shows that want to seem new, cool, and cutting edge.

Rarely if ever, meanwhile, will shows attack the edifice of consumer capitalism (see Chapter 4). Over time, then, the networks have become experts at toeing the line of the status quo – they may take more risks when the political climate is itself more progressive, but otherwise, they will often err on the side of the status quo. Thus, for example, when the liberal group Moveon.org tried to place an ad challenging President George W. Bush's fiscal policies in the 2004 Super Bowl coverage, CBS refused to take it, for fear of controversy (ironic when controversy in the form of Janet Jackson's bared breast sought them out that year!), whereas the company regularly took ads from Bush to promote those same policies. When media corporations behave as did CBS in determining who to accept money from, we can all too easily guess how similar policies and fear of rocking the boat feed into their programming practices.

For any show to be "commercially viable" requires not just audiences, but willing advertisers, and thus when progressive politics do not easily lend themselves to advertiser involvement, we are often left with the rather conservative status quo instead. Similarly, as Chapter 4 also discussed, certain issue-based political platforms struggle to see the light of day on television, whether on the news, entertainment, or otherwise. In particular, environmental politics are suspiciously absent from television, save for an occasional comment by Lisa Simpson or by teens who are coded as well-meaning yet naïve. With television receiving much of its advertising dollars from the oil and automotive industries, this political omission becomes more understandable. Or we might also notice a lack of working-class politics, with plenty of shows offering working-class heroes (see Kendall 2005), but few caring to discuss labor unions as much more than Mafioso fronts, inadequate wages as much more than the plight of illegal immigrants (who, it is sometimes suggested, should just be thankful for what they have), or quality health care, save for occasional *ER* B- or C-storylines. With television's ad dollars coming from big corporations and insurance companies, an earnest examination of such political issues could provoke the ire of a network's favorite clients, and so once more, omission and underplay prove more common strategies for commercial television. Thus, while corporate ownership and advertiser pressure have often been blamed for poor news ethics, they can also determine the political landscape of television entertainment's "realities."

Such moves have dire consequences for the practice and enabling of citizenship, for much of television reduces citizenship to being a consumer. Critics can at times overlook that consumption, at both the levels of purchase and use, is an important component of citizenship, but consumption cannot be the only component. A consumer "democracy" allows one vote *per dollar*, not one vote *per person*, and hence inevitably disenfranchises and outright ignores large portions of the population at the same time as it privileges others. A consumer democracy also looks to corporations for governance, bypassing elected officials and the democratic system to instead place all faith in corporations' ability to run the world. Thus, for instance, Laurie Ouellette argues that reality courtroom show *Judge Judy* subtly poses the benefits of a corporate democracy. The program invites legal combatants to take their case to television instead of the courts, allowing the irascible Judge Judy Scheindlin to preside. Sheindlin sees herself as a crusader fighting the problem of courts "overflowing" with ludicrous cases, and thus uses her show to encourage people to stop complaining, stop taking their problems to the courts, and be responsible individuals ("If you're a victim, it's your fault," she asserts (Ouellette 2004: 236)). In doing so, Ouellette observes, she espouses a worldview wherein all problems are personal and none institutional, and wherein state intervention, assistance, or service only spoil people, "female welfare recipients are cast as irresponsible nonworkers, [and] men lacking middle class occupations and salaries are routinely scorned for 'choosing' a life of poverty" (243). These politics are right wing and corporate, shunning social services as producing a nation of "babies," looking instead to noble corporations (such as the producers of the show) to straighten things out, and requiring individuals to make their own destiny. Of course, individual viewings of the show may offer various different options for identification, as Sheindlin may appear more villain than hero to some, but *Judge Judy* nevertheless offers a daily morality play on citizenship as corporate.

Dialogic spaces and cultural forums

Beyond shows such as Sheindlin's that offer explicit and largely uncontested messages, though, a considerably more common pattern visible in television entertainment's treatment of politics is to offer what Justin Lewis calls "ingenious ambiguity" (1991), whereby writers script a program that seemingly allows viewers from across the political spectrum to relate to and identify with their own political beliefs. The 2006 and 2007 seasons of *24* provide an example. On one hand, *24* has become notorious for its zealous love of torture. The eagerness of the show's Counter-Terrorism Unit and of hero Jack Bauer to torture someone after only ten seconds of interrogation is not only shocking, but disturbing at a time when the US' own policies on torture have been called into question in the wake of leaked photos from the Abu Graihb prison facility in Iraq, of photos and stories from its Guantanamo prison facility, and of President Bush's cavalier (mis)reading of the Geneva Convention agreement on the treatment of enemy prisoners. The 2007 season on *24* also began with a series of terrorist attacks on American soil that provokes the internment of Arab Americans. When one character is sent to interview men in an internment camp, he finds proof that they are indeed terrorists and terrorist sympathizers. Meanwhile, one of the president's national security advisers implores the president to approve more such measures, espousing a line of supposed realpolitik in a time of crisis. Thus the show is rife with conservative sentiment on racial profiling and on torture, and with racial fearmongering. However, the 2006 and 2007 seasons also told the story of an incompetent president led by a secret organization that is complicit with numerous terrorist activities, and in 2007 the vice president was painted as a dark and sinister figure pulling many of the strings behind this network. And while Arab Americans are being rounded up, the president as moral authority voices his displeasure, as do other likeable characters. Consequently, among the conservative messages, we also have liberal counter-arguments offered, and a storyline that rather obviously alludes to the (real) US president and vice president, and to concerns that the former was a puppet of the nefarious latter, both of whom may in turn be in the pocket of corporate interests. *24* refuses to resolve these varying strands, instead keeping to an ambiguous line whereby neither conservative nor liberal viewers could in good faith and full knowledge allege clear "bias." Such a strategy of ingenious ambiguity is therefore common in television, for producers can argue that they are by no means depoliticizing their dreamworlds, but they also protect themselves from controversy and complaint.

A strategy of ingenious ambiguity risks being disabling, by offering two steps forward and two steps backward, regardless of one's political leanings. But to see it as such would be to expect television programs to offer us only answers and proclamations; instead, a more helpful view might be to ask television to provide *resources* for arriving at our own answers, and *testing grounds* in which we can see various answers interplay. This returns us to Newcomb and Hirsch's notion of the "cultural forum," a place where different programs, characters, and events offer different politics that will then enter into dialogue and debate. As discussed in the above section, prominent voices may well be lacking from this dialogue, so we must avoid characterizing the cultural forum as complete or wholly open, but it nevertheless can often offer a space for the (limited) rehearsal, vigorous testing, and development of political beliefs.

Such discussion is most easily evident in shows that build dialogue or debate into their very structure. Talk shows, most prominently, offer a dialogic zone of education and debate, wherein various "experts" and common people share opinions, stories, and information about the topic under discussion. Talk shows often feature a host who attempts to frame discussion within certain moral–political terms of evaluation, but audiences are free to employ their own terms. Talk shows have also provided a rare space for working-class and everyday people to be heard on television, hence broadening the range of the dialogue, de-emphasizing the (often white middle-class male) expert paradigm of which many news stations are so fond (see Glynn 2000), and in so doing, actively *welcoming* audiences to make up their own minds, rather than have it made up for them. Such programs are talkback television, encouraging viewers to yell at the screen, to fume to fellow viewers during the next commercial break, or to debrief with friends later. For these reasons, many scholars have seen talk shows in particular as bastions of a nascent public sphere (see Livingstone and Lunt 1994). Other shows and genres build debate into their structure, too, though. The legal dramedy *Boston Legal*, for instance, offers two or three cases per episode, each usually based around a provocative moral or political issue. As opposed to *Law and Order*, though, in which guilt and innocence, right and wrong, are often heavily presumed from the outset, *Boston Legal* will frequently present impassioned arguments for both sides. Moreover, while *Law and Order* posits its public prosecutors as the ultimate good guys, hence imploring audiences to identify with them and their cause, *Boston Legal*'s lead characters are all flawed and comically odd beings, so the show does not ask for us to agree with even favorite characters. Rather, it presents various arguments and leaves the audience member to broker the peace between them.

John Hartley (1999) sees such dialogic space as offering "democratainment," and he applauds some shows' ability to make democracy a reality by circulating ideas, ideals, beliefs, opinions, and information that many viewers would otherwise never encounter. And from this grand mélange, Hartley observes, audiences can engage in "DIY citizenship," piecing together not only their own ideas, but also a better idea of the range of ideas in their surrounding society. Furthermore, citizenship to Hartley involves more than simply governmental politics, but also identity, interpersonal, and cultural politics, and he notes that entertainment has frequently been better at addressing such issues than has the news. If, as argued in Chapter 4, debates over representation and depiction are common with television entertainment, this is because television entertainment is often the key genre in which cultural politics are taken seriously and are habitually addressed. Entertainment, then, might play a constitutive role in fashioning *cultural* citizenship.

Taking politics personally

Moreover, Hartley and others have argued that by embedding politics into entertainment, and by showing how the political exists at the personal level, many television shows can model a more fluid interaction between the personal and political. In his examination of young people seemingly disaffected by and disinterested in politics, David Buckingham concludes that "[t]heir alienation was from politics *as conventionally defined* – that is, from the actions of politicians" (2000: 206), but that significant potential existed for television to lure these youth to politics through the personal. Van Zoonen echoes that "Politics has to be connected to the everyday culture of its citizens; otherwise it becomes an alien sphere, occupied by strangers no one cares and bothers about" (2005: 3). The governmental politics of the news can seem so peculiarly foreign, and thus entertainment that deals with political issues in the personal, private realm may hold the best chance of making politics real, relevant, and important to many viewers. As Jeffrey Jones argues, "It is this intimacy between public and private life that occurs with, through, and because of the medium of television that deserves our attention here" (2005: 24), for it is when the private is seen as political, and the political seen as private that we often feel most emboldened to participate in "Politics" (26).

Here, though, we must leave Habermas and his desire for a rational politics behind. Entertainment politics can never be truly rational, after all, unless they fail to entertain. To entertain is to capture one's imagination and affective investment, and to appeal to one's emotional center. Talk shows might win us over with a sobbing mother's tale, or *Boston Legal*'s lawyers may convince us with tricky rhetoric and spectacle. By contrast, Habermas hoped that a rational public sphere would stay clear of such dangers. However, in doing so, he grossly undervalues both the importance and the inevitability of emotion in making rational decisions. As was argued briefly in Chapter 2, though, emotion and affect always involve cognition and some form of rational deliberation. Studying neuroscience's understanding of the brain, for instance, political scientist George Marcus challenges the received wisdom that emotion and rationality are separate. Whereas Western culture has long distinguished between the heart and mind, passion and reason, Marcus shows that emotions actually enable rationality, and that "rationality is a special set of abilities that are recruited by emotion systems in the brain to enable us to adapt to the challenges that daily confront us" (2002: 7). Going beyond the mere science, though, Marcus argues that emotions are deeply involved in the most "rational" of political decisions. For instance, "Emotion plays an explicit role in bonding citizens, party, party platform, and elected officials. Caring about problems, caring about the nation, and caring for political parties [is] the glue that enable[s] a nation to organize and direct its politics" (37). Any one of us likely has opinions on thousands of issues, but it is our emotions that make us *care* about these opinions, and that make us want to fight for them, or do nothing about them. Hence, as much as rationality may be idealized as "pure" or "uncluttered" thinking, we only choose to think about things or to act upon them because of emotions and affect.

Consequently, Marcus argues for a reappraisal of the "sentimental citizen," and for the presence of emotions in politics. His argument is not that any and all emotions are to be celebrated, for emotion often replaces logic and information. Such is many critics' fear, then, that the sobbing mother's tears or the rhetorical fireworks on *Boston Legal* might disable viewers' inclination to seek out actual information on the issue at hand. Rather, Marcus notes that emotions might also be a powerful political ally, and an important component of the practice of citizenship. Van Zoonen applies this logic to television and popular culture, suggesting that emotional involvement and the affective powers of fandom in particular may enable and layer citizenship, and may play an important role in politics. As such, television entertainment's ability to make us care, its narrative capacities to hook us in, and its characters that occasionally become as friends to us may prove precisely the connection required to make an otherwise seemingly distant political issue become one that matters to us.

Such was the stated goal of *West Wing* creators Aaron Sorkin and Thomas Schlamme. On *The West Wing*'s DVDs, Sorkin notes his frustration that many citizens have effectively given up on the realm of politics, cynically seeing everyone involved in politics as in it for their own personal gain. Sorkin's own interactions with public servants suggested that even if misguided they cared deeply, often sacrificing better-paying jobs and richer family lives for the love of the country and for a dedication to the public good. Thus, *The West Wing* introduced us to the fictional White House staff of a fictional president, and followed their various political and personal travails, driven by their passion for governance and social justice. Sorkin's scripts proved remarkably topical at times, taking on not only "big" political issues such as capital punishment, the appointment of justices to the Supreme Court, or policies on terrorism, but also how the census works, how party candidates are chosen in small ridings, and so forth. Thus, viewers were treated to a weekly "visit" to the halls of American power and to otherwise unseen areas of politics (see Figure 5.1), in ways that not only offered some of network television's smartest, quickest dialogue to date, hence often offering significant raw information, and that not only created a dialogic sphere for the discussion of these issues, but that also asked viewers to care about them. Some of the show's speeches stand out as impressive, passionate calls to action, causing some fans even to regard the fictional administration as the team they wished would actually run the country. For instance, while addressing a college group, C. J. Cregg, then the show's White House Press Secretary, offered that:

> Twenty-five years ago half of all 18–24-year-olds voted. Today it's 25 per cent. 18–24-year-olds represent 33 per cent of the population but only account for 7 per cent of the voters. Think government isn't about you? How many of you have student loans to pay? How many have credit card debt? How many want clean air and clean water and civil liberties? How many want jobs? How many want kids? How many want their kids to go to good schools and walk on safe streets? Decisions are made by those who show up.

Here, then, a very explicit call to citizenship is issued, as the show attempted a crafty sleight-of-hand trick, turning fandom into citizenship, and *West Wing* consumers into American citizens.

Figure 5.1 Offering what the news cannot: a very human moment of presidential regret on *The West Wing*

Moreover, *The West Wing* provides examples of how overflow and televisual expansion have allowed its discussion of politics to continue well beyond the screen. Fan discussion groups grew quickly, yet the show also enjoyed cross-over appeal, frequently being mentioned in political blogs and other online communities dedicated to specific political issues. In particular, for instance, when President Barlet handily blasted a homophobic radio commentator (an obvious stand-in for real-life Dr Laura Schlessinger) for using the Bible to justify her bigotry, the dialogue was widely quoted on sites dedicated to gay rights, and on numerous liberal blogs and websites. The DVD release of the show also allowed further parsing of certain speeches, and of the producers' stated intentions behind such shows, and such transcription, decoding, and information similarly went out across a large network of websites. Thus *West Wing* characters, dialogue, and plot-lines found themselves both generating political discussion, and contributing to discussions that were already ongoing, stoking the fires of citizenship. Of course, its left-leaning politics did not always sit well with some viewers, and thus many anti-fans also felt the need to respond, engaging with its apparent messages in yet more political discussion, and concerned that its politics might color those of television as a whole. And particularly because the program occupied a reasonably unique place in television's panoply of political shows – being the only fictional show at the time set in the White House – television critics, newspaper columnists, and political scientists alike often waged in with various criticisms and compliments of its depictions, strategies, and messages. Whether being applauded or attacked, though, it succeeded in encouraging political debate and discussion. Moreover, as a fictional program, it could propose provocative scenarios different from real life that occasionally helped unmoor surrounding political discussion from the anchoring of the real life here and now to examine a more general issue at a conceptual level.

Politics: the show

To some, the fact that viewers consume politics through entertainment represents a particular failure of the news and a great pity. Certainly, to substitute *The West Wing* and *Boston Legal* for reading and viewing the news is unlikely to make one a fully functioning citizen. However, while we wait for the news to be reformed, and while other books than this discuss how this should happen, we should be careful not to discount the significant contributions to citizenship and political education that television entertainment offer us. As Jones (2005) notes, bemoaning the "textualization" of politics, and the degree to which politics have become something to watch, seemingly not something to participate in, has become a competitive sport in the fields of political science and public punditry. As Jones glosses, "For better or worse, the most common and frequent form of political *activity* – its actual practice – comes, for most people, through their choosing, attending to, processing, and engaging a myriad of media texts about the formal political process of government and political institutions as they conduct their daily routines" (2005: 17). Following on from this, then, concerns about politics becoming mere spectacle and citizenship a televisualized entity are common, given voice in many a tome, whether it be Robert Putnam's bestseller, *Bowling Alone: The Collapse and Revival of American Community* (2000), suggesting that we are all isolating ourselves from politics and social engagement via television, or Neal Gabler's *Life: The Movie* (2000), suggesting by its title alone that we have reduced ourselves to being spectators of life, not actors of it. However, as Jones points out, to see the textualization of politics and active citizenship as dichotomous is to misunderstand how politics work. Surely individuals need not be carrying a placard and marching on Congress, or campaigning for a candidate, to "count" as citizens; rather, in large nations with millions of people, we should expect that many will conduct their citizenship in less visually stunning a manner.[2] A key and significant duty for citizens is simply to be aware of and thinking about politics, so that they can then pick their spots for more active participation down the road.

Once citizenship is recognized to be frequently "textualized," we can therefore criticize simplistic notions of active citizenship that require obvious and overt participation to qualify as citizenship. Jones insists that there are "a multitude of ways in which people exchange, process, and engage political material in their day-to-day lives, ways that just as easily can be crude, limited, dismissive, trivial, playful, and emotional as they can be thoughtful, wide-ranging, generous, complex, rational, serious, and high-minded," and that people often "attend" to politics "in passing, cursorily, mixed in with other activities, from various media and across numerous subjects" (18). Thus, for television to encourage true participation in politics, and to enable an active citizenship, it needs to address politics in a wide variety of manners, through serious exposition *and* dramas, talk shows, comedies, reality shows, etc. Rather than penning politics and citizenship off in one small portion of the schedule, and hence in one small segment of our lives, television would do best to treat politics in a variety of ways in multiple locations. Speaking realistically, we may struggle to see that which is politically enabling in much of television's lineup, and thus neither Jones nor I argue here that television is currently living up to this aim, but he nevertheless provides us with a rationale for valuing the political where we do see it. When, as he writes, television makes it "much easier to 'bump up against' the political in one's daily life" (20), then interaction and involvement with the political becomes more intricately rooted in our everyday lives.

In a study of how Americans avoid talking about politics, Nina Eliasoph offers a sobering reminder of how little many people care to discuss politics. She paints a picture, based on considerable ethnographic work, of everyday Americans holding political beliefs and values that "lie in the closet gathering dust" (1998: 19) because they do not feel at liberty to talk about them. Politics has become a taboo topic for many, a conversation ender not starter, and hence, she speculates, "probably for most Americans, the public sphere is a dry and dismal place, from which intelligence, curiosity, and generosity have evaporated" (260). She even notes how at public meetings where politics might seem par for the course (such as PTA or community meetings), many of her subjects would apologize for "getting political" and would quickly try to change the topic if they did so. A major challenge for the US and for many other countries with similar seemingly dwindling rates of political involvement, is to find ways to make politics matter. Interestingly, though Eliasoph says little about the media in her book, in one provocative admission, she notes of one group that "When they allowed themselves to express opinions and not just repeat facts, the authorized opinions came from an entertainment show" (146). On one level, this comment illustrates Hermes' point that many popular culture-infused performances of citizenship remain hidden in mundane moments of everyday life, hence necessitating media ethnography to uncover just how often popular culture and citizenship work hand in hand (2005: 13). But more forcefully, as the example from Chapter 4 of the furor that surrounded *Celebrity Big Brother* illustrates, Eliasoph's observation suggests that television entertainment might at times provide an alibi and an excuse for talking about politics, an exception to the taboo to avoid politics, and thus a way to get political discussion rolling. A browse through fan discussion boards of any television show following an explicitly political episode quite often reveals active and engaged conversation about the political issues in question. Demands that politics be rational, that participants be highly educated about the issues, and that people take it seriously have so thoroughly alienated the realm of governmental politics from many citizens, that reforming the news alone cannot wholly "rescue" politics for everyday life: rather, entertainment may serve an important role in making politics emotive, playful, accessible, interesting, and thus vital.

Politics as a joke: *The Daily Show with Jon Stewart* and *The Day Today*

A key genre that deals with political discussion in such an emotive, playful, accessible, interesting, and vital manner is satire. As Jones notes, political talk in the news, news journals, and pundit shows "has always assumed one crucial point: that those doing the talking should have direct 'insider' knowledge of what they are talking about," hence also assuming outright that the goal is "to inform or educate, not fulfill other functions of political communication" (2005: 35). Education and the relaying of information must, of course, play a role in activating citizenship, but the risk with much news is that positing the viewers as unknowing outsiders and the newscasters, pundits, and guests as all-knowing insiders produces a stark binary that can reduce viewers to the status of children in a classroom. As with schoolchildren, viewers are encouraged to take notes and listen carefully, but not to participate in the production of knowledge as anything beyond being receptacles for it. The news can therefore be both patronizing and alienating at times, ironically reducing politics to a spectacle much more than do many of the entertainment shows that provoke more condemnation for textualizing politics. The power dynamics of news become all the more troubling when so many of its experts, whether guests or newscasters, are middle-aged, middle-class white males. Not only does such a news constituency replicate power imbalances in the world, where women, racial and ethnic minorities, the young, and the working class may be tired of being lectured to by great white fathers, but it also creates the semblance of an insider's club that includes politicians, pundits, and newscasters. No wonder, then, that so many feel disaffected by politics, since its presentation in the news quite often places much of the population on the outside of politics. Satire, by contrast, often offers ways in which the news' outsiders can feel and be engaged.

Whereas newscasters can tend to speak *to* the people, satirists labor to speak of and *for* the people. Much satire is about talking back to power, and about criticizing the edifices, practices, and decisions of power. As Critchley writes of good humor, satire aims to be therapeutic, and hence has an almost "messianic" and "redemptive" quality (2002: 16). Satire begins when a satirist smells bullshit and artifice, and when s/he attempts to reveal that bullshit and artifice. As comedians, too, satirists frequently speak in an everyday manner, not with the elevated poise and diction of the news or of politicians: they curse, they rant, they fume, and so forth. Thus, immediately, their mode of discourse is more mundane and everyday, of the people. Or satirists will parodically adopt the elevated poise and diction of politics and news, but only to criticize it from the inside, to point out its lunacy, and hence they are truly speaking in the language of "us," proposing to work on our behalf. Satirists accept outright that they are outsiders like us, not insiders like them. As such, satire as genre is often considerably more welcoming than is the news.

Bakhtin has written of the liberatory powers of laughter, and these are powers that satirists employ. Laughter, he writes:

> has the remarkable power of making an object come up close, of drawing it into a zone of crude contact where one can finger it familiarly on all sides, turn it upside down, inside out, peer at it from above and below, break open its external shell, look into its center, doubt it, take it apart, dismember it, lay it bare and expose it, examine it freely and experiment with it . . . Laughter is a vital factor in laying down that prerequisite for fearlessness without which it would be impossible to approach the world realistically. As it draws an object

to itself and makes it familiar, laughter delivers the object into the fearless hands of investigative experiment – both scientific and artistic.

(1981: 23)

To satirize in particular is to scrutinize, and to encourage one's audience to scrutinize too. Thus, whereas the news too often posits politics as something to learn, ideally satire will encourage viewers to play with politics, to examine it and test it, and to feel enabled to question it, rather than simply consume it as raw information. As Bakhtin suggests, moreover, by playing with the political, one can gain a greater sense of ownership over it, and can feel more empowered to engage with it. Sigmund Freud's seminal account of humor and jokes (1960) noted that many jokes perform a momentary act of aggression directed toward that which has power over us, whether a person, an idea, or an institution, for in that moment we free ourselves from that power. Similarly, then, satire can create for us a zone in which alongside the satirist we can render "common sense" as nonsense, and in which we can analyze and interrogate power and the realm of politics, rather than remain simple subjects of it.

One of today's most prominent and famous satirical programs is Comedy Central's *The Daily Show with Jon Stewart* (see Figure 5.2). Broadcast nightly Monday through Thursday in the US, and available in an increasing number of other countries, the show examines the news of the moment, but with satire, comic silliness, and play. In doing so, it offers a nightly response to the news, as the show is particularly adept at analyzing and parsing political speeches and reinterpreting them. During the course of any given episode, the show usually provides a significant amount of information as well as actual news footage gleaned from other channels, and its researchers have proven a smart lot, often unearthing speeches made years earlier by politicians that directly refute a recent speech, for instance. They have also scooped the news proper on many occasions, as for instance in 2004, when they offered more coverage of the Democratic and Republican conventions than did ABC, CBS, and NBC combined (Jenkins 2006: 225). Moreover, Jon Stewart wears a suit and tie, his set resembles a news program's, and camerawork and news graphics mimic the news too. But he is also prone to expressions of frustration and disgust, to comic facial expressions, and to making nonsensical asides. Thus the show is news like, but definitely not the news. Instead, it offers information, but then response and criticism, frequently mixing serious points with comic overstatement. For instance, one episode discussed various strategies being discussed by Congress for reforming immigration policies. After providing a fair overview of various strategies, Stewart then contrasted these with the conservative Republican stance, which, he stated, demanded that illegal immigrants be reduced to food-stuff, or "soylent verde" as he calls it. While absurd, the joke refers to the gist of the hardline Republican desire for immigrants to be done away with. Hence the segment provides information, calls on audiences to analyze the various proposed strategies for immigration reform, and then passes comic judgment on the coldness of one such strategy.

Important for *The Daily Show* and other satirical programs, though, is that while challenging official versions of the truth, and while encouraging audiences to do likewise, they do not set themselves up as rival mouthpieces of truth. As Hermes notes of popular culture's engagement with politics, its very strength "is that it is not a manifesto. Popular culture suggests, it implies, it ironizes" (2005: 11). When Stewart likens the Republican plan for immigration reform to *Soylent Green*, the comment has comical effect, but he also refuses to establish his opinion here as the

Figure 5.2 "Fake news" from *The Daily Show with Jon Stewart*

new truth, for it is too absurdly stated to lay claim to being a declaration of truth. Hence, good satire can *suggest* but ultimately requires the audience to produce "truth." As Jenkins notes, *The Daily Show* thereby presents the news as "something to be discovered through active hashing through of competing accounts rather than as something to be digested from authoritative sources" (2006: 227); it wants an active citizenship, not a passive one. Jones' audience research into *Politically Incorrect*, a show that encouraged satirical commentary on the news from its various debating guests, leads him to observe that:

> The point here that audiences understand, yet critics of these types of shows seemingly don't, is that what is discursively produced on television is not a *product* to be chosen (i.e., the most intelligent thought or rationally correct idea). Instead, what they desire is simply the *process* of being able to speak and hear others speak, of bringing about public thinking in a language they understand and that . . . is heartfelt and sincere, despite the possibility that such thinking might be misguided. The audience implicitly asserts that it is within *them* that truth and meaning will be made, not selected from choices developed by "experts."
>
> (2005: 176)

The Daily Show and other notable satires challenge official truths, frequently positing alternative options, yet ultimately they *demand* that viewers make up their own minds, and they posit news and the political as dynamic, not simply as a list of factoids. Moreover, as both Jones found of *Politically Incorrect* audiences (167), and as I found of *Simpsons* audiences wrestling with its satire (Gray 2006), good satire can often provoke considerable discussion away from the television set too. As a response to the news proper, satire can play a vital role as court fool (see Gray 2006, Jones 2005: 113), involving audiences as thinking, active citizens. Increasingly, too, good satire rides the peak of the waves of televisual expansion and overflow, so that, for instance, Jon Stewart's appearance on and destruction of CNN's *Crossfire* in 2005, or Stephen Colbert's Swiftian 2006 White House Press Correspondents Dinner address, circulated on Youtube, Ifilm, and so forth to thousands if not millions of viewers who had not seen them in their original context.

More than simply provide a response to the news, though, good satire can model ways of interacting with the news, and can thus inspire a DIY ethic of satire and parody. Jenkins (2006) charts the proliferation of such DIY projects online, examining a central genre of television news overflow: Photoshop'd parodies and remixed political speeches. British satirist, Chris Morris, for instance, edited one of George W. Bush's State of the Union addresses, available on Youtube[3] so that Bush now calls on Iraqis to "go home and die," and promises, "this year, for the first time, we must offer every child in America three nuclear missiles." If satire works well, though, it will not even need Youtube to provide evidence: rather, if viewers can sit through the news with a Stewart-like voice of cynicism, and thus leave eager to research further the "truths" on offer from that broadcast, then its political powers are working in full force.

To this end, news parody can similarly improve one's ability to watch the news critically. Long before editing State of the Union addresses, Chris Morris cut his teeth on the brilliant *Day Today* and *Brasseye*, the former a news parody, the latter a news journal parody. Both served as scathing attacks on the news, asking viewers to regard the genre not as a window to the truth, but as an active and at times worrying mediator. For instance, one episode of *The Day Today* followed the supposed outbreak of war between Australia and Hong Kong. Morris, as on-screen anchor, first plays an important part in making the war happen when, in interviewing Australian and Hong Kong officials, he goads them into hostilities. When war is then declared, Morris turns to the camera smiling and announces with glee, "Yes, it's war!" before excitedly promising the best coverage the viewer has ever seen. He nonchalantly rattles off, in convincing newspeak, that fighting has broken out "on the upper cataracts of the Australo-Hong Kong border," and we then cut to a field reporter, who peppers his speech with hyperbolic (and comically mixed) metaphors: "the stretched twig of peace is at boiling point," "this is literally a nation about to blow up in its own face." With the newsroom in full commotion, Morris then peacefully announces, "but first, the weather with Sylvester Stewart." Later on still, the show cuts to a commercial for a CD for the "Best Of" the supposed news program's war coverage, playing war scenes with pop music overlaid. In stark and yet very funny terms, the episode calls the news to task for its lust for war ("Yes, it's a war!"), for its eagerness to blow everything out of proportion, even to the point of actually *causing* a war, for its commodification of suffering (through the CD), for its callous disregard for the seriousness of the war ("But now the weather . . ."), and yet also of how easy it is for newspeak to lure us in (posing a border between Australia and Hong Kong!). *The Daily Show* deals in similarly wonderful moments of news parody, as do *The Simpsons* (see Gray 2006, Chapter 4), *South Park*, *The Colbert Report*, and occasional other shows. While rare on television, such moments of scintillating news parody can encourage active viewership of the news. As was said earlier, genres are political and ideological, but parody can destabilize their politics as common sense, rendering them instead as nonsense, and thus whether of the news or of other genres, parody can talk back to genre and recontextualize it and its politics (Gray 2006, Chapter 2).

To some critics of parody and satire, though, herein may lie the danger of the forms, for rather than lead to critical news viewership, some argue that they might lead to *no* news viewership, and instead to cynical disengagement. Furthermore, some allege that by "making fun of everything," such shows can promote an ethic of nihilism and withdrawal (see Matheson 2001, Wallace 2001). Such was the fear expressed in the American popular press in 2004, when various critics suggested that many youths were getting their news solely or predominantly from late-night talk show hosts such as Stewart, David Letterman, Jay Leno, and Conan O'Brien. As Michael Kalin worried in *The Boston Globe*:

> Stewart's daily dose of political parody . . . leads to a "holier than art thou" attitude toward our national leaders. People who possess the wit, intelligence, and self-awareness of viewers of *The Daily Show* would never choose to enter the political fray full of "buffoons and idiots." Content to remain perched atop their Olympian ivory towers, these bright leaders head straight for the private sector.
>
> (2006: n.p)

Such criticism cannot easily be dismissed, for certainly, parody and satire may alienate when they mean to welcome. However, little to no audience research exists to give evidence to the assertion. Rather, both Jones (2005) and I (2006) have found evidence to the contrary: that news satire, parody, and play can energize political citizenship, getting people interested, not disinterested, and passionate about the news and politics, not disaffected by them. Inevitably, some viewers will see such shows as substitutes for, not supplements to, the news and political citizenship, but such shows' positive potential seems to far outweigh their negative potential. As William Savage, Jr. notes of another criticism of satire – that some audiences just won't "get it," and hence may take it seriously – to a certain degree, we should ask, "so what?" (2003: 220). No text or genre will ever be interpreted in one way by all audiences. Satire and parody may "fail" politically, just as may *The West Wing* if audiences only care about the characters, or as may talk shows if audiences only want to see confrontation, but just as the news' own failures should not lead us to castigate hastily the genre, so too might we realize the immense potential of satire, as a pre-eminent form of political entertainment, to address citizens as citizens, talking to some audiences that the news avoids, encouraging audiences to engage with the news and the political, and welcoming audiences into the public sphere.

Doing citizenship

While this chapter has seemingly moved toward optimism, and while indeed the presence in the television line-up of programs such as *The West Wing*, *The Daily Show with Jon Stewart*, *South Park*, and so forth should limit and challenge the utter pessimism with which some commentators look upon television entertainment's engagement with politics, admittedly a few good programs alone do not create a vibrant public sphere. As Zygmunt Bauman writes in his somber treatise, *In*

Search of Politics, any agora or public sphere must be a "noisy, unruly and rowdy marketplace of complaints and demands" (1999: 94), not simply populated by a scant few opinionated individuals. A public sphere or a cultural forum is only as strong as the variety and energy of voices within it, and thus in assessing the capacity of television entertainment to foster citizens' engagement with all manner of policies and ideas, we must not only look to those programs that are leading the way, but must also demand more of the sometimes vast number of programs that are doing nothing. Of course, addressing viewers as citizens is not television entertainment's only task, and so we should avoid a stark political utilitarianism that demands that *all* programs be explicitly political at all times, but given television's almost unique powers to reach huge numbers of citizens and to broadcast widely information and ideas, and given television entertainment's popularity, television entertainment is simply too powerful and too vital a tool for the creation, maintenance, and enabling of citizenship for us not to call for yet more politics.

"Yet more politics" can sound, to some, like a synonym for "yet more boredom," yet as I hope to have shown, rather than entertainment and politics being incommensurable, entertainment can enliven politics and make it meaningful *while* entertaining. Politics remains a dirty word to many people, and it is for this reason that television entertainment can be so important, since in its more successful instances, it can show that politics need not be boring and otherworldly. Writing of attempts to present the news to youth, Buckingham notes that arguably more important than the specific information that the news offers is "how it enables viewers to construct and define their relationship with the public sphere" (2000: 18), and though we should not discount entertainment programs' abilities to relay pure information, their skill often lies in how they encourage viewers to engage with the public sphere. Or, as van Zoonen argues, of importance is not necessarily "what entertaining politics does to citizens, but what citizens do with entertaining politics, for citizenship is not something that pertains if it is not expressed in everyday talk and actions, both in the public and the private domain. Citizenship, in other words, is something that one has to do, something that requires performance" (2005: 123). What we must ask of television entertainment is that it offers multiple ways in which citizens can use it – starting dialogue, not finishing it, welcoming citizens into discussion of issues, not merely presenting them as distant and sealed topics. Television entertainment may offer scripts for citizenship and modes of performing citizenship that more traditional critics frown upon and deride, but when national elections in many democratic nations struggle to bring out voters, when many anti-democratic nations or governments in supposedly democratic nations struggle to keep certain voters at home, and when many individuals feel alienated from the realm of politics, creative and imaginative responses are required.

Eliasoph reminds us that:

> power works, in part, by robbing the powerless of the inclination or ability to develop their own interpretations of political issues. With active, mindful political participation, we weave reality and a place for ourselves within it. A crucial dimension of power is the power to create the contexts of public life itself. This is the power to create the public itself.
>
> (1998: 17)

Thus television entertainment can prove a key tool in both the reification of others' power over the public, or the public's power over itself. Television entertainment can play a central role in the creation of social reality, and hence the nature of those realities, their ideological underpinnings, and their inclusion or exclusion of a broad public in turn either grant or deny citizenship. As Eliasoph's quotation also renders clear, though, politics and the presentation of politics channel both personal and societal power, and thus the next and last chapter turns to further examination of power and television entertainment.

Chapter 6

Channel interference: television and power

The media . . . have social effects on a large scale not only because centralised mechanisms of broadcasting are in place, but also because we believe in the authority of media discourse in countless local contexts, because we believe that most others believe the same, and because we act on the basis of these beliefs on countless specific occasions.

Nick Couldry (2000: 5)

Any attempt to hear and learn what another culture wishes to say works toward equalizing power relations, particularly when what is said may not be what the listener wishes to hear. Listening is the opposite of representation, which is why the first act of the power-bloc on rising in the morning is to insert its ear plugs.

John Fiske (2003: 277)

As one of the central institutions in contemporary society, television's powers are many. Certainly, each of my previous chapters has focused on various powers of television entertainment: it can act as an expressive art, and hence a means to tell stories, communicate ideas to others, and amuse millions. It can allow its viewers to relax, engage in imaginative play or speculation, and create spaces for reflection. It is also powerful because it has moved beyond television, "overflowing" and expanding into popular culture as a whole, into everyday conversations and decisions, into community and individual identity building projects, and into multiple other media and technologies, from the Internet to cell phones. It is powerful because its programs either pretend to represent reality, because they are interpreted as such, or simply because they are feared to be interpreted as such. Hence it is also powerful because it not only shows us a world around us, but creates many of the parameters for our subsequent interactions with that world. Of course, television entertainment is not alone in holding such powers, but it is a rare entity for holding such powers *to such a degree*. It is possible, even unfortunately common, to overstate television entertainment's powers in *any given situation*, but it is difficult to overstate its *potential* powers. Moreover, as the previous chapters have shown, television does not just hold power – it can also give, network, arrange, defuse, refuse, or channel other powers within society, and thus it is both a medium of entertainment and a medium with which others can seek, maintain, deny, or exert control. Ultimately, the instances of television entertainment's involvement with powerplays are too numerous to list, but this chapter will chart several prominent ways in which television entertainment channels power, on both personal and global levels. The chapter asks us to consider who has power over television entertainment, what nature that power takes, and how it is or is not used, while also asking how television has been used in battles for power between citizens, media corporations, governments, advertisers, consumers, artists, regulators, and cultural elites.

John Fiske poses a difference between representation and listening, noting that listening and its correlate of allowing others to speak fundamentally challenges those in power, since power is often exerted through controlling and limiting knowledge and the right to share that knowledge. This chapter will therefore chart various ways in which television entertainment represents, thereby holding significant power over use, but it will also examine ways in which television entertainment can listen, and ways in which viewers can force television to listen, and can challenge its representational powers. First, I will examine television as an agent of normalization. Due to its powers to represent reality, and due to its mass viewership, television entertainment often holds the power to dictate – to represent – which people, ideas, and behaviors are "normal," and which are decidedly abnormal. As Nick Couldry suggests above, television often manages to convince us that it is a crystal ball that can show us all things in the world, and hence one can easily end up regarding many of its images and characters as "the way things are" in the world at large. After examining how television entertainment can normalize, though, I will also study how it can challenge prevalent scripts of normalization both endemic and external to television, posing new norms and/or interrogating old ones. At such moments, television entertainment may prove its most successful at encouraging us to listen and at providing something important to listen to. To challenge truly television's representational powers, though, also involves us recognizing how it and its programs construct themselves as our crystal ball accessing the world in the first place, and thus I will then, following Couldry, examine how television lays claim to the powers of representation, most notably through speaking not listening.

Television's powers are by no means wholly symbolic, though, and thus the chapter next examines how television's owners have amassed their power through financial acquisition and through masterful manipulation of television regulators. When the preponderance of media outlets in the US belong to or work under the wing of a very small list of companies, and when large swathes of world media offer similar images and programs, and/or are owned by many of those same companies, power is horded, and the privileges to represent or to decide to represent or listen belong to an elite few. The chapter will therefore turn to a discussion of the spatial configuration of power whereby television's powers become located in a few boardrooms in a few global capitals, and I will pay particular attention to the resulting charges of cultural imperialism. However, lest the powerplays of television all appear to be happening at a corporate level, and beyond our control as their own forms of spectacle to be admired or bemoaned, I will close the chapter by analyzing the significant powers of consumers and citizens to assert their own powers over television entertainment, both in the act of viewing but also as citizens whose television regulatory bodies must at least in theory act in their name.

"You sure are strange": entertaining normalization

As was discussed in Chapters 4 and 5, television entertainment holds substantial power to tell us of the world, people, and ideas around us, but in doing so, it can all too easily provide the images, manners, and thoughts to which we feel we must conform. The urge to conform, to belong, and to fit in is hardwired into many if not all humans, but the tele-vision of television creates for us even larger, otherwise-unseen communities to which we must conform, so that instead of merely comparing ourselves to those around us, we also look to the thousands of characters we meet on television. And if we watch television with any regularity, the numbers work against the real world here: quite simply, most of us know many more televisual characters than real people, and see more televisual locations than real ones. Thus, television can create ideas of normality. Stuart Hall, for instance, writes of the BBC's remarkable powers to create the British nation, becoming "an instrument, an apparatus, a 'machine' through which the nation was constituted. It produced the nation which it addressed: it constituted its audience by the ways in which it represented them" (1993: 32). Since Britons could only "see" the nation through television, as one of the few institutions able to provide a picture of the nation, the tele-vision of television allowed the BBC to *construct* the nation. Herein lies the secret to why television developed at such a fast rate, since in nations such as the UK where public broadcasting developed first, governments realized the paternalistic powers of television to normalize, while in countries such as the US where commercial broadcasting developed first, advertisers realized the medium's potential to socialize audiences to buy, buy, buy. As James Carey famously noted, "reality is a scarce resource," and "the fundamental form of power is the power to define, allocate, and display this resource" (1989: 87), and hence television entertainment, among a very few other powerful media, has the power to depict the "normal," "real" world that for whatever reasons its producers would like to exist. Building on Carey and others, then, Couldry notes "Any theorization of the media's social impacts must start from their privileged role in *framing* our experiences of the social, and thereby defining what the 'reality' of our society is" (2000: 14). The media, television entertainment amongst it, can tell us what is normal.

As a result of such power, we will often find television entertainment giving us odd notions about the world around us. In their study of *Cosby Show* audiences, for instance, Jhally and Lewis found audiences speaking of the Cosbys' wealth as "normal," and families living below the upper-middle-class televisual standard as somehow not normal. "In the TV world," they observe, "normality is attached to being comfortably middle class, being average means being above average. To be outside this world is, by implication, to be out of the mainstream, marginal, and, in a socioeconomic sense, conspicuously unsuccessful" (1992: 74). They therefore heard audiences talk of *Roseanne*'s working class family as unusual, even though census figures would suggest the Conners represent an American average, the Cosbys an American elite. Similarly, Diana Kendall (2005) writes of class framing in the media that often places the middle class as normal, and even as the moral core of the nation – from 7th *Heaven* to *Full House*, *The Cosby Show* to *The Gilmore Girls*, middle-class family values are often proposed as the gold standard by which all should live and to which all should aspire. Moreover, since many of these programs are then exported, whereas the actual incidence of families that fit television entertainment's more usual bill in the US itself is limited, these images risk becoming an international norm too, as I will discuss later in this chapter.

Herein lies the power of commercial influence, for while an audience member is marveling at the seemingly wonderful life that many of television's upper middle-class families enjoy, an ad break can cut into the program and offer images of how to achieve such happiness: maybe having skin like Rory Gilmore, a car like Lieutenant Horatio Caine, or a fully decked apartment like Frasier Crane would make one happier, advertisers want us to think. If happiness and normality are believed to lie at the end of a long credit card statement, advertisers become the truly satisfied consumers (see Jhally 1987). Commercial broadcasting has long been criticized for caring more about upscale audiences, and some might see the very unreflective world that American television presents as a function of producers' interests in offering images of characters "just like you" to such upscale viewers, but, rather, television entertainment has often avoided average lower-middle and working-class families as subjects since advertisers cannot use such people to sell as much product. In the face of such commercial normalization, a public broadcasting system may appear all the more attractive. However, given the long history of paternalism and elitism that runs as a backbone through many public broadcasting systems worldwide, often they too are complicit in a normalization of upper-middle-class life and values, and a pathologization and/or marginalization of working-class life. Many public broadcasters have done little to address the concerns of the working classes, even at times relishing their role as the cultural safe haven for the upper middle classes from the perceived tyranny of mass tastes (see Ouellette 2002). In both commercial and public broadcasting systems, then, upper-middle-class life is often normalized.

Meanwhile, as was discussed in Chapter 4, television entertainment is often produced by whites, for whites, and about whites, and by, for, and about heterosexual men, thereby often rendering television's public sphere white, heterosexual, and male (see Morley 2000). Thus if a masculine, heterosexual, and/or Western male perspective is so commonly taken as "normal" in all aspects of society, and other ways of thinking or acting are regarded as those of "special interest groups" or "the political correctness police," television entertainment's considerable role in marginalizing such perspectives is complicit.

Rebuilding your life: *Extreme Makeover: Home Edition*

To examine normalization in action, we could study the hugely popular ABC show *Extreme Makeover: Home Edition* (*EM: HE*), though many other makeover shows work in a similar manner. Each episode of *EM: HE* begins with a sad story of an afflicted family – either a death or sickness in the family, a natural disaster, or some other "problem" is shown to have brought them to their knees. However, either one of the family members (usually a child) or a neighbor informs ABC of the family's predicament, and the rest of the show follows the *EM: HE* production team's attempt to ease their suffering through completely rebuilding and redesigning their home. The family are sent away for one week, often to ABC parent company's Disneyland or Disneyworld, and we follow the design team's efforts to build a new house from scratch in a way that directly addresses their predicament. For instance, the team has added elevators for family members in wheelchairs, or voice-activated electronics for the blind. The show ends with the set-piece of the family returning from their vacation, standing behind a huge bus that blocks the sight of their new home, with neighbors aplenty cheering them on, before the bus is finally moved to reveal the beautiful new house and a tearfully thankful family (see Figure 6.1). As with many makeover shows, the program aims to be as much about changing lives as changing furniture, and has been a huge success in both ratings and image terms for ABC and Disney, a rare instance of a television program that simultaneously serves as formidable corporate PR. What is being normalized, though?

Keeping first with the spirit of the program, our analysis should note that *EM: HE* purports to send a message of inspiration and of philanthropy to viewers, with many implicit and occasionally explicit calls for audiences to "get out there" and help those around them. The inclusion of neighbors in the final set-piece, cheering the family's return as if rock stars, the seemingly magnanimous act of Sears to donate all the furniture and appliances, the building companies' donation of their time and often mortgage waivers, and of course ABC's screening of the entire

Figure 6.1 The *Extreme Makeover: Home Edition* design team receive thanks for "changing another life"

affair, all seemingly normalize philanthropy and the ethos of being a good neighbor. *EM: HE* has an upbeat, cheerful, earnest tone and charm to it that help broadcast a message of helping others, knowing your neighbors, and lending a hand.

At the same time, however, the program is built on many worrying assumptions, all of which normalize other power structures in society. First, *EM: HE* confines this magical world of philanthropy and neighborliness almost entirely to suburbia, and hence it risks implying that city or country dwellers have not even bothered to write in for help, wrapped up in their own individualistic worlds, or that they are less worthy recipients. Second, the show firmly espouses a conservative notion of what a family should look like: a mother, a father, and children. Extended families are regarded as odd, even pitiable, as the design team struggle to partition off nuclear family from nuclear family (since "they don't even have their own space!"), as though sharing space with an extended family member is automatically pitiable. Gay or lesbian families are nowhere to be seen. Meanwhile, single-parent households are subject to endless paeans to the nobility of the single parent "trying to get by" without the other, admittedly celebrating *certain* single parents in the process, but also rendering single-parent living in general as a social problem. Third, *EM: HE*'s overwrought pity for anyone with a disability often borders on the offensive, as host Ty Pennington's hushed tone when speaking about, for instance, a person in a wheelchair, renders differential abilities and body types pitiable yet little more.

As with many media depictions of disability, we as viewers are invited to feel lucky and thankful that we are not like these people, not to understand or appreciate them actually on their own terms. *EM: HE* treads very close to making disability a circus spectacle, as a leaked memo from the *EM: HE* production team to ABC affiliates in 2006 rendered clear in grim manner: the memo called for affiliates to be on the lookout ("let me know if one is in your town!" it pleaded) for people with various types of disability, including those with advanced aging disorder and those with multiple children with Downs syndrome.[1] Fourth, the show operates on the naíve assumption that a huge infusion of capital will "solve" the family's problems, offering, for instance, a flatscreen television and a themed room to a child whose parent has died: nice gifts, to be sure, yet once more we see the normalization of consumption as the path to happiness. Who needs something more practical, such as free grief counseling, the program seems to ask, when one has a new HDTV?

At a broader, structural level, too, *EM: HE* normalizes notions of how charity should be dispersed. The *EM: HE* world is one in which corporations, not governments, help the needy, and despite its ideal platform to do so, *EM: HE* has never criticized the lack of available social services or assistance, instead working on the assumption that such help need come only from wealthy benefactors (see McMurria 2005). This conforms to a markedly conservative vision of governmental responsibility and social welfare, one that therefore gets a free ride from the feel-good aura of *EM: HE* (and one that partially explains First Lady Laura Bush's declared love for the program). Yet corporations get a free ride, too, most notably Disney. While the laborers' volunteerism is touching, it is also completely unnecessary, since the show draws in top-ten advertising rates, regularly wins its time slot, and has few other big-ticket expenditures. The show confuses audiences into believing that Sears and the laborers are giving charity to the family and that such acts make the show possible, when in fact, as the *highly paid* organizer of the renovation efforts, ABC is in fact receiving the charity, not the family. The profitability of the show means that ABC could easily pay for all costs without volunteerism, and thus the working-class laborers' act of donating their time and expertise, while symbolically notable, otherwise only works to save ABC money. Sears meanwhile benefits in the same way that companies donating prizes to game shows do, receiving product placement in scenes full of screaming, happy people. As such, the show normalizes an ethically disturbing notion of charity and corporate citizenship, whereby profiting from charity becomes an acceptable norm, a feat replicated by Oprah Winfrey when she gave away 276 cars on her show in 2004, hence becoming front-page news and promising herself, her program, and Pontiac considerable advertising and PR points. As the case of *EM: HE* illustrates, then, especially when a show is particularly successful, we must interrogate what it and its success normalize, how they feed into power differentials and politics in the world outside television, and what is left unsaid and unrepresented.

Script edits: challenging normalization

However, if television entertainment can normalize ways of living, thinking, and being, it can also challenge scripts of normalization, or, rather, since television entertainment is not a monolithic entity programmed by one devious individual, various shows within the broad field of television entertainment can do battle. As has been said, one of television's great powers is its ability to offer cross-demographic communication (Hartley 1999), broadcasting an at times eclectic mix of ideas, and thus television may introduce us to difference as well as familiarity, and in time may render that which was once "different" as now normal. Television can render nonsense as common sense, offering spurious "common knowledge" about others, but it can also render ideas, lifestyles, or individuals that may be odd or threatening in one's regular life less strange and more comprehensible through televised interactions, hence proving some "common sense" and "common knowledge" to be nonsense.

In particular, as alluded to in previous chapters, comedy regularly plays with common sense, challenging us to rethink the rules and conventions of everyday life. On one hand, comedy can be a powerful tool for solidifying the status quo, as many comedy programs encourage us to laugh at the supposedly abnormal, thereby reifying the distinction between normal and abnormal. For instance, when the stock effeminate, flamboyant gay character of many comedy shows elicits laughter for his walk, talk, and desires, the show contributes to the disciplining of masculine behavior, laying out a clear set of norms for how men *should* walk, talk, and desire. On the other hand, though, the carnivalesque nature of comedy frequently allows a zone in which characters can test or brazenly violate expected norms. Whether it is Lucy Ricardo or Roseanne Conner, for example, some of comedy's bold women have gleefully violated expectations of gendered behavior, and through their star power and through audience identification, they carry significant power to destabilize prevailing norms, or at least to create competing norms (see Mellencamp 2003, Rowe 1995). What is more, since comedy is a relatively free space for action, and audiences are generally more accepting of a range of behaviors in the realm of comedy, sometimes comedy becomes one of the only spaces where certain discourses, ideas, and individuals *can* be challenged. Given the American news media's supposed reverence for "bias"-free reporting in particular, rebellion and dissension are often voiced most resolutely in shows such as *The Daily Show with Jon Stewart* or *South Park*. Admittedly, any given viewer might regard this rebellion and dissension as pure spectacle – something to be laughed at and appreciated for its edginess, but nothing that requires much time or thought – but good comedy might also move one to reflection.

In his book, *Tabloid Culture*, Kevin Glynn (2000) examines the strategic challenges to prevalent scripts of normal behavior that are lodged by much of "trash" culture, such as tabloid journalism and talk shows with their comic play. Glynn focuses particular attention on an elitism in hard news that declares what is truth, and that sees an upper-middle-class power bloc as guardians and producers of truth. Much tabloid culture, though, casts doubt on officialdom, expressing skepticism of its claims, rejecting its authority and instead valorizing the opinions of regular folk, and producing its own fantastic knowledges and truths that comically overturn official truth. Thus, for instance, tabloid culture is a realm in which supposed alien autopsies question the government's secretive nature, in which a *Jerry Springer* guest's outrageous behavior rejects the expectations of both Jerry and "polite society," and in which lascivious gossip about politicians or celebrities displaces journalists as truth-tellers and the politicians and celebrities themselves as moral authorities. Tabloid culture, Glynn writes, is a realm of "hypervisibilization" (2000: 23) whereby regular viewers are offered powers of surveillance (and hence of judgment) over institutions and individuals who regularly have control over those viewers. This power is momentary and symbolic, likely to dissipate as soon as the channel is switched off, but nevertheless holds the potential power either to create seeds of resentment that one takes away from the screen, or to feed those seeds, leading to a broader rejection of societal "norms" that have disempowered the viewer.

Thus, television entertainment's scripts of normalization may often work in contrast to or competition with one another. And just as Chapter 5 argued that all programs have an ideology, similarly all programs contribute to different scripts of normalization in one way or another. To some readers, the idea that *Jerry Springer*, *Roseanne*, or any item of television entertainment for that matter might contribute meaningfully to renewing or challenging real-life power structures may seem outlandish, but as Morley reminds us, "macro-structures can only be reproduced by micro-processes" (1992: 18–19). Television entertainment's capacity to present us with an army of subtle suggestions and implicit comments may therefore often prove more powerful in changing or reaffirming an audience member's mind than will more obvious and explicit statements or instructions in the news or from other real world authorities.

The myth of the mediated center

At the same time, we must be careful not to overstate television's powers of normalization. Declarations of the media's powers often accompany moral panics, sometimes grossly exaggerated, sometimes as little more than excuses to avoid searching for more deep-seated answers to social problems, and sometimes so that the person declaring the media's power can perform a supposed moral superiority. Therefore, television entertainment can often find itself in a firestorm of criticism and blame. Nevertheless, as Nick Couldry's work on what he dubs "the myth of the mediated center" reminds us, if television's powers are exaggerated, television producers are behind many inflated claims themselves. As Couldry defines the myth of the mediated center, it is "the belief, or assumption, that there is a centre to the social world, and that, in some sense, the media speaks 'for' that centre" (2003: 2), yet since the media stand to benefit in terms of symbolic power from being crowned the center of the social world, mediated narratives and rituals commonly repeat the message of a mediated center. Couldry observes that "Every media claim to speak 'for us all' naturalises the fact that generally we do not speak for ourselves" (2003: 29), assuring not simply that the media has power, but that we *give* it that power, at our own expense. The media's symbolic power, he states, "is far from automatic; in fact, it has to be continually reproduced through various practices and dispositions at every level of social life" (2000: 4).

In his two books *The Place of Media Power* (2000) and *Media Rituals* (2003), Couldry therefore charts numerous rituals by which the media lay claim to power, and he pays particular attention to moments, programs, and genres that draw a firm line between a seemingly mundane real world and a magical media world. Media rituals, he notes, are often most notable at those sites where the two worlds seemingly meet each other. Thus, for instance, fans who wish to meet celebrities or to get near a site of television production will often have their actions strictly managed. Attending the filming of *The Daily Show with Jon Stewart* or other late-night talk shows, ticket-holding would-be live audience members are regularly required to stand for up to two hours before being let into the theater, and are then given strict instructions on how to behave, so that, for example, fans attending *The Dave Letterman Show* are even told not to cheer in a high pitch. All the while, in other words, audience members are told how special it is to be witnessing media in action, how lucky they are to be allowed in the doors, and how much they must behave. Couldry found visitors to the Grenada Studios set of *Coronation Street* similarly entranced by the experience of being on the set, as though they were touching magic, and some were keen to get home and tell friends, while others spoke of being on the set as an achievement. Television entertainment presents us with magic worlds, and the correlate of this, Couldry reminds us, is that we often regard "television" as a magic-land, somehow "more 'intense' than the 'ordinary world'" (2000: 113). Hence we might understand why some people want to air their dirty laundry on daytime talk shows, admit to being a horrible person on *Dr Phil*, or sign a release form to allow such shows as *Cops* to depict their worst moments: being on television, television tells us again and again, is *special*, even in moments of humiliation.

Couldry also applies this framework to make sense of the intense popularity of reality-television shows such as *Big Brother* or *Popstars* that promise to make an "ordinary person" into a celebrity. Of the British *Popstars* (similar to the *Idol* franchise), he writes that contestants' "'ordinariness' confirms the 'reality' of what is shown" (2003: 107), their bad singing voices, emotional turbidity, and behavioral quirks a performance of being "regular people"; but then "that 'ordinariness' is the status from which the contestants compete to escape into another ritually distinct category, celebrity," in the process confirming that "the media (whether as the frame through which we see 'social reality,' or as the space into which we want to go to escape our 'ordinary reality') is special, higher than the 'ordinary world'" (107). Another key set of rituals of many competition reality shows, then, are the prolonged spectacles when a contestant is voted off. In the British *Big Brother*, Couldry notes, a basic point of the eviction ceremony "is to enact a transition for each housemate from ordinary person to media person" (2004: 60).

Similarly, in *American Idol*, the voting-off has become its own nightly show, separate from the previous night's competition. First, host Ryan Seacrest hyperbolically announces that "America" has voted, as if the entire nation was polled to choose its avatar (see Figure 6.2). Then Seacrest announces the week's loser . . . except the ensuing ritual proves that they are anything but a loser. The studio crowd are invited to cheer madly for the "loser" while s/he is shown a highlight reel of their journey from anonymity to fame, often accompanied by cuts to crying and/or

Figure 6.2 American Idol host Ryan Seacrest informs a contestant how "America" voted

screaming fans, and the "loser" is then asked for final words, and lastly to serenade the crowd one more time. In short, the "loser" is now a star, and is treated as such, his or her transformation complete. And in an instance of overflow further solidifying reality contestants' and shows' supposed place in the mediated center, commercial breaks following each episodes' completion regularly promise an upcoming news or morning show interview with the ousted contestant that will tell "what really happened": having purportedly been to the mediated center, the contestant promises to relay stories and juicy tidbits from that world for the dedicated viewer. Of course, competition shows are often stunning amalgams of game show, talent show, and group psychology session as well, but they prominently illustrate how carefully television entertainment works to insist on its placement at the center of the social universe.

The great French philosopher and social theorist Michel Foucault (1981) noted that societal power is often embedded in the power to speak and the power to divide up and classify the social world. Thus power comes to reside in certain sites. Television entertainment's continual reproduction, through media rituals, of the myth of the mediated center offers the medium rare powers to codify not only experiences and interactions with television as magical, but also experiences and interactions away from television as mundane and quotidian. We will return, then, at the chapter's end to an examination of how such powers might be challenged or revoked.

Owning the podium and yielding the floor: ownership and regulation

Behind symbolic power, though, must lie tangible power to control media of communication, and to circulate messages. In Foucauldian terms, we should ask who controls the valued sites of discourse, who has a place at the podium, and who is left on the outside. Foucault notes a rarefaction of speaking subjects, observing that power works by determining that "none shall enter the order of discourse if he [sic] does not satisfy certain requirements or if he is not, from the outset, qualified to do so. To be more precise: not all the regions of discourse are equally open and penetrable" (1981: 62). The performance and creation of symbolic power through media rituals is a key force by which television aims to determine who is "qualified" to speak, but we must also look to the legalities of ownership, whereby qualification and ability to speak are determined through control over culture. As Table 3.1 illustrates, the past twenty years have seen rapid conglomeration and expansion of the media industries, whereby much of the media universe has come under the control of a few large multinational corporations.

Whereas broadcasting regulatory policy in most countries was originally based on the notion that the airwaves are a public good, and hence that their allocation to would-be broadcasters should be contingent on the broadcaster using their portion of the radio or TV spectrum to serve the public, how best to serve the public and even how to conceive of the public have been causes for significant debate. Thus, in the UK, Canada, Australia, Japan, and the majority of other countries, broadcasting developed as state run. In the US, however, the successive regulatory documents of the 1912 Radio Act, the 1927 Radio Act, and the 1934 Communications Act favored the allocation of radio frequencies to large commercial broadcasters, marginalizing non-profit broadcasters and rejecting the notion of a state-administered public service broadcaster in the process (see McChesney 1994, Streeter 1996). Broadcasters were awarded licenses on the understanding that they serve "the public interest," and the Federal Radio Commission – later, and now, the Federal Communications Commission – was set up to regulate the licensing and to ensure diversity and public service.

By the 1980s, however, and following Ronald Reagan's appointment of Mark Fowler as Federal Communications Commission Chairman in 1981, a "deregulatory" fervor hit Hollywood, New York, and Washington, DC, with CBS News president William Leonard remarking that "there was a sense that you [in the broadcast industry] could do whatever the hell you wanted" (quoted in Holt 2003: 12). Fowler infamously noted that "Television is just another appliance. It's a toaster with pictures," and hence he failed to see the need for many regulations on the glorified toaster's ownership and practice. Technological advances had allowed for a significant growth in available channels via cable or satellite, and thus following the rationale that more channels equates to more diversity, and guided by a conservative philosophy that an "open" market with little government interference would better allow the television industry to serve the public, Fowler struck down many a broadcast regulation. Jennifer Holt observes that by the end of Fowler's "first four years as chairman, the FCC had reviewed, changed or deleted 89 per cent of the agency's approximately 900 mass media rules" (2003: 12). Fowler's laissez-faire attitude would be continued by his successors, eventually setting the stage for the Telecommunications Act, a major set of (de)regulations for the telecommunications industry passed by the US Congress in 1996.

In particular, the FCC toggled ownership rules to allow corporations to own yet more. For instance, the four decade-old Seven Station Rule that limited a corporation or individual to seven AM, seven FM, and seven television stations, was expanded to a twelve station rule in 1984. Though the 1984 Report and Order added a prohibition on ownership of stations that reached more than 25% of the nation's television households, the 1996 Telecommunications Act changed this number to 35%, and after legal action from the broadcast industry and significant lobbying, the Senate Appropriation Committee upped the limit to 39% in 2003. All the while, in 2002 and 2003, broadcasters spent $220 million lobbying the US government, and contributed another $25.5 million to federal candidates and lawmakers (Kunz 2007: 70). Other key ownership regulations that have been eased or allowed to be violated include the dual ownership rule that restricted ownership of two or more television stations in any given local market,[2] and the Newspaper/Broadcast Cross-Ownership Prohibition that sought to limit a corporation or individual's ability to own a television station and a newspaper in the same market, and that is now in question.

In addition, in 1995, the 1971 Financial Interest and Syndication Rules (known as "Fin-Syn") expired without renewal. These rules had prohibited networks from owning the syndication (rerun) rights to shows, thereby allowing and encouraging a greater diversity of television producers, by ensuring that they could profit from their own shows and that ABC, CBS, and NBC did not have a stranglehold on production. The expiration of Fin-Syn opened the doors to greater conglomeration. Thus, in anticipation of and following Fin-Syn's expiration and the Telecommunications Act, in 1996, Disney arranged to buy Capitol Cities/ABC, Westinghouse acquired CBS, News Corp. bought all of New World's stations, and Time Warner and Turner Broadcasting System merged. Ted Turner had already been wheeling and dealing to construct his media empire, though, having bought MGM/UA's film library in 1985, Hanna Barbera's library in 1991, and gradually extending his cable channel ownership to eventually include HBO, CNN, TBS, TNT, the Cartoon Network, and the WB, among others. Not to be outdone, in 1985 Rupert Murdoch's News Corporation had bought Twentieth Century Fox and six major broadcast stations from Metromedia, allowing him to create the fourth broadcast network, FOX, later in 1986. Then, in 2000, CBS merged with Viacom, and though they have since separated, Sumner Redstone pulls the strings for both companies. In 2004, NBC welcomed Universal to the GE-owned fold, and in 2006, former upstart networks WB and UPN merged to form CW, under the joint ownership of Time Warner and CBS. Moreover, the FCC's complete deregulation of ownership rules in radio (allowing Clear Channel to own over 1,100 stations by consequence) may predict future deregulatory efforts and FCC allowances for conglomeration within the US television industry.

While this brief history seems to detail only the American picture, these corporations and their properties also represent many of the world's major media owners, and their ability to move into foreign markets is predicated upon their relative power and ensuing financial success domestically, and hence on the regulation that has ensured such success. Thus, just as, in terms of *global reach*, there is nothing purely American about CNN, MTV, FOX, NBC, or Disney, so too has "American" regulation via the FCC impacted the world media picture.

The nitty-gritty details of who makes decisions within such corporate giants, and how streamlined they are or are not is open for debate, for with great holdings come great confusion and even internal battles over how best to operate (see Simone Murray 2005, Jenkins 2006: 7). But at least in principle, the consolidation of many of the world's key media corporations places an inordinate amount of broadcasting power into a few hands, thereby limiting potential entrants to the television production industry. Horizontal integration (collaboration with or outright purchase of companies in neighboring industries, such as film and television production companies) and vertical integration (collaboration with or outright purchase of companies upstream or downstream in the same industry, such as television production and distribution) is about control. Michael Eisner, for instance, has often spoken of Disney's purchases as attempts to "protect the mouse" (see *Milwaukee Journal Sentinel* 1998). Or as Edward Herman and Robert McChesney explain:

> When Disney, for example, produces a film, it can also guarantee the film showings on pay cable television and commercial network television, and it can produce and sell soundtracks based on the film, it can create spin-off television series, it can produce related amusement park rides, CD-Roms, books, comics, and merchandise to be sold in Disney retail stores. Moreover, Disney can promote the film and related material incessantly across all its media properties. Even films which do poorly at the box office can become profitable in this climate.
>
> (1997: 54)

The flip side of this corporate synergy is that Disney has a greater chance of ensuring that its media products will beat others in head-to-head battles, and its various wings can collude to kill competition from sources other than NBC Universal, News Corp, and the few other media corporations that can play the same game. "Protecting the mouse" (or the peacock or fox) is as much about limiting competition and hording speaking platforms as it is about allowing inhouse products to thrive.

Consequently, a significant task for all multinational corporations has been to lobby domestic and foreign governments for the repeal of laws that would limit their ability to horde such power, and for the creation of new laws to guarantee their continued control. Looking beyond Hollywood's success in DC, Herman and McChesney, for instance, examine how the rhetoric of calls for the "free flow of information" around the globe became a strategy for American multinationals to force open foreign markets whose culturally protectionist policies hampered their progress, and to replicate their success from Sydney to Stockholm. "Free flow was at once an eloquent democratic principle and an aggressive trade position on behalf of US media interests. The core operational idea behind the principle was that transnational media firms and advertisers should be permitted to operate globally, with minimal governmental intervention" (1997: 17). Thus the US State Department has often negotiated for "free flow" that would allow its companies freedom to operate as they wish (see also Miller *et al*. 2005), redefining "freedom" and "the public interest" in their wake not as citizens' or individuals' freedom to access a wide variety of material, nor citizens' freedom to create and circulate media themselves, but as "the mere absence of constraints on business (i.e., economic, or market, freedom), thus pushing political freedom into a subordinate category" (Herman and McChesney 1997: 35).

In response, other nations have often attempted to push through international agreements that would protect cultural products and exempt them from other trade laws, by restricting foreign ownership or by limiting foreign imports. In particular, the New World Information and Communication Order (NWICO) debates at UNESCO in the 1970s and 1980s (see Thussu 2006) represented a major push to establish guidelines for international expansion and communication. But first through the General Agreement on Tariffs and Trade (GATT) and the General Agreement on Trade in Services (GATS), and then with the World Trade Organization (WTO)'s advent in 1995, the US has applied continual (and often significantly more) pressure on the world to open up its cultural markets. As Toby Miller *et al*. dryly observe:

> The US has been like a child with a toy in the WTO, proud that it has filed more complaints than any other country and has prevailed so often (Barshefsky 1998). And just in case it should fail to destroy cultural policies through international trading institutions, it has lodged the EU on its internal Special 301 "Priority Watch List" for sanctions (USIA 1997). Again, there is a sense of a child, this time keeping a list of most-hated peers and real or imagined "meanness."
>
> (2005: 89)

As David Hesmondhalgh (2002: 109) observes, though, even the media corporations' success in framing the relaxing of ownership restrictions as "deregulation" represents a major PR coup, when in fact major communications laws such as the 1996 Telecommunications Act should more accurately be referred to as "reregulation": true "deregulation" and a true "free flow of information" would discontinue the media corporations' state-sanctioned oligopolistic control, allowing anyone to lay claim to the networks' restricted, FCC-apportioned, yet in theory *publicly owned*, domain of the broadcast spectrum.

These various attempts to keep state scrutiny at bay are important in power terms, since they allow media corporations to gobble up speaking platforms, and they represent particularly the FCC's eagerness to yield the floor to corporate interests. As will soon be discussed, they also locate media power in a few specific locations worldwide. But an equally worrying development in global media regulation is the media corporations' concerted attempt to rewrite intellectual property rights to strictly limit how consumers and citizens may use their products (see Miller *et al.* 2005, Vaidhyanathan 2001). These efforts, and the accompanying croc-odile tears from the media multinationals about lost profits and victimized artists, are deeply hypocritical on two levels. First, while Disney, for instance, complains about others retelling or using "their" stories and characters, Disney came to prominence partly on the back of retellings of Hans Christian Andersen and Grimm Brothers' tales. Second, while the media multinationals argue vociferously that culture must be allowed to "move freely and unfettered" by governmental restriction, they have proven remarkably fond of yet *more* governmental restriction and yet more *barriers* to movement at the level of intellectual property.

At heart, though, their fear with regards television is of the chaotic, uncontrol-lable nature of overflow and televisual expansion. Between YouTube, a host of BitTorrent sites, fan fiction, fan film, vidding, mashups, and even the simple VCR, television viewers today have countless platforms for watching, playing with, repurposing, and outright creating television or television culture. Media corpora-tions might therefore understandably feel that they are losing their vice grip on television culture. Some producers and even some companies have realized the possibilities for their shows to thrive in such an era, and have welcomed participa-tory interventions (see Jenkins 2006: 167). But many corporate legal teams have instead tried to set up a hard perimeter around products that they see as theirs, and have tried to dictate exactly how audiences can watch and enjoy their products. Tales of Hollywood's excesses in threatening or taking legal action against "copy-right violators" abound, whether it be Disney ordering several pre-schools with Disney figures on their walls to take them down or go to court (cited in Miller *et al.* 2005), or Time Warner sending cease and desist letters to several teenagers writing Harry Potter fan fiction (Jenkins 2006: 186). Both Hartley (1987) and Gitlin (1994) detail how the television industry has long regarded its consumers as (naughty) children, and now many within the industry are trying to play headmas-ter, not only owning the podium and the floor, but also telling us where to be, how to behave, and how to watch. Thus, beyond concerns over ownership of media outlets, we should also be concerned with media corporations' attempts to own and curtail the powers of consumption, use, and affect. As was examined in Chapter 2, consumption is often also about creation and identity; hence, if, *pace* Foucault, a rarefaction of speaking subjects exists, legal restrictions on modes of consumption inevitably become legal restrictions on speaking and simply on being.

The spatial configuration of power

The current practices of the television industry have therefore led to the shifting of power to several predominant "media capitals" (Curtin 2004) and away from many other regions. Within the US, for instance, the relaxation of ownership restrictions has meant that more and more television stations are owned and operated by a few companies with corporate offices far removed from their broadcasting area. A commitment to localism was written into much early FCC regulation, attempting to ensure that owners had a stake in a local community, so that they would best know how to serve it. Following the ownership deregulation of the eighties and onwards, and with the repeal of anti-trafficking rules that prohibited the fast sale, or "flipping," of television stations (see Streeter 1996: 239–40), committed local ownership has frequently become a thing of the past, and today much of a television station's product is centralized and differentiated from station to station, community to community, only by superficial means. The public good becomes computed only (if even) at a national or global level, not at an intimate, local level. Yet media capitals have long existed in public broadcasting systems too, as many countries' broadcasters have traditionally been located in a capital or major city, sending messages out to the nation as a whole. In the UK, then, the BBC has been roundly criticized for being London centric. In Canada, the CBC has similarly been criticized for caring first and foremost about Torontonians, with Tinic noting "the paucity of CBC regional production and the lack of regional representation on sitting funding committees," that produces a situation in which "the current funding-broadcast structure has more often served as a source of frustration rather than a source of support for the Vancouver production community," or other regional would-be producers (2005: 86). Certainly, a browse through much television worldwide often shows inordinate interest in the lives and concerns of dense urban communities, so that New York, London, Toronto, Los Angeles, Hong Kong, and their peers are not only sites of media governance, but also the locations that most frequently appear on screen, and whose inhabitants form the backbone of television's fictional communities. Television by no means began the marginalization of non-capitals, as transport, economic, and political networks tilted in big cities' favor long before television's invention, but broadcasting has often played a role in exacerbating or at least maintaining such power differentials.

Meanwhile, if media capitals bask in the light at a national level, the expansion of television on a global scale raises concerns over differential power between nations. In particular, as was examined in Chapter 3, the big American six of CBS, Disney, NBC Universal, News Corporation, Time Warner, and Viacom have sizeable holdings internationally, and they are often joined by one or more regional powerhouses in any given country. Ultimately, then, concerns of local issues being ignored or downplayed are writ large onto the globe. And just as Vancouverites or the Cornish worry about Toronto and London respectively filling the airwaves with stories by and about Torontonians or Londoners, so too now are many in the world concerned about the avalanche of American and other foreign content. Watching television in Taiwan often means watching a lot of American, Japanese, and Korean programs, many Middle Easterners watch a significant amount of Indian television in addition to *The Simpsons* and other American favorites in Arabic, and huge swathes of Australian television are American, especially with one-time Australian media mogul Rupert Murdoch sharing his new American patriotism with his former countrymen through FoxTel, Australia's premier satellite broadcaster. Foreign ownership, foreign programs, and foreign style form a triple threat to many cultures, giving rise to frequent complaints about cultural imperialism (see, for instance, Gans 1985, Herman and McChesney 1997, Mattelart 1983, Ritzer 1998, Schiller 1976).

American multinationals are fond of boasting that their material is simply better than what most of the rest of the world can muster. But frequently this boast refuses to acknowledge the success of those multinationals at ensuring there is no competition in the first place, so that, for example, when CBS or NBC can sell an hour-long drama at a fraction of the cost required to produce a local drama (see Chapter 3), many broadcasters worldwide do not even bother making much television, opting instead for the financial benefits of importing (see Miller *at al.* 2005). Also, with many multinationals owning local broadcasting, cable, and/or satellite, again they can flood a country with their own product, giving local shows few outlets wherein they could launch meaningful competition. However, even when American shows do "open" battle with foreign shows, the sheer size and hence wealth of the American market has often ensured that the American show has a much greater infusion of capital. Moreover, as Hollywood turns its eye to the overseas market with greater interest and intensity as discussed in Chapter 3, it is becoming increasingly successful at poaching foreign talent and co-opting foreign production. In such an environment, many foreign shows simply do not have the resources to compete with Hollywood. And while I write here of the US and Hollywood, other regional power-players similarly play the role of cultural imperialist at times. Both American and regional multinationals have often benefited from one another's presence, as each can play on fears of cultural incursion by the other to parlay greater viewer loyalty and policy interventions and governmental assistance.

Admittedly, charges of cultural imperialism are often broad and alarmist, and thus many critics have attacked the simplicity of the model. Several audience researchers, for instance, have shown that audiences often read against the "American" meanings in the programs (see Fiske 1989c, Katz and Liebes 1990, Lull 2007, Strelitz 2003), variously domesticating or defusing them, so that, for instance, Katz and Liebes' research found numerous Arabs watching *Dallas* as a spectacle of the decadence of American capitalism (1990: 119). Drawing on Ang's work with *Dallas* viewers that also suggested savvy (here, Dutch) viewers, John Tomlinson argues that "The complex, reflective, and self-conscious reactions of her correspondents suggest that cultural critics who assume this sort of [culturally imperialist] effect massively underestimate the audience's active engagement with the text and the critical sophistication of the ordinary viewer/reader" (2003: 123).

Elsewhere, too, I have examined how international reception of *The Simpsons* suggests that some American shows are far from, and are *read as* far from, über-patriotic and chauvinist in outlook (Gray 2007). Meanwhile, Tomlinson (2003) and Annabelle Sreberny-Mohammadi (1997) insist that culture comes not only from the media (as was discussed in the section on the myth of the mediated center above), and since media will be interpreted through one's own cultural lens, we should be careful not to assume that the *presence* (or even dominance) of foreign culture on television will equate to its dominance *in the culture*. Also, lest we think world television is all American all the time, in fact, American product is still in the minority in many countries, and numerous studies suggest that local shows will often outperform American alternatives when present (see Tunstall 2007, Waisbord 2004: 369). Clearly, then, cultural imperialism as a way of making sense of the world's television flow involves exaggeration and overstatement of the power of American television shows, and understatement, even patronization, of the strength and vitality of foreign cultures.

Nevertheless, most challenges to theories of cultural imperialism argue that audiences are not defenseless, and that foreign cultures are resilient. Even when accepted, though, neither point changes the fundamental power imbalance over who gets to share its stories with the world. Residents of Perth, Taipei, or Sao Paolo may not be at risk of "turning American" just because they watch *Friends*, *ER*, or *CSI*, but Hollywood is still not telling stories about Perth, Taipei, or Sao Paolo, and Hollywood's and other multinationals' dominance over foreign broadcasting limit the outlets available for truly local stories. Not only does such a state of affairs restrict other nations' ability to tell local stories, but they also have decreased chances of sharing those stories with other nations. Hence, representative augmentation notwithstanding, citizens of Perth, Taipei, and Sao Paolo can see what life and culture are like in New York or Los Angeles, but as yet television provides few opportunities for a return cultural exchange. Or, alternately, when such opportunities to "see" or "hear" the rest of the world arise, they are often heavily exoticized accounts of other countries circulated by American or other multinationals, not produced by the people being represented. Thus, for instance, CBS's popular reality show *The Amazing Race* sees teams race around the world, but its depiction of local cultures is often reduced to gross caricatures, as when the only Tanzanians one sees are Masai warriors leaping up and down, or when a trip to Kuwait results in a camel-jockeying challenge. When we see and hear the world on television, too often it is a local construction of the world, allowing Hollywood the right to speak for, classify, define, interpret, and translate other cultures, rather than letting them hold such powers themselves.

As Fiske's quotation at the outset of this chapter reminds us, a true act of sharing power would require listening. Given power differentials between nations, and particularly between the US and the rest of the world, that extend well beyond telecommunications into the military–industrial complex, global television's limitations on cultural flows therefore contribute to exacerbating global power inequities. The US and other industrial nations with well-developed television industries can speak at volume, but much of the rest of the world is left either to listen, to ignore, or to speak in hushed tones. A continuing challenge for the television industry, and for global television audiences, will thus be to find ways to let other cultures speak to one another, and to ensure that the US and other industrial nations find ways to listen. Television is not solely responsible for existing power imbalances between nations, but given that it plays its roles in exacerbating and reifying those imbalances, whether through more creative methods of producing and distributing media, through renewed efforts at instilling regulation on media flows, and/or through active citizenship (not just active audiencehood), citizens, consumers, and producers of television could play an important role in redistributing global power, at domestic, regional, and international levels.

Changing channels, changing programs

For much of this chapter, we have examined television entertainment's powers over us, but what of our powers over television entertainment? What powers do we have to guide television, and make it the medium that we want?

The most knee-jerk response to such questions is that if we don't like what we see, we have the power to turn the television off, or to change the channel. However, under closer analysis, neither of these powers prove to be as awesome as some would think. First, turning off the television or changing the channel in any given instance only stops the television flow to the individual(s) watching, and thus if I turn from my television in disgust at its misrepresentation of a community, its poor aesthetics, and/or its worrying politics, the show does not magically become better. In aggregate, admittedly, numerous viewers turning off might eventually convince a station or network to cancel the program, but importantly, cancellations are made without precise knowledge of why viewers did not watch. Ratings systems only measure who watches (from a small sample, no less), not *why* they watch or why they do not, and thus while cancellation deals with particularly egregious or offensive programs, no guarantee exists that the station or network will divine the reasons for viewer exodus and will learn from them. Maybe, they might pose, the timing was wrong, maybe it needed more stars, or maybe it needed to be more like program X; however, none of these may be the accurate reason, or the reasons may be more complex and varied. Once again, then, we return to issues of listening and speaking, since television has a remarkably poor apparatus for listening to audiences, preferring numbers over voices, and demographics over opinions. Communication from viewers to producers frequently vanishes into thin air or gets garbled in the process.

Second, though, the directive to "just change the channel if you don't like it" assumes optimistically that television is a complete medium, offering something for everyone, and that something on another channel is bound to satisfy us, when in fact our reason for turning off or changing the channel may point to a more endemic problem in the medium. As such, turning off or changing the channel are stark solutions to what might be more complicated issues. The offending program may be important or even enjoyable to a viewer for other reasons. If one finds much or all of television problematic, opting out of television is rarely a realistic, or even a helpful option. As Jenkins notes, debates over television keep "getting framed as if the only true alternative were to opt out of the media altogether and live in the woods, eating acorns and lizards and reading only books printed on recycled paper by small alternative presses" (2006: 248–9). Rather, though, precisely because television entertainment is powerful, and because it is one of our society's premium storytellers, creative venues, political forums, and windows to other areas of society, we must care about television enough to fight for it. Turning off the television is often an empty gesture, understandable and even the proper response in given moments, but politically disconnected from any meaningful resistance at many other moments.

As was discussed in Chapter 2, though, another power we have is to read against a program's grain. De Certeau notes that consumption and the consumer are often regarded as receptacles (1984: 167), but as his and others' work has shown, consumption is a nuanced, productive activity, with which we can *give* meaning, not solely wherein we *receive* prefabricated meaning. Certainly, just as we would be naïve to believe that turning off television deals with its problems, as Radway reminds us, "The act of purchase [or of viewing] does not always signify approval of the product selected; with a mass-production system it can just as easily testify to the existence of an ongoing, still only partially met, need" (1987: 50). Audiences will commonly pick and choose from programs, taking what they want, yet also rejecting that which they do not. All too commonly, critics have seen the audience–text interaction as beginning with a producer encoding messages into a text that an audience member is then left to consume as is or go elsewhere; instead, audiences come to texts with certain desires and inclinations to watch in certain ways, and they will often, if possible, bend a text around to get what they want out of it. Just as texts have power over us, we too have significant power over them.

Moreover, many television programs are open, in that they come to us incomplete, the producers making more episodes and continuing to craft the storyline while we watch the current episode. Here, then, Fiske notes, viewers often "feel they have the right and the ability to influence the future narrative" (1989a: 67). As was detailed in Chapter 2, Fiske, Jenkins, and other fan scholars' optimism that fans could sway the direction of a narrative was roundly criticized by many in the early 1990s; however, the television industry's slow move towards affective economics and the advent of the Internet may now give renewed justification to their optimism. Given the fragmentation of the viewing audience (see *Economist* 2002: 8, Lotz 2007b: 13), fans, it has been noted, are becoming more important to producers, and at the same time, Internet fan discussion sites are allowing a more direct form of communication between programs' creators and their consumers. Thus multiple show-runners, especially of serial narratives, have been well-known to frequent fansites to gauge viewer interest and/or faith in recent developments, *Battlestar Galactica*'s Ron Moore, *Lost*'s Damon Lindelof and Carleton Cuse, and *Veronica Mars*' Rob Thomas among them. Even actors are often popping by sites to see how their performance is being evaluated, and how their character is being interpreted, with, for instance, *Lost*'s Terry O'Quinn having been a frequent guest at online site *The Fuselage*, where he and the fans discussed his character John Locke. As viewers have more and more leisure options, many producers are realizing the utter importance of overflow, and of making their programs at least seem responsive and immersive, and frequently such a move requires opening up actual lines of communication – not just a language of ratings and shares – to talk to, and *listen* to fans.

Even without such lines of communication, though, viewers can watch and interpret programs as they wish, repurposing characters and themes as they go. That said, just as turning my television off doesn't succeed in turning yours off, my act of creative viewing doesn't entail your act. And just as the act of turning the television off doesn't necessarily communicate the reasons for my displeasure to the television industry, barring an open dialogue between myself and a receptive and responsive producer on a fan site (still a remarkably rare occurrence), the act of creative repurposing doesn't change the program on offer. Morley observes a fundamental difference "between having power over a text and having power over the agenda within which that text is constructed and presented" (1992: 31). For example, while gay or lesbian viewers have for a long time been forced to queer characters themselves, and read homosexuality into characters and storylines that are ostensibly straight, such an act does not produce actual gay or lesbian characters, and hence the abnormalization and marginalization of homosexuality continue; if anything, "speaking" through the bizarre mode of communication that is the Nielsens, their viewership of shows that lack gay or lesbian characters could easily be interpreted by the industry as widespread acceptance of the relative absence of gay or lesbian characters in television programming. Thus while creative interpretation, excorporation, poaching, and active audiencehood allow viewers some powers, we also need to find ways to be active citizens of television.

The viewer speaks

To a limited degree, some television and television-related venues are opening up space for viewers' participation or involvement. The more celebrated instances of viewer involvement come from the multiple reality shows that rely upon viewers at home to vote contestants off, with, for instance, *Big Brother* and *X-Factor* becoming phenomenal successes in the UK, and *American Idol* ruling the Nielsen rankings for several years in a row. Such shows seemingly allow viewers to choose who they want on the show, and who should go home, and their success has arguably sent a clear message to television producers that viewers appreciate opportunities to participate. Other shows have solicited viewer-created content (see Green 2008), making this the backbone of the program. *America's Funniest Home Videos* and numerous international versions have long succeeded on the back of viewers' own home recordings. MTV News' "Unfiltered" segment began in 1995, calling for viewers to pitch stories about their lives that would then be filmed. Or, seeking to surround their program with an aura of fan accessibility and ownership, in 2007, *Battlestar Galactica* producers Sci Fi Network made audio and videoclips for the show available, encouraging fans to mash up and re-edit the clips with their own material, sending the clips back to the network with promises of a prize for the best clip. To date, one of the more creative experiments in soliciting viewer-created content can be found in Current TV. Aimed at young viewers, and launched in 2005 on cable and satellite, Current TV promised to "democratize" television, and to this end solicits short "pods" rather than playing half- or full-hour programs. Pods are uploaded to Current TV's website, then voted upon by visitors to the site, with high vote-getters making it onto the channel alongside other pods made by Current TV itself. Current TV's voting process also seeks to fuzz the line between watching television online and on television, so that, for instance, Current viewers are encouraged to spend as much if not more time online – in order to screen would-be television pods – than they would watching the television. All such experiments are open to the criticism that television channels are funneling viewers' creative energies into contained spaces, and away from activities that might challenge the channels' bottom line and/or control, and they might also be accused of exploiting viewer labor. But we might also see such experiments as initial challenges to television's ways of doing business and ways of speaking that might be opening up a can of worms that the television industry will not be able easily to close.

Meanwhile, after all, viewer created content and participatory culture are thriving at web venues such as YouTube, Veoh, or IFilm. Here, using a fairly easy-to-use collection of software, people can either create and post their own videos, repurpose and mash up existing television (and film), and/or simply rip television clips away from their commercial surroundings and post them as such. YouTube and its corollaries thereby grant users and viewers multiple powers. With YouTube, one can avoid ads, one can be introduced to video from other countries that is otherwise unavailable, and one can see video from a more diverse collection of producers – all powers of consumption that are further supplemented by BitTorrent download sites that allow one to receive (and to own) longer clips or entire episodes. But one can also create video oneself, be less hampered by traditional television gatekeepers, and receive an audience – all powers of creation. Thus our abilities both to listen and to speak are increasing. Of course, such abilities require a fast computer and a fast Internet connection, and watching on even the best computer screen is still a vastly inferior experience for many viewers, and thus we must avoid the temptation to exaggerate the power-shifting skills of YouTube and BitTorrent. Nevertheless, and despite the industry's impressive feat of keeping up with most developments, and of finding new revenue sources in many of them, as does viewer-created content on television, television off-television is reconfiguring some of the industry's long-held powers. In certain instances, such sites have even been powerful platforms for media activism, "culture jamming" (Harold 2004, Lasn 2000), and for waging outright battles with the television industry.

Indeed, our powers as viewers and as citizens are by no means solely contained within the acts of consumption. Rather, we also have powers outside the television frame to call directly for change. Hence, was the case in 1999, for instance, when the National Association for the Advancement of Colored People (NAACP)'s Kweisi Mfume heard of the upcoming shows to be added to the American networks in autumn. Of the twenty-six new shows, none had a minority lead character, a situation that Mfume, the NAACP, and a coalition of other minority advocacy groups found unacceptable in a nation where the African-American and Latino/a populations alone each numbered close to 40 million at the time. Compounding the problem, later the Writers Guild of America reported that only 8.66 per cent of staff writers hired were minorities, only 6 of the 117 showrunners (5.17 per cent) were minorities, only 1.3 per cent of writers were Latino/a, and 77 per cent of the African-American writers who had been hired were working on the junior networks WB and UPN (NAACP 2003: 12). So the NAACP and its coalition partners held Television Diversity Hearings in Los Angeles in November of 1999. After press involvement and public shaming, the major networks all agreed to a series of sweeping changes that would integrate minorities at all levels both on-screen and behind the scenes. While their success and their commitment to change can certainly be debated, subsequent NAACP reports noted improvement, and post-1999, the industry now knew that it was being watched more closely. The NAACP and its partners did not magically correct television with their efforts, but they did exert significant pressure on the industry, showing how successful advocacy can be. Television producers are notoriously skittish about public criticism, aware of how easily such criticism can build, and thus advocacy remains a key power for citizens, both as groups and individuals.

Another example of a successful advocacy initiative reminds us of how some such initiatives can result in new regulation. In the late 1960s, Massachusetts homemaker and mother Peggy Charren was dismayed by the increasing incidence of children's television shows that hawked toys and other merchandise, and that appeared to be mere vehicles for advertising. Where, she wondered, was educational or informational programming for children? Thus, Charren assembled a small group of similarly concerned parents and citizens, forming Action for Children's Television (ACT) in 1968. First, ACT pressured the Federal Communications Commission (FCC) to act, but eventually took their requests directly to Congress. Ultimately, in 1990, Congress passed and introduced the Children's Television Act, further bolstering it in the 1996 Telecommunications Act. The CTA and its later revisions limited host selling in children's programs, but also required that all television stations broadcast a modicum of three hours of programming per week "specifically designed" to meet educational/informational purposes. "E/I" or "core" programming, as it is known: (a) must be produced with education as the primary goal; (b) must be regular programming (not last-minute substitutes) between 7 a.m. and 10 p.m.; and (c) must run at least thirty minutes long to count. Stations must declare to the FCC which programs satisfy their core quota. Sadly, since the passage of the CTA, the bill has been watered down, the television industry has often made a mockery of its spirit, claiming all sorts of entertainment programs to qualify as core (from *That's So Raven* to *Beverly Hills 90210* reruns), and the FCC has proven weak in demanding that broadcasters live up to the CTA's spirit. So the passage of the CTA is not a utopian story of the housewife versus the industry, but it still suggests both the powers of advocacy, and the need for continued advocacy.

As the CTA case also proves, often the regulatory bodies whom we have entrusted with the duties of regulating television in "the public interest" have vastly different conceptions of what is best for the public, or of whom they serve – citizens, consumers, or corporations. Advocacy is therefore required, and regulatory bodies need to be told in no uncertain terms what the public wants. In the US, citizens were even forced to lay suit against the FCC to demand that public complaints be taken into account in broadcast license renewal decisions. Throughout the 1950s and 1960s, civil rights groups and the United Church of Christ regularly petitioned the FCC to revoke the license of the Jackson, Mississippi NBC affiliate, on the grounds that its racist, segregationist agenda failed to serve its local community. Eventually, the UCC laid suit against the FCC, and it was only a US Court of Appeals decision in 1971 that compelled the FCC to revoke the station's license.[3] By the 2000s, though, Des Freedman (2006) notes that both the FCC in the US, and Ofcom in the UK still regularly shut the public out of meetings to discuss regulation, restrict access to information, and generally prove either indifferent or outright hostile to public sentiment. Once again in 2004, then, it was a court case – *Prometheus Radio Project* vs. *The FCC* – that required the FCC to listen to the concerns of a broad coalition of citizens and community groups from across the political spectrum, and halt its latest round of media ownership deregulation.[4] The court's ruling found that the FCC had not adequately considered the effects that its next wave of deregulation would have on broadcast diversity.

While 2004 proved a victory for the media reform movement, the results are potentially short-lived, and the FCC and Congress' deregulatory fervor remains, as evident in many other recent decisions and debates (see, for instance, Anderson 2008). Just as we must care about our immediate communities, and care enough to get involved when need be, the media reform movement's struggles leading up to the 2004 decision were motivated by the notion that we must care enough about our mediated communities, and about the media's significant role in connecting us to all manner of communities, local or global, to get involved (see Kunz 2007, McChesney *et al.* 2005). And just as the television industry has often needed forceful nudging by advocacy groups, so too do regulatory bodies require similar compulsion. Regulation will always be an important part of assuring a television system that is responsive to the needs of citizens, precisely because other interests (whether commercial or paternal) can too easily control television and television regulation, and thus advocacy becomes a key power that citizens wield, even if history has proven it to be a rarely used power.

Conclusion: the values of television entertainment

To conclude this chapter and the book, I return to an observation from Antonio Gramsci, noted in Chapter 5, namely that ideology works by becoming common sense, and hence by becoming invisible. Often power works similarly. We might be more attuned to spotting acts of power when they are grandiose and explicit, but power is given, traded, taken, and/or yielded in the most subtle of acts too. Thus, if we wish to have more power over television, first we must analyze what subtle powers it has over us, and what power we grant it every day. We must displace its place as "mediated center," and realize our own significant powers over and in spite of the medium. L. S. Kim notes that "Media culture is contradictory: on one hand it is hegemonic, on the other hand, because hegemony is a social existence that people are not coerced into but consent to, it is contestable. Media culture needs to be contested" (2008: 458). Part of this contestation requires that we must consider what we would like television to do better, differently, or not at all – we must take television's hegemonic common sense and subject it to analysis and scrutiny, rendering it anything but common sense. And then we must purposively work towards creating television entertainment anew. Many of those acts of re-creation will themselves be subtle, not necessarily loud or conspicuous, but our true power over television begins when we realize that we *ought* to have power over television, and when we deliberate on what we want television to be and how we propose to guide it toward that goal.

Every year, the Academy of Television Arts and Sciences meet to hand out Emmys for excellence in American television, and the British Academy of Film and Television Arts meet to hand out BAFTAs for excellence in British television, ceremonies that are repeated with small variations worldwide by other local television industries. For a few days beforehand, audiences, entertainment journalists, actors, producers, and many others eagerly anticipate, debate, and hype the ensuing awards, and the inevitable complaints and congratulations follow soon thereafter from the same voices. But the Emmys, the BAFTAs, and many of their international iterations are voted on by those within the television industry, purely inhouse affairs. A continuing challenge for us as television *viewers* is to find our own ways to evaluate television. What is good television, and what is bad television? Why do we want good television and what does it offer us, or how/why do we suffer under bad television and how might we reform it? In this book and divided into its six chapters, I have offered several key means by which we can evaluate television, and with which we can answer such questions. I pose that how television entertainment withholds, networks, and/or channels creativity, innovation, and industry, affect, fantasy, and meaning, expansion, overflow, and synergy, reality and representation, politics and citizenship, and power, all determine its success and its value to us as viewers and as citizens, as individuals and as communities. These are the scales on which we should measure its impact on and usefulness to society.

All of these dimensions of television come together in the deceptively simple question, "Is this entertaining?" but I hope to have shown how varied and complex a process television entertainment is. Entertainment may often appear to be light, frivolous, and devoid of meaning by its very nature, but rather it is through entertainment that we interact with, discuss, debate, learn from and about, and make sense of much of the world around us. As a premier site for entertainment, then, television has become a vital site for the witnessing, enacting, participation in, and questioning – or even contestation – of politics, of power, of reality, of art, of our relationships with others, of our hopes and worries for ourselves, and of everyday life in the twenty-first century.

Notes

Introduction

1 In mid-2006, John Q Public changed his on-screen name to John Q Republican, but by mid-2007, he and his library of reviews had vanished from Amazon.

I Art with strings attached: creativity, innovation, and industry

1 As Ien Ang (1991) notes, frequently even public broadcasters have internalized the ethos of commercial television, themselves peddling for audiences (or, simply, broadcasting shows created in a commercial context).

2 Increasingly, though, networks are also negotiating "repurposing" deals, whereby they can broadcast an episode once on the network, before moving it over to a corporate sibling cable channel for further immediate play (see Lotz 2007b: 124).

3 For more information on exactly how ads are sold, see Lotz 2007a.

4 Napoli (2003) notes that, on average, cable channels receive 60 per cent of their revenue from audience sales (ads) and 40 per cent from content sales, whereas cable providers receive 85 per cent from content, and only 15 per cent from audience sales.

2 Broadcasting identities: affect, fantasy, and meaning

1 Within fan studies, the definition of "fan" is contested, with some regarding fans as those with a *communal* engagement with a text (i.e.: belonging to fanclub, attending conventions, posting regularly online, etc.), not simply those who like a text. Thus Tulloch and Jenkins (1995) distinguish between "fans" and "followers," the latter being more casual, less involved fans. However, following common usage outside fan studies, here my use of the word "fan" incorporates followers too.

2 In the early 2000s, Nielsen announced its intent to double its national sample size to 10,000 households (Napoli 2003: 154). By 2007, its website boasted a sample of 25,000, but this number includes local people meters. Given the nature of their business, Nielsen is often not forthcoming in the specifics of its science.

3   Television unboxed: expansion, overflow, and synergy

1   See www.driveshaftband.com
2   However, both Hesmondhalgh (2002) and Simone Murray (2005) point out that synergy is itself risky, and thus a synergistic business strategy represents a gamble for yet more profit, not a risk-avoidance strategy per se.
3   Moreover, these ads proved crucial to the ARG, hence "forcing" ARG viewers to consume the advertising.

4   Keeping it real: reality and representation

1   All statistics on the real-world American population are taken from the 2000 Census. See www.census.gov/prod/2001pubs/c2kbr01−1.pdf for race and ethnicity, and www.census.gov/prod/2001pubs/c2kbr01−9.pdf for gender (accessed 15 July, 2007).
2   After taking into account dispersion of the Latino/a population (who may also report as any other racial group), Census 2000 figures suggest a USA that is 69.1 per cent White, 12.1 per cent African-American, 12.5 per cent Latino/a, 3.6 per cent Asian or Pacific Islander, 0.42 per cent Middle-Eastern, 1.6 per cent Multi-racial. See www.census.gov/prod/2001pubs/ c2kbr01−1.pdf.
3   Most public broadcasters too, teeter on the edge of financial viability, and thus they must also heed the threat of widespread viewer complaints. Furthermore, since many public broadcasters regard the educated upper-middle-class viewer as their proper audience (see Ouellette 2002), they too have often given up on the working class.

5   Plugging in: politics and citizenship

1   Habermas' public sphere has been criticized by many (see, for example, Fraser 1987) for being historically inaccurate and for being limited to a select few, but here I write of it as an ideal for the future for all, not as a reality from the past, nor solely as Habermas' own version of it.
2   Certainly, many books bemoaning the state of citizenship stumble in equating civic participation with somewhat antiquated, limited, and/or class-specific practices, such as writing letters to a newspaper or taking part in a protest rally, and such books have thus come under heavy fire for their crude measurements of citizenship and blindness to issues of gender, class, and sociopolitical context (see Grant et al. 2005).
3   See www.youtube.com/watch?v=9FSpQLsUmVQ.

6   Channel interference: television and power

1   See www.thesmokinggun.com/archive/0327062extreme1.html.

2 As of 1999, dual ownership is allowed if a market has at least eight independently owned stations, and if only one of the dually owned stations is among the top four rated in the market (Kunz 2007: 73).

3 A few months later, control of the station was given to new management, a biracial non-profit foundation.

4 See www.fcc.gov/ogc/documents/opinions/2004/03–3388–062404.pdf.

Bibliography

Abercrombie, Nicholas and Longhurst, Brian (1998) *Audiences: A Sociological Theory of Performance and Imagination*, London: Sage.

Ahmed, Sara (2004) *The Cultural Politics of Emotion*, New York: Routledge.

Andersen, Robin and Gray, Jonathan, eds (2008) *Battleground: The Media*, Westport, CT: Greenwood.

Anderson, Benedict (1983) *Imagined Communities: Reflections on the Origin and Spread of Nationalism*, New York: Verso.

Anderson, Bonnie (2004) *News Flash: Journalism, Infotainment and the Bottom-Line Business of Broadcast News*, San Francisco: Jossey-Bass.

Anderson, Chris (2006) "The Long Tail," *Wired* (www.wired.com/wired/archive/12.10/tail_pr.html).

Anderson, Tim (2006) "At the End of the Day We're All 'End-Users,'" *Flow* 4.9 (http://flowtv.org/?p=183).

Anderson, Steve (2008) "Network Neutrality," in Andersen and Gray 2008.

Andrejevic, Mark (2007) *iSpy: Surveillance and Power in the Interactive Era*, Lawrence: University Press of Kansas.

Ang, Ien (1985) *Watching Dallas: Soap Opera and the Melodramatic Imagination* trans. Della Couling, London: Methuen.

—— (1991) *Desperately Seeking the Audience*, New York: Routledge.

—— (1994) "In the Realm of Uncertainty: The Global Village and Capitalist Postmodernity," in David Crowley and David Mitchell (eds) *Communication Theory Today*, Cambridge: Polity.

Bacon-Smith, Camille (1992) *Enterprising Women: Television Fandom and the Creation of Popular Myth*, Philadelphia: University of Pennsylvania Press.

Bagdikian, Ben (2004) *The New Media Monopoly*, Boston: Beacon Press.

Bakhtin, Mikhail Mikhailovich (1981) *The Dialogic Imagination* trans. Caryl Emerson and Michael Holquist, ed. Michael Holquist, Austin: University of Texas Press.

—— (1984) *Rabelais and His World* trans. Hélène Iswolsky, Cambridge, MA: MIT Press.

Barker, Martin and Brooks, Kate (1998) *Knowing Audiences: Judge Dredd, Its Friends, Fans and Foes*, Luton: University of Luton Press.

Barshefsky, Charlene (1998) Testimony of the United States Trade Representative before the House Appropriations Committee Subcommittee on Commerce, Justice, State, the Judiciary and Related Agencies, 31 March.

Barthes, Roland (1995) *The Pleasure of the Text* trans. Richard Miller, New York: Hill and Wang.

Baudrillard, Jean (1983a) *In the Shadow of the Silent Majorities or, The End of the Social and Other Essays* trans. Paul Foss, John Johnston, and Paul Patton, New York: Semiotext(e).

—— (1983b) *Simulations* trans. Paul Foss, Paul Patton, and Philip Beitchman, New York: Semiotext(e).

Bauman, Zygmunt (1999) *In Search of Politics*, Palo Alto: Stanford University Press.

Becker, Howard S. (1984) *Art Worlds*, Berkeley: University of California Press.

Bellamy, R. V., Jr. and Walker, J. R., eds (1996) *Television and the Remote Control: Grazing on a Vast Wasteland*, New York: Guilford.

Bennett, Tony (1979) *Formalism and Marxism*, London: Routledge.

Bhavnani, Kum-Kum (1991) *Talking Politics: A Psychological Framing for Views from Youth in Britain*, Cambridge: Cambridge University Press.

Bird, S. Elizabeth (2003) *The Audience in Everyday Life: Living in a Media World*, New York: Routledge.

Bjarkman, Kim (2004) "To Have and To Hold: The Video Collector's Relationship with an Ethereal Medium," *Television and New Media* 5.3: 217–46.

Blumler, Jay G. and Katz, Elihu (eds) (1975) *The Uses of Mass Communication: Current Perspectives on Gratifications Research*, London: Sage.

Boddy, William (2004) "Interactive Television and Advertising Form in Contemporary US Television," in Spigel and Olsson 2004.

Bonner, Francis (2003) *Ordinary Television: Analyzing Popular TV*. Thousand Oaks, CA: Sage.

Bourdieu, Pierre (1984) *Distinction: A Social Critique of the Judgement of Taste* trans. Richard Nice, London: Routledge & Kegan Paul.

—— (1998) *On Television and Journalism* trans. Priscilla Parkhurst Ferguson, London: Pluto.

Brooker, Will (2001) "Living on *Dawson's Creek*: Teen Viewers, Cultural Convergence and Television Overflow," *International Journal of Cultural Studies* 4.4: 456–72.

—— (2002) *Using the Force: Creativity, Community and Star Wars Fans*, New York: Continuum.

—— (2008) "Television Out of Time: Watching Cult Shows on Demand," in Roberta Pearson (ed.) *Reading Lost: Perspectives on a Hit Television Show*. London: I.B. Tauris.

Buckingham, David (1987) *Public Secrets: East Enders and its Audience*, London: BFI.

—— (1997) "Electronic Child Abuse? Rethinking the Media's Effects on Children," in Martin Barker and Julian Petley (eds) *Ill Effects: The Media / Violence Debate*, New York: Routledge.

—— (2000) *The Making of Citizens: Young People, News and Politics*, London: Routledge.

Caldwell, John Thornton (1995) *Televisuality: Style, Crisis, and Authority in American Television*, New Brunswick, NJ: Rutgers University Press.

—— (2004) "Convergence Television: Aggregating from and Repurposing Content in the Culture of Conglomeration," in Spigel and Olsson 2004.

Campbell, Christopher P. (1995) *Race, Myth, and the News*. Thousand Oaks, CA: Sage.

Cantril, Hadley (1966) *The Invasion From Mars*, Princeton: Princeton University Press.

Carey, James (1989) *Communication as Culture: Essays on Media and Society*, Boston: Unwin Hyman.

Castañeda, Maria (2007) "The Complicated Transition to Broadcast Digital Television in the United States," *Television and New Media* 8.2: 91–106.

Caughie, John (1990) "Playing at Being American: Games and Tactics," in Patricia Mellencamp (ed.) *Logics of Television: Essays in Cultural Criticism*, London: BFI.

Caves, Richard E. (2000) *Creative Industries: Contracts Between Art and Commerce*, Cambridge, MA: Harvard University Press.

de Certeau, Michel (1984) *The Practice of Everyday Life* trans. Steven F. Rendall, Berkeley: University of California Press.

Chaney, David C. (2001) "From Ways of Life to Lifestyle: Rethinking Culture as Ideology and Sensibility," in James Lull (ed.) *Culture in the Communication Age*, New York: Routledge.

Clickz.com (2007) "Global Online Populations" (www.clickz.com/showPage.html?page= stats/ web_worldwide).

Cohen, Elliot D., ed. (2005) *News Incorporated: Corporate Media Ownership and Its Threat to Democracy*, Amherst, NY: Prometheus.

Comolli, Jean-Louis and Narboni, Jean (1993) "Cinema/Ideology/Criticism (1)," in Anthony Easthope (ed.) *Contemporary Film Theory*, London: Longman.

Condit, Celeste (1994) "The Rhetorical Limits of Polysemy," in Horace Newcomb (ed.) *Television: The Critical View*, 5th edn, Oxford: Oxford University Press.

Consoli, John (2005) "CBS to Embed Impala Logo in 5 Premieres," *Mediaweek* September 1 (www.mediaweek.com/mw/news/networktv/article_display.jsp?vnu_content_id= 1001053570).

—— (2006a) "44 Mil. Watch TV in Unmeasured Places," *Mediaweek* April 21 (www.medi-aweek.com/mw/news/media_agencies/article_display.jsp?vnu_content_id=100238 3527).

—— (2006b) "CW Secures $650 Million in Upfront Business," *Mediaweek* June 23 (www.mediaweek.com/mw/news/recent_display.jsp?vnu_content_id=1002727487)

—— (2007) "Coen Downgrades '07 Ad Spend," *Mediaweek* June 26 (www. mediaweek.com/ mw/news/media_agencies/article_display.jsp?vnu_content_ id=1003603775).

Coontz, Stephanie (1998) *The Way We Really Are: Coming to Terms with America's Changing Families*. New York: Basic Books.

Corner, John (1995) *Television Form and Public Address*. London: Hodder Arnold.

Couldry, Nick (2000) *In the Place of Media Power: Pilgrims and Witnesses of the Media Age*, New York: Routledge.

—— (2003) *Media Rituals: A Critical Approach*, New York: Routledge.

—— (2004) "Teaching Us to Fake It: The Ritualized Norms of Television's 'Reality' Games," in Murray and Ouellette 2004.

Creeber, Glen (2004) *Serial Television: Big Drama on the Small Screen*, London: BFI.

Critchley, Simon (2002) *On Humour*, New York: Routledge.

Crupi, Anthony (2006) "FNC Tops CNN For 18 Straight Quarters," *Mediaweek* June 28 (www.mediaweek.com/mw/news/cabletv/aricle_display.jsp?vnu_content_id=1002 763658).

Crupi, Anthony and Consoli, John (2005) "Nets Testing VOD Waters," *Mediaweek* 14 November: 5.

Curtin, Michael (2004) "Media Capitals: Cultural Geographies of Global TV," in Spigel and Olsson 2004.

Dahlgren, Peter (1995) *Television and the Public Sphere: Citizenship, Democracy and the Media*, Thousand Oak, CA: Sage.

Deleuze, Gilles and Guattari, Felix (1988) *A Thousand Plateaus: Capitalism and Schizophrenia* trans. Brian Massumi, London: Athlone.

Descartes, Rene (1985) "The Passions of the Soul," *The Philosophical Writings of Descartes*, vol. 1, trans. J. Cottingham, R. Stoothoff, and D. Murdoch, Cambridge: Cambridge University Press.

van Dijk, Jan A. G. M. (2005) *The Deepening Divide: Inequality in the Information Society*, Thousand Oaks, CA: Sage.

Dyer, Richard (1992) *Only Entertainment*, New York: Routledge.

Economist (2002) "Power in Your Hand: A Survey of Television," 13 April, special insert.

Eliasoph, Nina (1998) *Avoiding Politics: How Americans Produce Apathy in Everyday Life*, Cambridge: Cambridge University Press.

Eliot, T. S. (1991)[1920] "Tradition and the Individual Talent," in Charles Kaplan and William Anderson (eds) *Criticism: Major Statements*, 3rd edn, New York: St. Martin's.

Ellis, John (2000) *Seeing Things: Television in the Age of Uncertainty*, London: I.B. Tauris.

Elsaesser, Thomas (2002) "The Blockbuster: Everything Connects, But not Everything Goes," in Jon Lewis (ed.) *The End of Cinema as We Know It*, New York: NYU Press.

Fanon, Frantz (1968) *Black Skin, White Masks*, New York: Grove.

Feuer, Jane (2001) "Situation Comedy, Part 2," in Glen Creeber (ed.) *The Television Genre Book*, London: BFI, 67–70.

Finkle, Jim (2005) "New Shows, New Marketing," *Broadcasting and Cable* 135.8 (21 February), 8.

Fiske, John (1989a) Hans Borchers, Gabriele Kreutzner, and Eva-Marie Warth "Moments of Television: Neither the Text Nor the Audience," in Ellen Seiter, *et al.* (eds) *Remote Control: Television, Audiences, and Cultural Power*, London: Routledge.

—— (1989b) *Reading the Popular*, London: Unwin Hyman.

—— (1989c) *Understanding Popular Culture*, London: Unwin Hyman.

—— (2003) "Act Globally, Think Locally," in Parks and Kumar 2003.

Fleming, Dan (1996) *Powerplay: Toys as Popular Culture*, Manchester: Manchester University Press.

Foucault, Michel (1981) "The Order of Discourse" trans. Ian McLeod, in Robert Young (ed.) *Untying the Text: A Post-Structuralist Reader*, London: Routledge and Kegan Paul.

Fraser, Nancy (1987) "What's Critical About Critical Theory? The Case of Habermas and Gender," in Seyla Benhabib and Drucilla Cornell (eds) *Feminism as Critique: The Politics of Gender*, Minneapolis: University of Minnesota Press.

Freedman, Des (2006) "Dynamics of Power in Contemporary Media Policy-Making," *Media, Culture and Society* 28: 907–23.

Freud, Sigmund (1960) *Jokes and Their Relation to the Unconscious* trans. James Strachey, London: Hogarth.

Gabler, Neal (2000) *Life: The Movie: How Entertainment Conquered Reality*, New York: Vintage.

Gans, Eric (1985). *The End of Culture: Toward a Generative Anthropology*. Berkeley: University of California Press.

Gauntlett, David (2005) *Moving Experiences: Media Effects and Beyond*, Eastleigh: John Libbey.

Gillespie, Marie (1995) *Television, Ethnicity and Cultural Change*, New York: Routledge.

Gitlin, Todd (1994) *Inside Prime Time*, revised edn, New York: Routledge.

Glynn, Kevin (2000) *Tabloid Culture: Trash Taste, Popular Power, and the Transformation of American Television*, London: Duke University Press.

Goldsmiths Media Group (2000) "Media Organisations in Society: Central Issues," in James Curran (ed.) *Media Organisations in Society*, London: Arnold.

Gomery, Douglas (2007) *A History of Broadcasting in the United States*, London: Blackwell.

Graham, David (1999) *Becoming a Global Audience: British Television in Overseas Markets*, London: DCMS.

Gramsci, Antonio (1971) *Selections from the Prison Notebooks*, New York: International.

Grant, Monica, Nisha Varia, Valerie Durrant, and Nelly Stromquist (2005) "The Transition to Citizenship," in National Research Council and Institute of Medicines, *Growing Up Global: The Changing Transitions to Adulthood in Developing Countries*. Washington, DC: National Academies Press.

Gray, Jonathan (2005) "Anti-Fandom and the Moral Text: *Television Without Pity* and Textual Dislike," *American Behavioral Scientist* 48.7: 840–58.

—— (2006) *Watching with The Simpsons: Television, Parody, and Intertextuality*, New York: Routledge.

—— (2007) "The News : You Gotta Love It," in Gray *et al.* 2007.

—— (2008) "Cinderella Burps: Gender, Performativity, and the Dating Show," in Susan Murray and Laurie Ouellette (eds) *Reality TV: Remaking Television Culture*, 2nd edn, New York: NYU Press.

Gray, Jonathan and Mittell, Jason (2007) "Speculation on Spoilers: *Lost* Fandom, Narrative Consumption, and Rethinking Textuality," *Particip@tions: Journal of Audience and Reception Studies* 4.1 (www.participations.org/Volume%204/Issue%201/4_01_graymittell.htm).

Gray, Jonathan, Sandvoss, Cornel, and Harrington, C. Lee, eds (2007a) *Fandom: Identities and Communities in a Mediated World*, New York: NYU Press.

Gray, Jonathan, Sandvoss, Cornel, and Harrington, C. Lee (2007b) "Why Study Fans?" in Gray, Sandvoss, and Harrington 2007a.

Green, Joshua (2008) "User-Created Content and Audience Participation," in Andersen and Gray 2008.

Gripsrud, Jostein (2004) "Broadcast Television: The Chances of Its Survival in a Digital Age," in Spigel and Olsson 2004.

Gross, Larry (2001) *Up From Invisibility: Lesbians, Gay Men, and the Media in America*, New York: Columbia University Press.

Grossberg, Lawrence (1992) "In There a Fan in the House?: The Affective Sensibility of Fandom," in Lisa A. Lewis (ed.) *The Adoring Audience: Fan Culture and Popular Media*, New York: Routledge.

Grote, David (1983) *The End of Comedy: The Sit-Com and the Comedic Tradition*, Hamden, CN: Archon.

Habermas, Jürgen (1989) *The Structural Transformation of the Public Sphere: An Inquiry into a Category of Bourgeois Society,* trans. Thomas Burger, Cambridge: Polity.

Haggins, Bambi (2007) *Laughing Mad: The Black Comic Persona in Post-Soul America*, New Brunswick: Rutgers University Press.

Hall, Stuart (1990) "Cultural Identity and Diaspora," in Jonathan Rutherford (ed.) *Identity, Community, Culture, Difference*, London: Lawrence & Wishart.

—— (1993) "Which Public, Whose Service?" in Wilf Stevenson (ed.) *All Our Futures: The Changing Role and Purpose of the BBC*, London: BFI.

Harold, Christine (2004) "Pranking Rhetoric: 'Culture Jamming' as Media Activism," *Critical Studies in Media Communication* 21.3: 189–211.

Harrington, C. Lee and Bielby, Denise (1995) *Soap Fans: Pursuing Pleasure and Making Meaning in Everyday Life*, Philadelphia: Temple University Press.

—— (2005) "Global Television Distribution: Implications of TV 'Traveling' for Viewers, Fans, and Texts," *American Behavioral Scientist* 48.7: 902–20.

Hartley, John (1987) "Invisible Fictions: Television Audiences, Paedocracy, Pleasure," *Textual Practice* 1.2: 121–38.

—— (1999) *The Uses of Television*, New York: Routledge.

Hellekson, Karen and Busse, Kristina, eds (2006) *Fan Fiction and Fan Communities in the Age of the Internet: New Essays*, Jefferson, NC: McFarland.

Herman, Edward S. and McChesney, Robert W. (1997) *The Global Media: The New Missionaries of Global Capitalism*, London: Cassell.

Hermes, Joke (1995) *Reading Women's Magazines: An Analysis of Everyday Media Use*, Oxford: Polity.

—— (2005) *Re-Reading Popular Culture: Rethinking Gender, Television and Popular Media Audiences*, London: Blackwell.

Hesmondhalgh, David (2002) *The Cultural Industries*, Thousand Oaks, CA: Sage.

Hills, Matt (2002) *Fan Cultures*, New York: Routledge.

—— (2005a) *How to Do Things With Cultural Theory*, London: Hodder Arnold.

—— (2005b) "Patterns of Surprise: The 'Aleatory Object' in Psychoanalytic Ethnography and Cyclical Fandom," *American Behavioral Scientist* 48.7: 801–21.

Hilmes, Michele (2003) "Who We Are, Who We Are Not: Battle of the Global Paradigms," in Parks and Kumar 2003.

—— (ed.) (2004) *The Television History Book*, London: BFI.

Hockley, Luke (2003) *Cinematic Projections: The Analytic Psychology of C. G. Jung and Film Theory*, Luton: University of Luton Press.

Hoffman, Alison R. and Noriega, Chon (2004) "Looking for Latino Regulars on Prime-Time Television: The Fall 2004 Season" (www.chicano.ucla.edu/press/reports/documents/ crr_04Dec2004_000.pdf).

Holt, Jennifer (2003) "Vertical Vision: Deregulation, Industrial Economy and Prime-time Design," in Mark Jankovich and James Lyon (eds) *Quality Popular Television: Cult TV, the Industry and Fans*, London: BFI.

hooks, bell (1995) "Feminism: It's a Black Thing," *Killing Rage: Ending Racism*, New York: H. Holt & Co.

Horkheimer, Max and Adorno, Theodor W. (1972)[1994] *Dialectic of Enlightenment: Philosophical Fragments*, trans. John Cumming, New York: Seabury.

Jenkins, Henry (1992) *Textual Poachers: Television Fans and Participating Culture*, New York: Routledge.

—— (2002) "Interactive Audiences?" in Dan Harries (ed.) *The New Media Book*, London: BFI.

—— (2006) *Convergence Culture:Where Old and New Media Collide*, New York: NYU Press.

—— (2007) "Afterword:The Future of Fandom," in Gray, *et al.* 2007.

Jensen, Joli (1992) "Fandom as Pathology:The Consequences of Characterization," in Lisa A. Lewis (ed.) *The Adoring Audience: Fan Culture and Popular Media*, New York: Routledge.

Jhally, Sut (1987) *The Codes of Advertising: Fetishism and the Political Economy of Meaning in the Consumer Society*, New York: Routledge.

Jhally, Sut and Lewis, Justin (1992) *Enlightened Racism:The Cosby Show, Audiences, and the Myth of the American Dream*, Boulder, CO: Westview.

Johansson, David (2006) "Homeward Bound: Those *Sopranos* Titles Come Heavy," in David Lavery (ed.) *Reading The Sopranos: Hit TV From HBO*, New York: I.B. Tauris.

Johnson, Catherine (2005) *Telefantasy*, London: BFI.

Johnson, Stephen (2005) *Everything Bad is Good for You: How Today's Popular Culture is Actually Making Us Smarter*, New York: Riverhead.

Jones, Gerard (1992) *Honey, I'm Home! Sitcoms: Selling the American Dream*, New York: Grove Weidenfeld.

Jones, Jeffrey (2005) *Entertaining Politics: New Political Television and Civic Culture*, Lanham, MD: Rowman and Littlefield.

Kalin, Michael (2006) "Why Jon Stewart Isn't Funny," *Boston Globe*, 3 March, 2006 (www.boston.com/ae/movies/oscars/articles/2006/03/03/why_jon_stewart_isnt_funny/).

Katz, Elihu and Liebes, Tamar (1990) *The Export of Meaning: Cross-Cultural Readings of Dallas*, Cambridge: Polity.

Kendall, Diana (2005) *Framing Class: Media Representations of Wealth and Poverty in America*, Lanham, MD: Rowman and Littlefield.

Kim, L. S. (2008) "Representations of Race," in Andersen and Gray 2008.

Klein, Naomi (2002) *No Logo*, New York: Picador.

Klinger, Barbara (2006) *Beyond the Multiplex: Cinema, New Technologies, and the Home*, Berkeley: University of California Press.

Kompare, Derek (2005) *Rerun Nation: How Repeats Invented American Television*, New York: Routledge.

Kraszewski, Jon (2004) "Country Hicks and Urban Cliques: Mediating Race, Reality, and Liberalism on MTV's *The RealWorld*," in Murray and Ouellette 2004.

Kubey, Robert (2004) *Creating Television: Conversations with the People Behind 50 Years of American TV*, Mahwah, NJ: LEA.

Kunz, William (2007) *Culture Conglomerates: Consolidation in the Motion Picture and Television Industries*, Lanham, MD: Rowman and Littlefield.

Lasn, Kalle (2000) *Culture Jam: How to Reverse America's Suicidal Consumer Bing — And Why We Must*, New York: Harper.

Lauzen, Martha (2005) "Boxed In: Women on Screen and Behind the Scenes in the 2004–05 Prime-time Season" (www.women-in-film.org/pdf/WIF-WEBboxedinhrfnl.pdf).

Lavery, David and Thompson, Robert J. (2002) "David Chase, *The Sopranos*, and Television Creativity," in David Lavery (ed.) *This Thing of Ours: Investigating The Sopranos*, New York: Columbia University Press.

Lefebvre, Henri (1991) *Critique of Everyday Life*, trans. John Moore, London: Verso.

Lembo, Ron (2000) *Thinking Through Television*, Cambridge: Cambridge University Press.

Lévy, Pierre (2000) *Collective Intelligence: Mankind's Emerging World in Cyberspace*, trans. Robert Bononno, New York: Perseus.

Lewis, Justin (1991) *The Ideological Octopus: An Exploration of Television and Its Audience*, New York: Routledge.

—— (2004) "The Meaning of Real Life," in Murray and Ouellette 2004.

Livingstone, Sonia (1990) *Making Sense of Television: The Psychology of Audience Interpretation*, New York: Routledge.

Lipsitz, George (1990) *Time Passages: Collective Memory and American Popular Culture*, Minneapolis: University of Minnesota Press.

Livingstone, Sonia and Lunt, Peter (1994) *Talk on Television*, New York: Routledge.

Lotman, Jurij (1977) *The Structure of the Artistic Text*, trans. Gail Lenhoff and Ronald Vroon, Ann Arbor: University of Michigan Press.

Lotz, Amanda (2007a) "How to Spend $9.3 Billion in Three Days: Examining the Upfront Buying Process in the Production of US Television Culture," *Media, Culture and Society* 29.4: 549–67.

—— (2007b) *The Television Will Be Revolutionized*, New York: NYU Press.

Lull, James (1990) *Inside Family Viewing: Ethnographic Research on Television's Audiences*, New York: Routledge.

—— (2001) "Superculture for the Communication Age," in Lull (ed.) *Culture in the Communication Age*, New York: Routledge.

—— (2007) *Culture-on-Demand: Communication in a Crisis World*, London: Blackwell.

Lyon, David (2007) *Surveillance Society: Monitoring Everyday Life*, Milton Keynes: Open University Press.

Magder, Ted (2004) "The End of TV 101: Reality Programs, Formats, and the New Business of Television," in Murray and Ouellette 2004.

Mandese, Joe (2005) "DVR Threat Gets Downgraded," *Broadcasting and Cable* 135.37 (12 September), 20.

Marc, David (1989) *Comic Visions: Television Comedy and American Culture*, Boston: Unwin Hyman.

Marcus, George E. (2002) *The Sentimental Citizen: Emotion in Democratic Politics*, University Park: Pennsylvania State University Press.

Matheson, Carl (2001) "*The Simpsons*, Hyper-Irony, and the Meaning of Life," in William Irwin, Mark T. Conard, and Aeon J. Skoble (eds) *The Simpsons and Philosophy: The D'Oh! of Homer*, Chicago: Open Court.

Mattelart, Armand (1983) *Transnationals and Third World: The Struggle for Culture*. South Hadley, MA: Bergin and Garvey.

Mayerle, Judith (1994) "Roseanne – How Did You Get Inside My House? A Case Study of a Hit Blue-Collar Situation Comedy," in Horace Newcomb (ed.) *Television: The Critical View* Fifth Ed., New York: Oxford University Press.

McAllister, Matthew (1996) *The Commercialization of American Culture: New Advertising, Control, and Democracy*, Thousand Oaks, CA: Sage.

McCarthy, Anna (2004) "The Rhythms of the Reception Area: Crisis, Capitalism, and the Waiting Room TV," in Spigel and Olsson 2004.

McChesney, Robert W. (1994) *Telecommunications, Mass Media, and Democracy: The Battle for the Control of US Broadcasting, 1928–1935*, New York: Oxford University Press.

—— (2004) *The Problem of the Media: US Communication Politics in the Twenty-First Century*, New York: Monthly Review.

McChesney, Robert W., Newman, Russell, and Scott, Ben, eds. (2005) *The Future of Media: Resistance and Reform in the 21st Century*, New York: Seven Stories.

McClellan, Steve (2005) "Ad Clutter Spikes," *Adweek* 31 October (www.mediaweek.com/mw/news/recent_display.jsp?vnu_content_id=1001392205).

McKee, Alan (2007) "The Fans of Cultural Theory," in Gray, et al. 2007.

McKinley, E. Graham (1997) *Beverly Hills, 90210: Television, Gender, and Identity*, Philadelphia: University of Pennsylvania Press.

McMurria, John (2005) "Desperate Citizens," *Flow* 3.3 (http://flowtv.org/?p=272).

Meehan, Eileen (1990) "Why We Don't Count: The Commodity Audience," in Patricia Mellencamp (ed.) *Logics of Television: Essays in Cultural Criticism*, Bloomington: Indiana University Press.

Mellencamp, Patricia (2003) "Situation Comedy, Feminism, and Freud: Discourses of Gracie and Lucy," in Joanne Morreale (ed.) *Critiquing the Sitcom*, Syracuse: Syracuse University Press.

Meyer, Thomas (2002) *Media Democracy: How the Media Colonize Politics*, Cambridge: Polity.

Miller, Mark Crispin (1986) "Deride and Conquer," in Todd Gitlin (ed.) *Watching Television*, New York: Pantheon.

—— (1988) *Boxed In: The Culture of TV*, Evanston, IL: Northwestern University Press.

Miller, Toby (1993) *The Well-Tempered Self: Citizenship, Culture, and the Postmodern Subject*, Baltimore: Johns Hopkins University Press.

Miller, Toby, Nitin Govil, John McMurria, Richard Maxwell and Tina Wang (2005) *Global Hollywood 2*, London: BFI.

Milwaukee Journal Sentinel (1998) "Entrepreneur's Success Translates to Boudoir," 4 May (findarticles.com/p/articles/mi_qn4196/is_19980504/ai_n10419302).

Mittell, Jason (2000) "The Cultural Power of an Anti-Television Metaphor: Questioning the 'Plug-in Drug' and a TV-Free America," *Television and New Media*: 1.2: 215–38.

—— (2004a) *Genre and Television: From Cop Shows to Cartoons in American Culture*, New York: Routledge.

—— (2004b) "Generic Cycles: Innovation, Imitation, and Saturation," in Michelle Hilmes (ed.) *The Television History Book*, London: BFI.

—— (2005) "An Arresting Development," *Flow* 3.8 (http://flowtv.org/?p=294).

—— (2006) "TiVoing Childhood," *Flow* 3.12 (http://flowtv.org/?p=194).

—— (2008) *Television and American Culture*, New York: Oxford University Press.

Modleski, Tania (1984) *Loving with a Vengeance: Mass-Produced Fantasies for Women*, New York: Methuen.

Morley, David (1986) *Family Television*, London: Comedia.

—— (1992) *Television, Audiences and Cultural Studies*, New York: Routledge.

—— (2000) *Home Territories: Media, Mobility and Identity*, New York: Routledge.

Mulvey, Laura (1989) *Visual and Other Pleasures*, London: Palgrave MacMillan.

Murray, Simone (2005) "Brand Loyalties: Rethinking Content within Global Corporate Media," *Media, Culture, Society* 27.3: 415–35.

Murray, Susan (2005) *Hitch Your Antenna to the Stars: Early Television and Broadcast Stardom*, New York: Routledge.

Murray, Susan and Ouellette, Laurie, eds (2004) *Reality TV: Remaking Television Culture*, New York: NYU Press.

Myers, Kathy (1986) *Understains: The Sense and Seduction of Advertising*, London: Comedia.

NAACP (2003) "Out of Focus, Out of Sync, Take 3: A Report on the Film and Television Industry, November 2003" (www.naacpimageawards.net/PDFs/focusreport1_master.pdf).

Napoli, Philip M. (2003) *Audience Economics: Media Institutions and the Audience Marketplace*, New York: Columbia University Press.

—— (2008) "Ratings," in Andersen and Gray 2008.

Neale, Stephen (2000) *Genre and Hollywood*, New York: Routledge.

Newcomb, Horace M. and Alley, Robert (1983) *The Producer's Medium*, New York: Oxford University Press.

Newcomb, Horace M. and Hirsch, Paul M. (1984) "Television as a Cultural Forum: Implications for Research," in Willard D. Rowland, Jr. and Bruce Watkins (eds) *Interpreting Television: Current Research Perspectives*, Thousand Oaks, CA: Sage.

Ouellette, Laurie (2002) *Viewers Like You? How Public TV Failed the People*, New York: Columbia University Press.

—— (2004) "'Take Responsibility for Yourself': *Judge Judy* and the Neoliberal Citizen," in Murray and Ouellette 2004.

Palmer, Jerry (1987) *The Logic of the Absurd: On Film and Television Comedy*, London: BFI.

Parks, Lisa (2004) "Flexible Microcasting: Gender, Generation, and Television–Internet Convergence," in Spigel and Olsson 2004.

Parks, Lisa and Kumar, Shanti (eds) (2003) *Planet TV: A Global Television Reader*, New York: NYU Press.

Pearce, Tralee (2006) "Wired Up, Plugged In, Zoned Out," *Globe and Mail* 14 January: F8.

Penley, Constance (1997) *NASA / TREK: Popular Science and Sex in America*, London: Verso.

Philo, Greg (1999) "Media and Mental Illness," in Philo (ed.) *Message Received: Glasgow Media Group Research 1993–1998*, New York: Longman.

Plato (1974) [390 BC] *Plato's Republic*, trans. G. M. A. Grube, Indianapolis: Hackett.

Postman, Neil (1986) *Amusing Ourselves to Death: Public Discourse in the Age of Show Business*, New York: Penguin.

Putnam, Robert (2000) *Bowling Alone: The Collapse and Revival of American Community*, New York: Simon & Schuster.

Radway, Janice (1987) *Reading the Romance: Women, Patriarchy, and Popular Literature*, London: Verso.

—— (1988) "Reception Study: Ethnography and the Problems of Dispersed Audiences and Nomadic Subjects," *Cultural Studies* 2.3: 359–76.

Raphael, Chad (2004) "The Political Economic Origins of Reali-TV," in Murray and Ouellette 2004.

Ritzer, George (1998) *The McDonaldization Thesis: Explorations and Extensions*. Thousand Oaks, CA: Sage.

Rosenstone, Robert A. (1995) *Visions of the Past: The Challenge of Film to Our Idea of History*, Cambridge: Harvard University Press.

Rowe, Kathleen (1995) *The Unruly Woman: Gender and the Genres of Laughter*, Austin: University of Texas Press.

Said, Edward W. (1979) *Orientalism*, New York: Vintage.

Sandler, Kevin (2007) *The Naked Truth: Why Hollywood Doesn't Make X-Rated Films*, New Brunswick, NJ: Rutgers University Press.

Sandvoss, Cornel (2003) *A Game of Two Halves: Football Fandom, Television and Globalisation*, New York: Routledge.

—— (2005a) *Fans: The Mirror of Consumption*, New York: Polity.

—— (2005b) "One-Dimensional Fan: Toward an Aesthetic of Fan Texts," *American Behavioral Scientist* 48.7: 822–39.

Savage, William J., Jr. (2003) "'So Television's Responsible!' Oppositionality and the Interpretive Logic of Satire and Censorship in *The Simpsons* and *South Park*," in John Alberti (ed.) *Leaving Springfield: The Simpsons and the Possibility of Oppositional Culture*, Detroit: Wayne State University Press.

Scannell, Paddy (1989) "Public Service Broadcasting and Modern Life," *Media, Culture and Society* 11.2: 135–66.

Schiller, Herbert (1976). *Communication and Cultural Domination*. Armonk, NY: M.E. Sharpe.

Sconce, Jeffrey (2004a) "See You in Hell, Johnny Bravo!" in Murray and Ouellette 2004.

—— (2004b) "What If? Charting Television's New Textual Boundaries," in Spigel and Olsson 2004.

Seaman, William (1992) "Active Audience Theory: Pointless Populism," *Media, Culture and Society* 14.2: 301–11.

Shields, Mike (2006) "ABC.com to Stream Hit Shows in Fall," *Mediaweek* 7 August (www.mediaweek.com/mw/news/recent_display.jsp?vnu_content_id=1002950193.

Shelley, Percy Bysshe (1991)[1821] *A Defence of Poetry*, in Charles Kaplan and William Anderson (eds) *Criticism: Major Statements* 3rd edn, New York: St. Martin's.

Shklovsky, Victor (1988)[1917] "Art as Technique," in David Lodge (ed.) *Modern Criticism and Theory: A Reader*, New York: Longman.

Silverstone, Roger (1994) *Television and Everyday Life*, New York: Routledge.

—— (1999) *Why Study the Media?*, Thousand Oaks, CA: Sage.

Simon, Richard K. (1999) *Trash Culture: Popular Culture and the Great Tradition*, Berkeley: University of California Press.

Sontag, Susan (1964) "On Camp," *Against Interpretation*, New York: Delta.

Spigel, Lynn (1992) *Make Room for TV: Television and the Family Ideal in Postwar America*, Berkeley: University of California Press.

—— (1995) "From the Dark Ages to the Golden Age: Women's Memories and Television Reruns," *Screen* 36.1: 16–33.

Spigel, Lynn and Olsson, Jan, eds (2004) *Television After TV: Essays on a Medium in Transition*, Durham, NC: Duke University Press.

Sreberny-Mohammadi, Annabelle (1997) "The Many Faces of Imperialism," in Peter Golding and Peter Harris (eds) *Beyond Cultural Imperialism*, Thousand Oaks, CA: Sage.

Steemers, Jeanette (2004) *Selling Television: British Television in the Global Marketplace*, London: BFI.

Streeter, Thomas (1996) *Selling the Air: A Critique of the Policy of Commercial Broadcasting in the United States*, Chicago: University of Chicago Press.

Strelitz, Larry (2003) "Where the Global Meets the Local: South African Youth and Their Experience of Global Media," in Patrick Murphy and Marwan Kraidy (eds) *Global Media Studies: Ethnographic Perspectives*, New York: Routledge.

Taylor, Paul (1988) "Scriptwriters and Producers: A Dimension of Control in Television Situation Comedies," in Chris Powell and George E. C. Paton (eds) *Humour in Society: Resistance and Control*, New York: St. Martins.

Thussu, Daya K. (2006) *International Communication: Continuity and Change*, London: Hodder Arnold.

——, ed. (2007) *Media on the Move: Global Flow and Contra-Flow*, New York: Routledge.

Tinic, Serra (2005) *On Location: Canada's Television Industry in a Global Market*, Toronto: University of Toronto Press.

Tomlinson, John (2003) "Media Imperialism," in Parks and Kumar 2003.

Tueth, Michael V. (2004) *Laughter in the Living Room: Television Comedy and the American Home Audience*, New York: Peter Lang.

Tulloch, John and Jenkins, Henry (1995) *Science Fiction Audiences: Watching Star Trek and Doctor Who*, New York: Routledge.

Tunstall, Jeremy (2007) *The Media Were American: US Mass Media in Decline*, New York: Oxford University Press.

Turow, Joseph (2006) *Niche Envy: Marketing Discrimination in the Digital Age*, Cambridge: MIT Press.

USIA (1997) "1997 National Trade Estimate Report – European Union." M2 Press Wire.

Vaidhyanathan, Siva (2001) *Copyrights and Copywrongs: The Rise of Intellectual Property and How It Threatens Creativity*, New York: NYU Press.

Waisbord, Silvio (2004) "Understanding the Global Popularity of Television Formats," *Television and New Media* 5.4: 359–83.

Wallace, James M. (2001) "A (Karl, not Groucho) Marxist in Springfield," in William Irwin, Mark T. Conard, and Aeon J. Skoble (eds) *The Simpsons and Philosophy: The D'Oh! of Homer*, Chicago: Open Court.

Wark, Mackenzie (1994) *Virtual Geography*, Bloomington: Indiana University Press.

Wasko, Janet (2003) *How Hollywood Works*, Thousand Oaks, CA: Sage.

Webster, James G. and Phalen, Patricia F. (1997) *The Mass Audience: Rediscovering the Dominant Model*, Mahwah, NJ: LEA.

Williams, Raymond (1975) *Television: Technology and Cultural Form*, London: Fontana/Collins.

Winn, Marie (1985) *The Plug-In Drug: Television, Children, and the Family*. New York: Penguin.

Winnicott, D. W. (1974) *Playing and Reality*, Harmondsworth: Penguin.

Zeitchik, Steven (2006) "Inside Move: It's a Shames: 'Lost' Finds Forgotten 'Twin,'" *Variety* 18 June (www.variety.com/article/VR1117945504.html?categoryid=14&cs=1).

Zillman, Dolf and Bryant, Jennings (1994) "Entertainment as a Media Effect," in Zillman and Bryant (eds) *Media Effects: Advances in Theory and Research*, Hillsdale, NJ: LEA.

Zillman, Dolf and Vorderer, Peter, eds (2000) *Media Entertainment: The Psychology of Its Appeal*, Mahwah, NJ: LEA.

van Zoonen, Liesbet (2005) *Entertaining the Citizen: When Politics and Popular Culture Converge*, Lanham, MD: Rowman and Littlefield.

Index

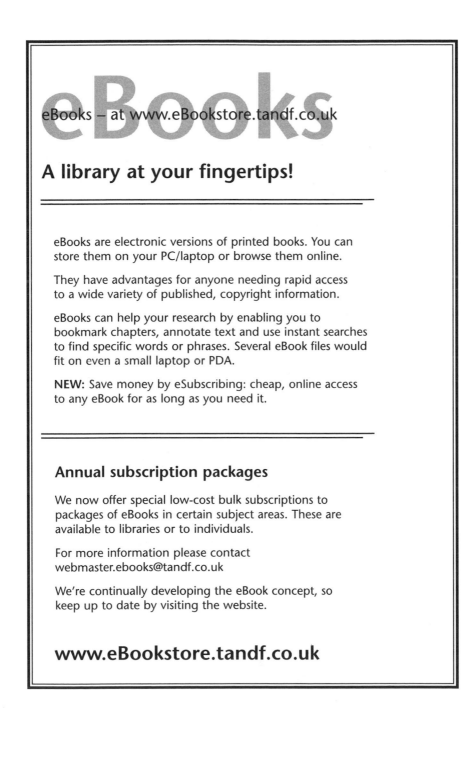